VOTING IN BRITAIN

VOTING IN BRITAIN

© 2001 John Hostettler, Brian Block and Barry Rose

ISBN 1 902681 23 1

M009695

By the same authors:

John Hostettler
The Politics of Criminal Law: Reform in the Nineteenth Century
Thomas Wakely: An Improbable Radical
The Politics of Punishment
Politics and Law in the Life of Sir James Fitzjames Stephen
Thomas Erskine and Trial by Jury
Sir Edward Carson - A Dream Too Far
At the Mercy of the State - A Study in Judicial Tyranny
Sir Edward Coke - A Force for Freedom
Lord Halsbury

Brian P. Block
Justice Matters
An Introduction to Judicial Decision-Making
The Pain and the Pride - Life Inside the Colorado Boot Camp

As Co-authors
Hanging in the Balance: A History of the Abolition of Capital
Punishment in Britain

Published by
Barry Rose
Chichester, England

Contents

Acknowledgement

We wish to acknowledge the useful comments and helpful suggestions of Professor Peter Catterall who read the first draft of this book. Any faults that remain, and the views expressed in the book, are entirely our own.

John Hostettler
Brian P. Block

Preface

Political representation has never been handed to people on a plate. Representative government has always had to be fought for over long periods of time. As a consequence, the securing of universal adult suffrage, which is one of the essential elements of democracy, is a vital issue for society and once achieved its maintenance demands constant vigilance.

This book is the first study to trace the underlying pressures for the franchise[1] in England from the embryo Parliaments in the twelfth century to the granting of the vote to 18-year-olds in 1969. It reveals a flame for liberty that, throughout our history, has sometimes flickered almost unseen and at other times has flared into violence.

The true origins of Parliament and the franchise are still somewhat obscure. It appears that their roots can be found in Anglo-Saxon kingdoms although some historians believe that the idea of parliaments was imposed from continental practice in the Holy Roman Empire and since the Angles and the Saxons came from northern Europe perhaps there is no contradiction. What is certain is that the native blossoming of Parliament and the franchise in England was a gradual process in the twelfth and thirteenth centuries when kings involved in expensive wars required frequent and heavy financial subsidies. These were easier to obtain if representatives of the people

---

1. Franchise is the right to vote for or against a measure, a candidate for office or a government. To be democratic it must involve a real choice.

to be taxed gave their consent. This financial aspect has remained a constant impetus for retaining the franchise in some form, although in modern times voters want also to press for particular legislation, have a say in how the country should be governed and secure measures to improve their conditions and quality of life.

In the early days of kingship monarchs consulted nobles and prelates as a matter of course. A new situation arose in 1265, however, when Simon de Montfort, in order to legitimise his fragile authority after defeating Henry III in battle, summoned to Parliament, not only traditional advisers who supported him, but also two knights from each county with two citizens and burgesses apiece from the large towns and cities. This precedent was followed subsequently by the dynamic but profligate King Edward I with the knights and burgesses elected in open shire courts by all those who were able to attend. It was a primitive form of representative democracy but it was later to lead to struggles to expand the franchise and enable electors to exercise a more direct influence on those who represented them. It also drew the knights closer to the burgesses and away from the unelected magnates, which was to point the way to the subsequent shaping of the House of Commons.

Although Parliament has produced many outstanding parliamentarians and statesmen over the centuries, power, corruption and undue influence deformed the electoral system from its early days until modern times. We indicate how such abuses arose and why they persisted and grew. As they fed upon the body politic there were sporadic upsurges of attempts to reform the franchise, only to be thwarted at different periods by royal and aristocratic interests as well as by MPs themselves. Moreover, only a very restricted male franchise existed until late in the nineteenth century.

In the seventeenth century some reforms were achieved during the Commonwealth but they were limited as a consequence of Oliver Cromwell's fear of losing power and they were rescinded on the Restoration of Charles II. Then, in the eighteenth century the American colonists made a strong impression in Britain when they demanded "no taxation without representation". Partly as a result, both inside and outside Parliament, reformers as diverse as Pitt the Younger and John Wilkes were busy advocating reform. But when the ideals of liberty, equality and fraternity began to spread across the Channel from France, accompanied by the execution of the French king and many aristocrats, Pitt himself conducted a reign of terror against reform organisations and their leaders in England and Scotland.

However, beneath the surface and largely unregarded at the time, the Industrial Revolution was changing not only the economic and demographic face of Britain but also its politics and its culture. As a result of this and the concepts of freedom and representation which flowed from the American and French Revolutions the growing middle class, encouraged by men like James Mill and Francis Place, began to see themselves as the natural leaders of a society they wished to inherit and conduct on their own lines. Once the Napoleonic Wars were over, reform Unions mushroomed throughout England. As for the nascent industrial working class, although they had no leaders in the higher reaches of society and despised a system of government that could ignore their poverty and distress and even countenance the brutality and moral insensibility demonstrated by the massacre at Peterloo and its aftermath, many of them were desperate for the vote which they believed would provide a means of improving their grim, soulless quality of life.

The pressure of public opinion meant that the achievement of an electoral system that would abolish the rotten boroughs[2] and give the franchise to the inhabitants of such large towns as Manchester, Birmingham and Leeds was by this time becoming a real possibility. By 1831 the Tory Party, led by the Duke of Wellington, was strife-ridden and it was at this point that Earl Grey and Lord John Russell began to lead the rising tide for reform. They believed that by introducing limited reform they would re-vitalise the fortunes of the stagnant and long-out-of-power Whig Party. But they were no democrats and for them reform had to be acceptable not only to the restless middle and working classes but also to the aristocracy, and, above all, introduced without precipitating a political revolution. The threat of revolution was a serious prospect which loomed large at the time. However, making their proposals acceptable to

---

2. Rotten boroughs were often left with few voters or none at all and their right to send two members to the House of Commons was usually "owned" by a wealthy and powerful patron.

the middle and working classes without conceding universal (male) suffrage or voting in secret by ballot was a Herculean task for these aristocratic Whig leaders. Furthermore, they had also to persuade the peers in the House of Lords that they had no cause for alarm and would lose none of their status or power if they accepted the 1831 Reform Bill. The response in the Upper House was expressed in howls of anguish at what was perceived to be a plan for the destruction of the Constitution and their privileged position within it.

The ensuing battles in Parliament and throughout the country for the Great Reform Act of 1832, which finally broke the deadlock of centuries, are the stuff of high drama, brought to life in the pages of *Hansard,* the contemporary newspapers and the memoirs of those who lived through the struggle. Yet the Act created very few new voters, failed at the time to give the middle class the leadership role in the country that it sought and did nothing to bring the working class into the electoral system. It also failed to settle the franchise for all time as its framers unrealistically promised, and it was not many years later before the Chartists were engaged in a bitter conflict with the authorities which heralded an explosive decade. What the Act did do, and this was its unintended but decisive achievement, was to show that widening the franchise was possible within the constitution. Subsequently, growing prosperity in Queen Victoria's reign brought to the fore the question of democracy and in 1866 Gladstone proposed to extend the franchise to urban male working class householders who were "fathers of families" and therefore responsible persons who could be trusted with the vote.

The Liberals were, however, in Lord Derby's word, "dished" by Disraeli, the Tory leader in the House of Commons, who, in an effort to retain power, to the surprise of Gladstone, the country and not least his own party, gave the vote to practically all urban rate-paying male householders in boroughs. His Reform Act of 1867, which was hammered out in an acute parliamentary struggle, instantly added 938,000 voters to an existing electorate of 1,056,000 in England and Wales. At a stroke the electorate was almost doubled but even then millions of men and all women were still excluded from the vote. In the following year Disraeli succeeded Lord Derby as prime minister and in his own words had "climbed to the top of the greasy pole" to power although the enlarged electorate ungratefully soon turned him out of office. Promoted by Gladstone, another Act, in 1884, extended to the counties the gains won in the boroughs.

Women were generally excluded from the demands for household or even "universal" suffrage, and this led to the inception of a women's suffrage movement and, in the early twentieth century, to the militant suffragettes. Their struggles resulted in levels of violence and self-sacrifice that were submerged only by the onset of the First World War. However, the issue remained merely dormant and women's role in the war and the growing desire for democracy and equality together were so potent that opposition dissipated and in 1918 women of 30 and over were finally granted the vote. The voting age was not 21 as was the case for men since it was argued (statistically correctly) that this would mean women voters outnumbering male voters, a situation that was unacceptable to an all-male Parliament. For 10 years statistics outweighed democracy until this anomaly was corrected in 1928 when all women over 21 were given the vote. Subsequently, what was at the time regarded as the final step in the achievement of a democratic suffrage, the vote for 18-year-olds, was granted on 12 May 1969. But was it the final step? In 1989 the Social Democratic Labour Party in Northern Ireland asked why stop at 18-year-olds and suggested votes at 16.[3] The pressure group "Demos" took a similar position in 1998.

However, democracy is not simply a matter of voting but of power since it is governments that are elected. Democracy can be seen as a form of government where the desires of the majority are met within a framework of constitutional restraints designed nonetheless to guarantee to the minority the enjoyment of certain individual and collective rights such as freedom of speech and religion. On this basis whilst Imperial Germany before 1914 had a wider franchise than the United Kingdom it was undoubtedly less democratic. Parliamentary democracy can also be said to require an opposition that could be not only an alternative to the government but also a focus for the discontent of those who do not support, or have become disillusioned with, the government of the day.

---

3. *The Times*, 13 June 1989, p.7. No doubt the SDLP calculated that it would benefit at the polls if votes at 16 were introduced.

At the turn of the millennium fresh struggles loomed. Spokesmen for the Labour government elected in 1997 quickly let it be known that they wanted changes in the electoral system. In April 1998, Peter Mandelson, at the time minister without portfolio, took part in a seminar in the British embassy in Bonn attended by prominent German political leaders. There he argued that "it may be that the era of pure representative democracy is coming slowly to an end". Despite the "may be" he then added quite clearly that political elites including intellectual, trade union and local authority elites were of "an age that has passed away". New Labour, he said, was responding to this challenge by using everything from the internet to referendums to close a democratic deficit which Europe was ignoring. Wolfgang Schauble, the Christian Democrat leader in the Bundestag, was not impressed, insisting that a political class was essential for leadership; a view many in the Labour leadership do not accept.[4]

The question might at this stage be asked, had an era of pure representative democracy ever begun? Furthermore, what is meant by representative democracy? It is much easier to demonstrate what is undemocratic than to pinpoint what is democratic. Other countries, for instance China, Israel and the United States, have systems that they consider democratic but which we consider inferior to our own; democracy has a cultural context and their systems will be looked at in chapter 18.

---

4. See John Lloyd. *A political class - who needs one?* In *The Times*, 20 March 1998, p.24.

Generally speaking, however, in the United Kingdom representative democracy is considered to mean a form of government where the citizens exercise the right to make political decisions not in person but through representatives chosen by them and responsible to them. They believe that they have the right to have their views taken into account in the determination of important measures on issues of state. Representative democracy is understood to be the expression of the will of the people through Parliament. Of course, such a form of democracy is not perfect and it cannot ever be "pure". It cannot reflect the views of all the people and, subject to constitutional restraints, a majority imposes its will on a minority who do not always agree with it. Sometimes the wishes of the people are thwarted as when a Conservative government imposed the "poll tax", although in this case in response to immense public outcry Parliament repealed the law. But a choice has to be made between different forms of government and, as Winston Churchill put it, representative democracy is "the worst form of government apart from all the others".

Most observers would probably agree that at least until the end of the rotten boroughs, in which under the guise of voting MPs were in reality appointed, popular representation was largely a fiction. This is not only because of the manner of the elections to the House of Commons but also on account of the power of the House of Lords. Nevertheless, by the nineteenth century the working classes, both industrial and agricultural, strongly believed that if only they had the vote they would elect members of Parliament who would act on their behalf to relieve their poverty and dire living conditions. Indeed, throughout the centuries people suffering from economic hardship have engaged with the franchise question in the hope that a change of representatives would bring prosperity. As it happens, during the nineteenth and twentieth centuries the conditions of the working class (and the middle class) have improved beyond anything that could have been prophesied and although this had a great deal to do with the economic improvement throughout the country as well as global technological advances, representative democracy also played a significant part.

The landslide election of the Liberal government in 1906 is a prime example. This government greatly improved the legal position of trade unions and their members, took the first steps towards the welfare state from which millions of people have benefited and seriously curbed the veto power of the House of Lords. Again, in 1945 the Attlee-led Labour government created the National Health Service, took into public ownership ailing industries and implemented the proposals of the Beveridge Report on social security.

The vote, of course, is not a panacea. The Republic of Ireland, which since its independence has had parliamentary democracy with universal suffrage, was nevertheless one of the poorest countries in Europe until it began to derive economic benefits from European Union membership which led to a loosening of its economic ties to the United Kingdom. However, it was the elected representatives of the people who sanctioned the decision to join the EU. Contrast this with Singapore which since *it* became independent after the Second World War has had a voting system in which the constituencies are arranged to yield a permanent one-party elected dictatorship. Yet, it has become one of the most prosperous countries in Asia.

In the United Kingdom both men and women have benefited enormously from technology, improved living standards and advances in health and education that were a feature of the second half of the twentieth century. Agitation by pressure groups has played its part in securing some benefits but it is usually directed at persuading MPs to act. [And a great deal is owed to the MPs, who are the life blood of representative democracy]. The position of women is one example. As early as the 1920s Parliament improved women's property rights, provided pensions and child allowances for widows and by the Sex Disqualification (Removal) Act of 1919 abolished all extant restrictions upon the admission of women into the professions, occupations and civic positions including appointment as magistrates and selection as jurors. More recently we have seen Parliament enact the Equal Pay Act of 1970 and the Sex Discrimination Act of 1975.

The Labour government of 1997 embarked upon a vast programme of constitutional innovations dealing with the electoral system by which the franchise is exercised. According to the home secretary, Jack Straw, the changes are the "most intensive since 1689".[5] They include different systems of elections for Europe and for Northern Ireland, Scotland and Wales as well as changes in the composition of the House of Lords. Elections to the new Northern Ireland Assembly in June 1998 were by the single transferable vote method (STV), first used in the province under the Government of Ireland Act of 1920 although discontinued for Stormont at the end of the 1920s. (It was also used for university seats from 1918 to 1950). In Northern Ireland this has involved very large constituencies that vote for several members each. The result has been a deliberate balance between Unionists and Nationalists. Such a system, designed to achieve a balanced Assembly, was based upon expediency and was not really democratic. But, this shows how a less democratic method can be used to achieve a more democratic end.

Professor Peter Catterall is of the opinion that because of Northern Ireland STV has become stigmatised in the United Kingdom as an electoral system designed to deal with communalism. However, he says, that is not considered its principal virtue where it is used in the Irish Republic, for the Australian Senate and in Tasmania.

Elections to the Scottish Parliament were held in May 1999. The method used was a modified version of the German-style Alternative Member System (AMS) in which

---

5. Jack Straw. Interview with *The Times*, 29 December 1998. In fact, the Glorious Revolution of 1689 did indeed introduce significant constitutional changes but it achieved little by way of reforming the corrupt electoral system of the time.

the number of top-up members was deliberately restricted in order to minimise the proportional representation effect. In a low turn-out of voters some members were elected by constituencies and the rest from party lists. This has produced a Parliament that broadly matches the percentages of the vote achieved by each party and has resulted in a coalition instead of one-party government. Party lists are a less than democratic form of franchise, however, and members elected from them may tend to be regarded as second-class MPs. The lists also mean that some 30 to 40% of MPs owe their places to their party machines. The Welsh Assembly elections in May 1999 also used a similarly diluted version of AMS which in another low turn-out also resulted in no party having a clear majority.

As if that were not confusion enough, the system of voting for the new mayor of London was the Supplementary Vote (SV). Electors were asked to indicate a first and second preference among candidates. If none of them won an overall majority the top two contenders were to receive the second preferences of the eliminated candidates.

Furthermore, most hereditary peers have lost their right to sit and vote in the House of Lords. The prime minister, Tony Blair, pledged on television on 30 July 1998 that Labour's plans for a reformed House of Lords would include holding "democratic elections". Subsequently he changed his mind and Labour's submission to the Royal Commission on Lords Reform recommended that all members of the second chamber should be nominated by an independent appointments commission who would vet members to ensure that no one party has an overall majority. For the European elections in June 1999 the UK was divided into huge regional constituencies each of which provided several members for the European Parliament. Ballot papers listed only political parties and it was not possible to vote for individual candidates or for a mixture of parties. Indeed, those at the top of the lists secured their seats without the electors being able to vote for them on their merits.

Into this maelstrom has been thrown the Jenkins Report. New proposals, which are by no means a system of proportional representation, have been put forward in this Report for future general elections to the Westminster Parliament and are considered in chapter 17. For some people a form of proportional representation may be a fairer system of voting and may be seen as the culmination of the franchise struggles of the past. On the other hand, the introduction of voting for party lists controlled by party leaders instead of for an individual candidate may be regarded as an erosion of meaningful democracy. It should be recognised that with even a diluted form of proportional representation a new Lib-Lab coalition might rule out a Conservative or Labour government for the foreseeable future.

As similar methods of elections in other countries have often produced coalition governments with small parties exercising excessive and non-mandated power, they may be perceived as something to be resisted. At the least such proposals are likely to stimulate a vigorous debate and cause a good deal of soul searching.

CHAPTER 1

Origin and Abuse of Parliamentary Representation

Some Victorian historians, seeking to show that the "Mother of Parliaments" at Westminster has a pedigree of more than a thousand years, represented the Anglo-Saxon Witan as a quasi-democratic body made up of all freemen who chose to attend. It was a myth. In reality the Witan was a council of bishops and noblemen, the so-called "wise men", to whom kings, who always needed counsellors, looked for advice.

The Elusive Constitution

Genuine political representation in England came about slowly and in a piecemeal manner. Its actual origin is still largely shrouded in mystery, not least because no monarch attempted to establish parliaments as a matter of policy. After all, they were likely to impinge on royal power, as indeed they did from the start. But the insatiable desire for money to finance lavish living at home and expensive wars abroad was the crucial factor that led inexorably to the calling of Parliaments. Complex interactions of massive royal expenditure (and its

1

mismanagement) with hostile baronial power nurtured the seed as with the *Magna Carta* of 1215 and its many offspring. Nonetheless, the growth of the franchise was a slow process. It started in the shires and spread in a ragged form to the towns where no similarity of electoral process was achieved since the boroughs had no uniform system of voting and often the franchise there was in the gift of the monarch who granted it where and when it suited his interests.

Furthermore, as we shall see, after 1430 very little change of substance in either the principle or the methods of elections occurred for centuries and by some mystique the whole static fabric became perceived as the Constitution which made England wealthy, civilised and powerful. This perception was far from the truth and it was not until the Industrial Revolution that the illusion was shattered. So widely believed was the fallacy, however, that exposing it brought the country to the verge of revolution in the early nineteenth century.

Birth and Growth of Parliament

The idea of representation has a long history. In Anglo-Saxon times the custom of using representatives was established by the Teutonic races who conquered Britain and was reinforced under the rule of the Normans and Angevins. At one time or another the councils of the Church were attended by representatives from each diocese; spokesmen for the towns gave evidence before the

Domesday commissioners; representatives of the hundreds and townships sat in the shire courts and on early presenting juries; representatives of each vill attended the justices in eyre; and other itinerant judges were assisted by knights elected by the counties under article 18 of *Magna Carta*. In the Middle Ages the word "parliament" (the French *parlement*) meant "discussion", and in that sense Parliaments of a kind were to be found as early as the reign of Henry II (1154-89), although at the time they were more like conferences between the king and representatives of notables in the Great Council. By the middle of the thirteenth century, however, the character of the Council was changing and its more important sessions were commonly being referred to as Parliaments. Here the king would discuss with magnates, who were summoned as individuals, important affairs of state such as the levying of taxation, legal disputes and petitions submitted to him. Nevertheless, it would be a mistake to see the Council or Parliaments at this time as established institutions with clear-cut membership and functions and, indeed, they have left behind few records.

Significantly, in a rebellion in 1258 similar in many ways to that against King John (1199-1216) in 1215, the great barons imposed on Henry III (1216-1272) the Provisions of Oxford which set up a Council of 15 of their representatives with powers to supervise government and restore justice. They agreed to consult three times a year with a committee of 12 magnates in a Parliament and, as they insisted on the king consulting them on all important matters, they severely restricted his dominance. However, despite the importance of the Provisions there is no record of them beyond a copy in the chronicle of Burton Abbey.[1] Perhaps Henry had them destroyed but in any event no constitutional principle was involved on the part of the barons who were simply reacting to the king's misgovernment and reasserting their own power in society. They were quite unconcerned with what the future results of their actions might be which is why the birth of Parliament was a process and is something of a mystery.

However, only six years later, a new procedure was adopted after Simon de Montfort, a French aristocrat but also Earl of Leicester, defeated Henry III in battle at Lewes in 1264 and took him prisoner. In an attempt to obtain wider support and legitimacy for his rule in place of the deposed monarch, de Montfort summoned an innovative assembly at Westminster in January 1265. This was made up not only of barons and bishops but also, for the first time two knights elected in the shire court of every county together with two citizens and burgesses from each of the large towns and cities to represent the urban freemen and taxpayers. Henry was forced to submit to Simon's creation, to accept a modified version of the Provisions of Oxford and to allow his own son, Prince Edward, to be held as a hostage in Dover castle.

De Montfort also contended that Parliament could sit even if not called by the king or against his opposition.

---

1.   M.T. Clanchy. *Early Medieval England.* 194. Folio Society edition, 1997.

However, he was killed in battle with the army of the escaped Prince Edward at Evesham in August 1265 after which Henry to a large extent allowed his son to take control of affairs of state until Henry's death in 1272. And when the prince became king himself he restored his father's principle that Parliament could meet only in the king's presence after being summoned by him. Nonetheless, the calling of Simon's Parliament had set a precedent.

Thirty years on, in 1295 with war against France imminent Edward I (1272-1307), known as the "English Justinian", and always in desperate need of finance, called a Parliament made up of the higher clergy, noblemen, two knights from each county, two citizens from each city and two burgesses of each borough to which the king's writ was granted. The writs calling the Parliament referred to a prospective devastating invasion by the king of France and commanded the attendance of the prelates and clergy and "other inhabitants of our realm" to determine how the danger should be averted. These "other inhabitants" were the knights from the counties, and the citizens and burgesses from 120 cities and boroughs[2] who were elected to represent their "respective communities". Together they became known as "the commons" and they met apart to discuss and vote financial assistance to the king, although they did not regularly sit separately from the nobles and clergy until

---

2. This figure is drawn from the sheriff's returns to the 1295 Parliament in 1 *Parliamentary Writs*. 34 *et seq.*

1340. By this time it had been recognised by a statute of Edward II in 1322 that the supreme legislative power of the kingdom rested in the king, lords and commons assembled in Parliament. Statutes had also required that Parliaments should be held annually but this was not always observed.

The main purpose of the 1295 Parliament was to provide various financial aids to enable the king to wage war against France. To this end, and because taxes were to be higher than ever before, the king had to ensure that decisions made were taken back into the country to be carried out and the taxes which had been agreed, paid. It made sense for the king to have statutes enacted in Parliament where not only were his legal and other advisers present but also many barons and on some occasions representatives of the counties and boroughs, thus ensuring their widespread endorsement. For example, the preamble of the Statute of Westminster I of 1275 reads:

> "These are the establishments of King Edward, son of King Henry, made at Westminster in his first general parliament after his coronation, after the close of Easter in the third year of his reign, by his council and with the *assent* of the archbishops, bishops, abbots, priors, earls, barons and the community of the land summoned there."[3]

---

3.   William Stubbs (ed.) *Select Charters*. 442. 1921.

It was important for the king to have his statutes disseminated far and wide in order to strengthen his hand against the powerful feudal magnates and Church. Altogether during his long reign, Edward held 52 "Parliaments" and in 13 of them representatives were called from the counties and boroughs, generally when taxation was an issue. The reasons are clear. The ordinary revenue of the crown in the reign of Edward I was about £19,000 a year. The customs due to the king would bring in a further £10,000-£12,000 annually. But between 1294 and 1298, for example, the king spent a staggering £730,000 on war alone. Hence, even after massive extra grants from the clergy, he was obliged to raise in taxes from his subjects in excess of £40,000 a year, and this could be achieved only with their consent.[4] It became understood that grants to the crown were not to be extracted from the people without their agreement previously expressed by their representatives. Indeed, even earlier, in the year 1290, two Parliaments had been called, one comprised solely of prelates, barons and "great men" and the second including free men of the counties but not cities and boroughs. Each in turn granted aids drawn from the people they represented with the result that representation and taxation were seen to be co-extensive.

Only two years after the 1295 Parliament, a law was passed which provided that there was to be no taxation of

---

4.   For these figures see M.H. Keen. *England in the Later Middle Ages: A Political History.* 39. 1997.

the people without their consent. By this the king bound himself that "no talliage or aid shall by us or our heirs be imposed or levied in our kingdom without the will and assent of the archbishops, bishops, barons, burgesses, *and the other free men of our realm*.[5] (Our italics). As will readily be seen this landmark statute not only declared the rights of the people in regard to taxation but also defined the parliamentary suffrage. Along with the composition of the 1295 Parliament it made a crucial contribution to our history and future growth of the House of Commons.

Such huge demands for taxation by Edward and his immediate successors, all of whom were constantly at war in France, Scotland and Wales, meant the representatives from the counties and boroughs became an essential element of Parliaments which often came to be assembled at least once a year. County and borough members were elected in free elections if the sheriffs obeyed the commands of the royal writs. And as well as such members participation in Parliaments increasing they also gradually became insistent on their rights; they began to take advantage of the monarch's dependence on them for financial grants to expand their role and have statutes enacted that protected their estates and commercial and fiscal interests.

In a momentous move, in 1339 the Commons openly declared that they could not grant finance to King Edward III (1327-1377) without consulting the electors of

---

5.   Statute De Tallagio. 30 September 1297.

their counties. The Lords had already made a grant but the Commons responded to the king in writing, saying "As it was necessary that a great aid should be granted, they dared not give their assent till they had advised and consulted the commons of their counties; and therefore they desired another parliament to be summoned, and in the meantime they would return to their counties, and would do their utmost to obtain for the king a proper aid."[6] This was followed, in 1401, with the Commons informing the king that they wished to be told of the answers to their petitions before making any grant. The king refused to agree but in reality the Commons succeeded because it quickly became the practice to delay the grant to the last day of the session by which time the fate of the petitions would be known.[7]

Elections

In these early days both the county and borough electors registered their votes in the county court and this gave considerable leverage to the sheriffs who by this time had grown over-mighty and corrupt and sometimes ignored the king's writs requiring them to hold *free* elections. On occasion they are known to have falsified returns and even made returns of their own nominees without holding

---

6.   See Homersham Cox. *Antient Parliamentary Elections.* 87. 1868.
7.   William Stubbs. *The Constitutional History of England in its Origin and Development.* 267/8. 1884.

elections at all. Indeed, Edward III (1327-77) had set up a commission to investigate corruption among them and many were dismissed. But even after 1430 both Henry VI (1422-61) and Edward IV (1461-83) complained of some members being illegally returned without any election being held.

Misuse of their position by sheriffs was encouraged by the fact that many of the voters of the counties had failed to appreciate the privilege of being represented and often desired to forego it. After all, freeholders in dependent situations could seldom exercise a free choice. What this meant in reality was that the larger landlords often secured the election of their choice of county members by influence and direct bribery and since peers were among the most wealthy and powerful of them they exercised considerable control over the outcome of elections. A similar lack of interest was shown by voters in the boroughs that were taxed more heavily than the counties and had to pay wages of two shillings a day to any burgesses they sent to the Commons. For instance, in 1368 the borough of Torrington was able to persuade the king to excuse it from sending members. Others may have secured a similar release from the sheriff. Nevertheless, it must not be overlooked that most elections were free and open to a large number of voters.

County Franchise

Gradually the status of MPs and their influence in the

country and its affairs, increased particularly in wars in which lucrative possessions could be won overseas, and the opportunity to sit in Parliament became more sought after. In time, as the importance and prestige of Parliament and particularly the Commons grew in the early fifteenth century, the wealthy and powerful in the land began to view the franchise as a property. As Sir William Holdsworth has expressed it, "it often happened that a seat in the House of Commons became as hereditary as an estate or as a seat in the House of Lords."[8]

One consequence was that among the most wealthy landowners there grew up a concern about the types of electors, the conduct of elections and the making of returns by the sheriffs. The times were disturbed. Henry VI was a weak king and the bloody feuds between the Lancastrians and the House of York that were to lead to the Wars of the Roses had already commenced. A statute of 1406 had confirmed the established custom that elections for Parliament should not only be held in the shire court but also in plain view, and with the assistance of all who attended. But soon the feuds began to spill over into election meetings and so large were the numbers of those present that disturbances occurred which resulted in disputed elections.

This led to knights who were members of Parliament

---

8. *A History of English Law.* x. 557. 1938. Indeed, in 1703 chief justice Holt was to hold that the election of knights belonged to freeholders of the counties and was an original right vested in and inseparable from the freehold. *Ashby v. White.* Mich. 2 Anne.

and their patrons to press the king to curtail the franchise by means of a property qualification. The issue was brought to a head by a petition from the Commons that read:

"Pray the commons of this present parliament that, Whereas, the elections of knights of shires elected to come to your parliaments in many counties of England have lately been made by too great and excessive number of people dwelling within the same counties; of whom the greater part are by people of little or no means, of whom each pretends to have an equivalent voice so far as relates to such elections with the most worthy knights or esquires dwelling in the same counties; of which homicides, riots, batteries and divisions between the gentlemen and other people of the same counties probably will arise and be, if a convenient remedy be not provided in that behalf;

That it may please your gracious lordship to consider the premises, and to provide and ordain by the authority of this present parliament, that the election of knights of the same counties within your realm of England to be chosen to come to parliament hereafter be made in each county by people dwelling and resident therein, of whom each has freehold to the value of 40 shillings a year. And that those that be chosen be dwelling and resident within the same counties."[9]

---

9.   Rot. Parl. iv. 350.

As a result, in 1430 a regressive but durable statute[10] was passed which determined the county franchise for the next four centuries - that is until the Reform Act of 1832. It is sometimes presented as a progressive landmark in the history of the franchise in giving 40 shillings freeholders the vote. In reality it reduced to such landed property owners an already existing wider county franchise. It was the first statute to regulate the election of representatives by limiting the franchise and in doing so it took a serious step backwards. Before Henry's reign all free householders, and not only landed freeholders, could vote at the elections of knights in the counties.[11] To restrict the elections to a more limited class, this new Act provided not only that voters and representatives alike had to be resident in the county[12] but that the voters had also to be freeholders owning land to the value of at least 40 shillings - the famous 40 shillings franchise. "Freehold" was interpreted to include annuities and rentcharges issuing out of a freehold estate but these were insignificant compared with the loss of the household franchise.

The purpose of the Act was, in its own words following the Commons' petition, to keep out what it described as

---

10. 8 Hen VI, c.7 (1430).
11. Edward and Annie Porritt. *The Unreformed House of Commons. Parliamentary Representation before 1832.* i. 20. 1903. See also details of sheriffs' returns in the "Parliamentary Writs" which confirm elections of knights in various counties "by the whole community".
12. For voters this requirement was no longer operative by about 1620. Porritt. 24. For members it was abolished by statute in 1774. (14 Geo. III. c.58).

outrageous and numerous (our italics) people of small substance "who pretended a voice as to such election with the most worthy knights and esquires". In other words to restrict the county franchise to the gentry - after all, forty shillings was a substantial sum at that time. And even then, to make doubly sure, in 1445 it was decreed that those to be chosen were to be "notable knights, esquires or gentlemen able to be knights and not of the degree of yeomen or under". To achieve the aim of the statute, copyholders (originally tenants at will of the lord of the manor) were also excluded as well as leaseholders, however valuable their land. A leasehold was of course regarded as a chattel, and not a landed interest, but a lessee householder had formerly enjoyed the right to vote.

Clearly in initiating this change the king's advisers were not looking to the future but endeavouring to buttress their own power and that of the wealthy knights in particular. One consequence was that at this time Parliament became fixed in two Houses and began to adopt its modern procedures, including the initiation of legislation by bill instead of by petition. The House of Commons also reasserted its legislative and financial powers and insisted that grievances should be redressed before supplies (ie, money for the king) were granted.

When Henry VIII (1509-47) came to the throne, his first Commons consisted of 298 members, 74 from the shires and 224 from the cities and boroughs. Despite the numerical superiority of the boroughs it was from the shires that came many of the active and independent members, ie, the knights. Two members represented most of the counties, regardless of their size, but there was no rule for deciding which towns should return members. The king issued his writ where he thought it appropriate and in his interest. Nevertheless, the boroughs were important in the scheme of things, not least because many of them could often be purchased outright, thus strengthening the hands of the men of property.

Because at the time towns had reached different stages of development the following four types of boroughs existed. Indeed, they continued with only minor changes from the thirteenth century to the 1832 Reform Act. Between them they sent over 200 members to the Commons:

1. "Scot and Lot" and "Potwalloper" Boroughs:
There were 59 such boroughs ranging in population from six in Gatton in Surrey to populous places with thousands of voters such as Westminster. The qualification for the scot and lot vote varied from one place to another but generally depended on payment of minor poor or church rates (scot) or compulsory work done in person, such as acting as an alderman or constable (lot). The potwalloper, on the other hand, had to show that he provided his own sustenance and that he was master of a fireplace at which to cook it.[13] Although by custom this had long been the position, in the eighteenth century, in the case of Honiton in Devon, the House of Commons confirmed it and defined the potwalloper as "every inhabitant in the

---

13. *House of Commons Journals.* xi. 492.

borough who has a family and boils a pot there".[14]

Daniel Defoe, in his *A Tour through the Whole Island of Great Britain* in 1725 recounted his visit to Taunton in Somerset. The town had, he said, two MPs who were elected by potwallopers who included every inhabitant who cooked his own food. "To make out which", he continued, "several inmates, or lodgers, will, sometime before the election, bring out their pots, and make fires in the street, and boil their victuals in the sight of their neighbours, that their votes may not be called in question".[15] In 1838 a committee of the House of Commons confirmed that in Taunton a potwalloper was a householder or lodger who furnished and cooked his own meals at his own fireplace. Nevertheless, many of these boroughs fell to the control of landed aristocrats although in some, such as Westminster, the number of artisan voters was sufficiently large that in later years Radicals often succeeded in becoming elected in fiercely fought contests.

2. Burgage Boroughs:

In some 41 of these boroughs the electorate was small and this facilitated the abuse of their right to vote by the virtual purchase of the borough by some lord or country gentleman. Burgage tenure was attached to certain tenements, similar to a modern freehold but generally at a money rent. In a few places even someone resident

---

14. *Ibid.,* xx. 366.
15. Vol. ii. 19. Folio Society edn. 1983.

merely overnight could vote at an election the next day.[16] But not all burgages had the right to elect attached to them and where they did the right could easily be bought and, in a restricted franchise, a wealthy man could buy enough to control the borough. An example is found at Haslemere in Surrey where, in the reign of George III, the Earl of Lonsdale settled a colony of Cumberland miners to occupy the burgage houses and do as he told them at elections.[17] Clearly those who purchased the means of being represented in Parliament found it to their advantage and worthwhile as a stepping-stone to the kind of influence and power of MPs mentioned earlier. What is astonishing is the extent to which, over the years, and with such widespread corruption, the House of Commons contained so many independent spirits.

Nevertheless, tawdry and frequent disputes between the candidates of rival claimants to borough patronage constantly swamped the election committees of Parliament. And although several attempts were made in the Commons in the eighteenth century to reform the burgage borough electoral system, all were defeated by vested interests. An entertaining account of the election in Appleby in 1802 was given by Sir Philip Francis. Although Appleby had one hundred burgage holders, one of its MPs was nominated by the Earl of Thanet who had purchased the rights of many burgage voters for himself. "I was unanimously elected by one Elector" (presumably

---

16. *House of Commons Journal*. xxii. 796.
17. E. And A. Porritt. *Op. cit.* 34.

a nominee of the Earl), Sir Philip wrote, to Harriet Francis on 7 July 1802. "There was no other candidate, no Opposition, no Poll demanded, Scrutiny or petition. So I had nothing to do but thank the said Elector for the Unanimous Voice with which I was chosen ... On Friday Morning I shall quit this triumphant Scene with flying Colours and a noble determination not to see it again in less than seven years ... My elector intends to hang himself in November and then I shall elect myself: and that will do as well."[18]

The only slightly redeeming feature about burgage boroughs was that, as with freeman boroughs, women who were burgage holders had the right, not to vote themselves - that would have been too much - but to a "vote" which, whilst they could not exercise it, they could transfer to a male relative. Unfortunately, he in turn could sell it to an outsider. These "votes" were not lost until the Municipal Corporations Act of 1835 when women were actually disenfranchised totally; not that such "rights" could seriously be called a franchise.

3. Corporation Boroughs:

There were 19 of these boroughs where the franchise was restricted to members of the corporation including, for example, Buckingham and Bury St Edmunds. They were easy prey to the wealthy who could either join the corporation or insert their nominees by bribery.

In Northampton as early as the year 1381 members of

---

18. Quoted by G.S. Veitch in *The Genesis of Parliamentary Reform*. 9. 1913.

the municipal corporation are known to have usurped the right to elect members to the House of Commons in place of the general voters. In 1768 a scandal arose in the city of Oxford the reek of which penetrated to Parliament. The mayor, bailiffs and several aldermen wrote a letter under their common seal to the two sitting members saying that if they were paid £7,500 they would re-elect them at the next general election. The members concerned produced the letter in the Commons and the signatories were sent to Newgate Prison until they had apologised on their knees before the Speaker.[19] And in 1783 the borough of Tiverton in Devon had five thousand inhabitants, none of whom had the vote. The 25 self-elected members of the corporation chose their representatives for them.[20]

The eminent legal historian F.W. Maitland thought the decline of old municipal corporations was "curious, if not disgraceful". Writing of the boroughs of Oxford and Cambridge as they were before the Municipal Reform Act of 1835 he said that, "The Constitutions of Oxford and Cambridge were closely similar on paper. They weɪt to the bad in different ways. The freemen of Oxford were numerous; the freemen of Cambridge few. Too many of the Oxford corporators lived in the workhouse; too many of the Cambridge corporators lived near Cheveley. It is of beer and mob rule that we read in the one town; in the other of oligarchy and wine - "excellent wine", said an unregenerate alderman, "and plenty of it". "Morally", he

---

19. *Parliamentary History*. [16] (10 February 1768).
20. T.H.B. Oldfield. *History of the Boroughs*. i. 547. 1792.

said, "the town loses its sense of personality and sense of duty."[21] In both towns the corporations held control.[22]

Numerous attempts were made in the House of Commons to restore the franchise to all entitled to vote by law in the corporation boroughs but all were defeated, with the corporations defending their actions as being designed to avoid "popular tumults common at elections."

4. Freeman Boroughs:

In the fourteenth century some hundred boroughs had franchises which were available to every freeman who was a householder and undertook municipal duties such as watch and ward. "Watch" was the duty of constables and others to arrest rioters and robbers by night; "ward" by day. Nevertheless, the venal practices mentioned in connection with the three preceding types of boroughs were also imposed on this wider franchise when membership of the House of Commons became more sought after than in those early days when being an MP was often seen as a burden. For instance, in Norwich in the eighteenth century it was permitted by statute[23] for the returning officer to go to the city gaol to take the votes of prisoners who were freemen. And as late as 1835 Lord

---

21. *Township and Borough.* 94/5. 1898.
22. The Porritts give numerous accounts of abuses in many individual cities and towns in their *Unreformed House of Commons. Op. cit.* For claims that the Porritts overestimated the abuses and relied too much on the attacks on the political system by contemporaneous Radical and Whig campaigners see John A. Phillips. *The Great Reform Bill in the Boroughs.* 1992.
23. 3 Geo. II. c. 8.

Melbourne's attorney-general, Sir John Campbell, claimed that "in various places the majority of the freemen pay no rates, have no property, do not pay scot or bear lot." There were some instances of freemen having "no home except the common gaol, in which they pass the greater part of the year, and from which they are withdrawn on the approach of a contested election, municipal or parliamentary, for the purpose of giving their votes for a bribe."[24]

Moreover, in freeman boroughs outsiders who were not residents could be made freemen and residents bribed to vote for them. The classic example is that of Oliver Cromwell. Although he lived outside the borough of Cambridge he desired to represent it in the House of Commons. As he was not a freeman of the borough the mayor simply bestowed the freedom on him "gratis, on payment of one penny for the poor" and he was elected to the first Parliament of 1640.[25] This procedure became more frequently used in subsequent years, often to the dismay of resident freemen, particularly where a large number of outsiders flooded in to become freemen simply to serve a patron. As usual, reform proved elusive and attempts in Parliament to establish that only resident freemen could vote proved abortive. Only 24 freeman boroughs ever succeeded in excluding outsiders being made freemen and distorting and corrupting the franchise.

---

24. *The Mirror of Parliament.* ii. 1502. 1835.
25. Porritt. *Op. cit.* 61.

In all these types of boroughs, even for some time after the Reform Act of 1832, the corrupt practices continued in full rigour.

CHAPTER 2

Failure to Reform

When Henry VII (1485-1509) ascended the throne there were fewer than 300 MPs. On the death of Elizabeth I (1558-1603) there were more than 450. By this time all the numerous abuses in the electoral system mentioned above had become widely apparent and were seen for what they were. For instance, in the reign of Edward VI (1547-53) letters addressed by the king to the county sheriffs openly stated that, "Our pleasure is that where our privy council, or any of their jurisdiction in our behalf, shall recommend men of learning and wisdom, in such case their directions shall be regarded and followed."

And the sheriffs of several counties were required to return certain persons whom the king recommended by name.[1]

17th Century Attempts at Reform

Elizabeth's secretary of state, Thomas Wylson, wrote, "it is thought that there are overmany (burgesses) already and there will be a device hereafter to lessen the number

---

1. *Parliamentary History.* i. 599.

for the decayed towns."[2] In fact, the queen only made matters worse by creating 31 new rotten boroughs under the control of the crown and its nominees in an attempt to secure ascendancy in her sometimes less than docile Parliaments. On the other hand, in 1604 the queen's successor James I (1603-25)[3] charged his sheriffs not to direct, "a writ to any ancient town, being so ruined there were not residents sufficient" to make a choice of MPs.[4] However, no lasting reform was achieved.

Prestige of Parliament

As has been noted the many attempts to get rid of corruption, which generally merely tinkered with the problem, all failed and, indeed, hardly any reform at all was accomplished until 1832. But one should not lose sight of the growing influence and prestige of Parliament. Notwithstanding his power Henry VIII was always careful to have his Reformation and treason objectives endorsed by Parliament. The Parliaments of Elizabeth played a positive role in helping to establish the English nation state and the new culture of the age. And some

2. Porritt. *The Unreformed House of Commons. Parliamentary Representation before 1832.* i. 2.
3. James, on the advice of his attorney-general, Sir Edward Coke, granted representation to the universities of Oxford and Cambridge which dutifully elected his nominees. Coke, a former Speaker of the House of Commons, advised the vice-chancellor of Cambridge, his old university, that its two MPs should be professors of civil law.
4. Porritt. *Op. cit.* 1/2.

years later outstanding parliamentary patriots like Sir John Eliot, Sir Edward Coke and John Pym punctured the early Stuarts' doctrine of the "divine right of kings" and forced through the great Petition of Right.

The autocratic Charles I (1625-49) managed to rule for 12 years without a Parliament but when he needed money to finance war in Scotland he was impelled to call one early in 1640. Under the leadership of Pym the Commons decided to discuss grievances and refuse money to the king who promptly dissolved what was soon dubbed the "Short Parliament". With the necessity of obtaining finance still bearing down upon him Charles called another later in the year for which he gave directions as to which of the servants of the crown were to be provided with seats in the House of Commons. "I enclose by His Majesty's command," wrote Secretary Vane to Secretary Windebank on 27 September 1640, "a note of the names of such of his servants as he thinks should be provided with burgess-seats to attend this Parliament, and it is his pleasure that you speak with the Lord Chamberlain concerning it; His Majesty expecting some help from him for the others. You are to see them provided out of such places as are in His Majesty's and the Prince's gift."[5]

But this was to no avail since, with 505 members, many of them Puritans, the Long Parliament, as it became known, set about destroying the king's instruments of autocratic rule - the star chamber, the high commission and other prerogative courts. It then

---

5. *State Papers*. 1640/1. 104.

used its power of attainder to secure the execution of the king's adviser, the Earl of Strafford, and send William Laud, the archbishop of Canterbury, to the scaffold for allegedly attempting to subvert the religion and fundamental laws of England. It also proposed to disenfranchise a number of decayed boroughs and give the vote to every owner of land whatever his tenure. These plans were shelved, however, during the ensuing Civil War in which the parliamentary forces were triumphant. As the Rump Parliament, following "Colonel Pride's Purge", it then tried the king and secured his execution. With only 50 or so MPs remaining after the purge, the population in the towns and the squires in the countryside were largely unrepresented.

Cromwell's Changes

Although Cromwell and the army dominated Parliament, in 1647 when the army was in occupation of London, Cromwell endeavoured to reach a settlement with both the House of Commons and the king based on the "Heads of Proposals", in effect a new Constitution, produced by his son-in-law, Henry Ireton. These proposals included schemes for biennial Parliaments and a franchise based on contributions to taxation. Seats from rotten boroughs were to be allotted to large counties that were not adequately represented. However, Cromwell believed that anything approaching manhood suffrage would lead to the overthrow of property and the destruction of civil society and he was not about to relinquish power. Nothing was proposed therefore about fully enlarging the franchise despite the influential Colonel Rainborough and his supporters arguing that it should be extended downwards to all men save wage labourers and paupers.

In the famous Putney Debates held between the army council and the Levellers on the Levellers' "Agreement of the People" in October and November 1647, Rainborough said, in a sentiment that was to be repeated in succeeding centuries, "the poorest man in England is not at all bound in a strict sense to that government that he hath not had a voice to put himself under." Later, in the same debates, he continued, "I do not find anything in the law of God that a lord shall choose 20 burgesses and a gentleman but two, or a poor man shall choose none; I find no such thing in the law of nature, nor in the law of nations."[6] In fact, the army council voted in favour of giving the franchise to all adult males except servants. The Levellers, for their part also in some respects more than 200 years ahead of their time, wanted to abolish all property qualifications and allow men of twenty-one years and over, except servants and beggars, to enjoy the parliamentary franchise. Their desire for manhood suffrage was also implicit in their demand that constituencies be redistributed according to the number of their inhabitants. But Cromwell successfully insisted that the vote be tied to property after arguing furiously that all

---

6.   H.N. Brailsford. *The Levellers and the English Revolution.* Edited by Christopher Hill. 274/5. 1976.

the other suffrage proposals "did tend very much to anarchy."

Perhaps in an endeavour to win over Cromwell, in November 1648 a revised "Agreement of the People" proposed a different enlargement of the electorate. The vote was to be open to all citizens paying poor relief except for servants receiving wages and those in receipt of alms who presumably did not pay poor relief anyway. In a curious proposal coming from the Levellers one hundred and seventy boroughs were to lose their franchise rights with only 28 towns and cities retaining representation. The remaining 300 seats were to be allotted to the counties. These suggestions were accepted by the Rump Parliament in principle in 1649 - the year in which Charles I was executed. But on reconsideration in the 1653 "Barebones Parliament[7] (which itself had only 140 members selected by Cromwell and the army and was really a nominated assembly) it was decided that many of the boroughs should retain their rights and counties should be subject to a £200 property qualification. As it happens this Parliament, to which Cromwell had promised to resign his power, also proposed to abolish the Court of Chancery, ecclesiastical patronage and tithes. Cromwell regarded such measures as highly dangerous and he swiftly closed down the Parliament before

---

7.   So called after Praisegod Barebones an Anabaptist preacher who was appointed as member for the City of London. The name was intended to be a derisory comment on an assembly described by Clarendon in his *History of the Great Rebellion* as a "little daft parliament made up of old bottles of mean men."

anything could be done.

Despite the small number of MPs who sat during the Commonwealth and Protectorate (1649 -1660), Cromwell could not ignore the House of Commons. The languishing Rump Parliament was less than enthusiastic for any change but in 1653 it accepted the "Instrument of Government" drafted by General "Honest" John Lambert. This made Cromwell lord protector backed by a council of state, provided for triennial Parliaments with a minimum sitting of five months and made electoral districts more equal. It also disenfranchised a number of smaller boroughs with the result that in the 1654 parliamentary elections there were only 133 borough constituencies, including 30 each from Scotland and Ireland, compared with 398 in the Long Parliament. A number of villages, including Old Sarum near Salisbury, were deprived of their members. On the other hand, the number of county constituencies, where Cromwell expected support, was raised from 90 to 265. The Instrument of Government also substituted a £200 county franchise in place of the 40 shillings freeholder vote, although this extraordinary measure was reversed by the Parliament of the following year.

Royalists were disqualified everywhere as were "Papists", immoral and irreligious persons, profaners of the Lord's Day, profane swearers and cursers, drunkards and common haunters of taverns and ale-houses. University representation was reduced from four to two. Moreover, in Ireland not only Roman Catholics but everyone who had supported the recent rebellion were excluded from the franchise. As a consequence voters were confined to English and Scottish settlers and most of the MPs elected were army officers.[8]

Nevertheless, for Cromwell the effect of the changes was disappointing since English returns showed that many government supporters were defeated at the polls and the resulting Parliament came close to undermining the Instrument. This only reinforced his determination that ultimately he was not prepared to allow any serious reform of the franchise to succeed. He thereupon proceeded to disbar all members who failed to swear an oath to be true to the lord protector and the government. It was a precedent he was to follow with his last Parliament, called in 1656, when some hundred or so elected MPs were excluded from the House of Commons.

The Restoration

Although Parliament recovered some of its former power after the Restoration of 1660 the later Stuarts proved equally uninterested in improving the electoral system. However, the Parliament of March 1679 in the reign of Charles II drafted a Bill it claimed would regulate abuses at elections. It provided, *inter alia*, for:

---

8. S.R. Gardiner. *History of the Commonwealth and Protectorate*. iii. 6/10. 1901.

(i)   a return to the limitation of the county franchise to persons having a freehold estate worth £200 or more,

(ii)   a standard franchise in the boroughs consisting of all householders paying scot and lot provided they had resided in the borough for at least one year (London, York, Norwich, Exeter and Bristol were to be excluded),

(iii)   a penalty of £500 and disability from sitting in Parliament for anyone giving bribes or rewards for votes, and disenfranchisement of the borough where the bribery took place,

(iv)   no future Parliament to continue for more than two years.

Curiously the Bill made no provision to ensure that Parliaments would ever be called, a defect that was not remedied until the Mutiny Act of 1689 required William III to review the legal status of his troops annually. In the event the Bill did not become law.

Whigs and Tories

It was during the struggle in 1679 over a Bill to exclude James, Duke of York - later James II - from the succession that two factions formed. As terms of abuse each called the other Whigs or Tories. The term "Whig" originated in Scottish Gaelic and was applied to horse thieves and later to Scottish Presbyterians and was aimed at those who wished to exclude the heir from the throne, and thence at nonconformity. The Irish word "Tory" was applied to those who supported James despite his being a Roman Catholic.

The revolution of 1688 was a joint achievement which went some way to blurring the differences between the two factions and the Tories thenceforth accepted some of the Whig doctrines of limited constitutional monarchy rather than the previous divine absolutism. Later, in the reign of Queen Anne the Tories were resistant to religious toleration and foreign entanglements and were identified with the squires and the Anglican clergy, whereas the Whigs were more involved with the aristocracy and the wealthy middle class.

After Queen Anne died in 1714 George I was enthroned as a nominee of the Whigs and a year later the Tory leader Henry St John, Viscount Bolingbroke fled to France; these two events virtually destroyed the Tories as a political force at the time. Thereafter for the next half century rule was by those aristocratic groups who regarded themselves as Whigs and the remaining Tories were discredited as Jacobites who sought the restoration of the Stuarts. During this time, however, some hundred gentlemen who remained as members of the House of Commons regarded themselves as Tories. Notwithstanding the Whig hegemony these Tories were influential in local politics and administration and were not without importance.

It was during the reign of George III that the meanings of the two terms changed. At that time there was neither a Tory nor a Whig party as such. What there was, was on one hand aristocrats and families who operated in Parliament through patronage and influence: the Whigs; and a Tory tradition which survived among certain families and social groups. The "King's Friends" from whom the king drew his ministers came from both groups and from neither. It was only when important political issues that stirred public opinion arose, such as the War of Independence in America, that party alignments began to take shape, after 1784. Pitt the Younger emerged as leader of the Tories - a new Tory Party that broadly represented the interests of the gentry, the merchants and official administrators. The Whig Party, led by Charles James Fox, represented the interests of religious dissenters, industrialists and those in favour of parliamentary, electoral and other reforms.

During the French Revolution there was another blurring of the parties. Many moderate Whigs deserted Fox and supported Pitt, but after 1815 the confusion of party and nomenclature resolved itself with the emergence of the "conservative" Tories Sir Robert Peel and Benjamin Disraeli and the "liberal" Whig Lord John Russell and later William Ewart Gladstone by whose time the two party labels had become Conservative and Liberal. The label "Tory" has become synonymous with "Conservative" but the term "Whig" has long since lost all party political meaning.

The Glorious Revolution and the Bill of Rights

To avoid the Roman Catholic succession to the throne plotted by James II, leaders of both the Whigs and the Tories invited William, Prince of Orange, to replace the king and to enforce both the law and the Protestant religion in England. Already prepared, William landed at the small fishing port of Brixham in Devon in 1688 and brought to pass a Revolution without a single shot being fired. A convention was then called in London which offered the throne to William and Mary in February 1689. This was accompanied in both the Commons and the Lords by a *Declaration of Rights* which was soon embodied in the *Bill of Rights* which ranks second only to *Magna Carta* as a charter of liberty.

This "Glorious Revolution" of 1689 signalled the partial triumph of the propertied Whigs over royal despotism, although this was not always apparent during the subsequent reigns of the four Georges. Nonetheless, the king (or queen) had become a constitutional monarch no longer above the law and Parliament, although still retaining considerable influence through patronage. And the *Bill of Rights* did award the monarch an annual sum to meet the expenses of the civil list, although all the remaining revenue was left in the hands of the Commons to support the armed forces and defray the cost of government. It also provided that election of members of Parliament should be free, that there should be freedom of speech for MPs in the House of Commons and that the House was to meet frequently. The Revolution also produced efforts to reform the procedure at elections. For this purpose, three Bills were passed in 1696. The first made it illegal to give money or other bribes to electors;[9] the second attempted to reduce the number of double or false returns[10] whilst the third provided for the quicker return of election writs and that no one under 21 was allowed to vote.[11] All three proved to be ineffective as was an attempt to prevent revenue officers from interfering in elections.

One problem was how to ensure that Parliament met frequently. In 1664 a Triennial Act had provided that there should not be more than a three years interval between Parliaments but Charles II had ignored it and James II had seemed likely to do the same. Yet the later Triennial Act of 1694 went no further than providing that Parliament should be summoned at least once in three years and should not last more than three years, although William III saved the situation by calling frequent Parliaments as the *Bill of Rights* required.

Two years later, in 1696, the Tories commenced a movement to restrict membership of the House of Commons to men of the landed classes - clearly aimed at securing them a majority. In that year they introduced a Bill to give effect to this restriction and immediately provoked a flood of petitions in opposition. Plymouth, for instance, petitioned that as the borough chiefly subsisted

---

9.   7-8 Wm. III. c. 4.
10. *Ibid.* c. 7.
11. *Ibid.* c. 25

by trade if the Bill became law the people of Plymouth might never "send one of their own inhabitants who knows their circumstances, though wise and rich in personal estate" and "must choose a stranger to represent them."[12] The City of London claimed that the Bill would restrain the ancient privileges of its citizens "by rendering many eminent and fit merchants and traders of great personal estate incapable to serve in Parliament."[13]

The third reading of the Bill in the Commons was carried by 200 votes to 160 but surprisingly was rejected by the Lords, who might have been expected to welcome it, by 62 votes against 37. However, when the Tories came to power in 1710 they again attempted to secure their rule by introducing a Bill that a county candidate should possess an income of £600 a year from land and a burgess an income of £300. On this occasion the Bill was enacted although candidates giving fictitious information or "borrowing" land until their election was secured often avoided it. Nevertheless, the Act was not repealed until 1858.

As it happens, although the Revolution changed the political order it produced little to improve the franchise or secure popular influence on members of Parliament. After all, the victorious Whigs also believed in political representation by men of property although they were more flexible about the meaning of property than the Tories. However, in the succeeding two centuries it was

---

12. *House of Commons Journals*. xi. 598.
13. *Ibid.* 599.

a widely held belief that the Revolution had reformed the franchise, although this did not prevent nineteenth century reformers being confronted with appeals from those in power to regard the flawed and corrupt system as the embodiment of centuries of "venerable tradition". Tradition was a powerful force in inhibiting attempts at reform which consequently proved sporadic. Coupled with the power of the aristocracy, both in the country and Parliament, it produced a structure of politics from which ordinary people felt remote.

Stirrings for Reform

After the Glorious Revolution little more was heard of reform until 1745. But in the ruling echelons of society the Whigs and Tories[14] were so bitterly divided that in the year of Queen Anne's death (1714) there were at least 110 seats fought in the general election in England and Wales which returned a Whig government. By 1722 the number of contests had grown to 156. Subsequently, after having impeached the Tory leaders and created a fever of fear of a Jacobite rebellion to place a Catholic Stuart on the throne, the Whig ascendancy was so strong that there were only four county contests in 1741, three in 1747, five in 1754 and four again in 1761.

---

14. According to the Whigs the Tories were, "monsters with large foreheads, prodigious mouths, supple hams and no brains." For good measure the Tories retorted that the Whigs were, "demure, conscientious prick-eared vermin."

But Not Too Fast

In the early days of these electoral doldrums the question
of franchise reform was raised on 17 October 1745 by Sir
Francis Dashwood, an opposition Whig. He moved in the
House of Commons that Bills should be framed to secure
to the people the right to be freely and fairly represented
in Parliament by members frequently chosen and free of
undue influence.[15] William Pitt the Elder opposed the
motion, pleading that with an expected invasion from
France such reform would make ministers odious in the
eyes of the people. Although his reason for rejection
scarcely held water the motion was defeated without a
division. Nevertheless, outside of Parliament a radical
demand for major reform of the system of representation
was growing.

Then, in 1768, shortly before the North American
colonists refused to pay taxes imposed by a Parliament in
London in which they were not represented, the
libertarian John Wilkes was sent to the House of
Commons by the electors of Middlesex. Five years earlier,
prompted by Pitt, he had in his journal the *North Briton*
branded the King's Speech of the Grenville government
as dishonest. Grenville chose to treat this as a personal
attack on the king and secured a general warrant for the
arrest of Wilkes whom the government then concealed in
the Tower of London in an attempt to evade a writ of
habeas corpus. This ruse did not succeed, however, and

---

15. *Parliamentary History*. [13] 1337/42.

the liberal-minded, Charles Pratt, Earl Camden, lord chief justice of the court of common pleas, released him. In doing so he also ruled that general warrants, which neither named the person to be arrested nor even his or her offence, were illegal, as they have remained ever since.

Then, after Wilkes' election in 1768, in further retaliation a corrupt royal court and government acted promptly to prevent him from taking his seat by expelling him from the House of Commons. They continued to do so when he was re-elected on three further occasions. In the end they not only declared that Wilkes was ineligible but the House of Commons proclaimed as duly elected Colonel Luttrell whom Wilkes had defeated at the poll by a majority of 1,143 votes to 296. There was no statutory authority for such a move, which could involve the dangerous threat of MPs being appointed instead of elected, and it made a resolution of the Commons equal in effect to a law made by both Houses of Parliament and the king, and thus this ploy was unconstitutional. Such blatant interference with the will of the electorate gave Wilkes great popular support, expressed in the cry of "Wilkes and Liberty", and triggered a widespread interest in the franchise in both Britain and the American colonies.

The distinguished historian W.E.H. Lecky considered that the Wilkes affair gave birth to the movement for parliamentary reform in England.[16] However, Parliament

---

16. *A History of England in the Eighteenth Century.* iii. 174. 1882.

itself was to remain largely indifferent to such reform until the effects of the Industrial Revolution began to be felt with the rapid growth of new industries and a population shift from south to north which transformed both the face of the country and the class structure of society. But even then, what was being achieved in terms of the franchise?

When George I had come to the throne in 1714, 5.5% of the population, some 300,000 men, were entitled to vote, but derisory as that was it compares well with the 3.1% on the eve of the Reform Act of 1832 and 4.7% after the Act. Whilst the population had risen rapidly by 1832 the proportion of electors was in the meantime actually decreasing. However, the real and lasting effect of the 1832 Act was not a substantial addition to the number of electors but rather the revelation that popular pressure could ensure franchise reform - a lesson that was duly learnt.

Perhaps in 1745 Pitt's reason for opposing reform may in his mind have appeared to be sound. In any event, it was only after the Wilkes' affair, by which time he had become the Earl of Chatham, that on 22 January 1770 he felt able to concede to the House of Lords that, "The constitution intended that there should be a permanent relation between the constituent and the representative body of the people. Will any man affirm that as the House of Commons is now formed, that relation is in any degree preserved? My Lords, it is not preserved; it is destroyed."

Nevertheless, he still desired no serious change since he continued,

"Let us be cautious, however, how we have recourse to violent expedients. The boroughs of the country have, properly enough, been called the rotten parts of the constitution ... But in my judgment, my Lords, the boroughs, corrupt as they are, must be considered as the natural infirmity of the constitution. Like the infirmities of the body, we must bear them with patience, and submit to carry them about with us. The limb is mortified but its amputation might be death.

Let us try, my Lords, whether some gentler remedy may not be discovered. Since we cannot cure the disorder, let us try to infuse such a portion of new health into the constitution as may enable it to support the most inveterate diseases.

The representation of the counties is, I think, still preserved pure and uncorrupted."[17]

A little over a year later, on 22 April 1771, he was to explain in a letter to Lord Shelburne that he believed the county members "approached nearest to the constitutional representation of the country because they represent the soil."[18] Apart from that, the purity of the counties as against the boroughs was widely accepted until 1832 when most of the rotten boroughs lost the franchise. They were seen to be more independent and indeed office seekers would often find it easier to find a patron who owned or could buy a borough than fight a

---

17. *Parliamentary History.* [16] 752/3.
18. PRO. *Chatham Correspondence.* iv. 157.

county election. Even Fox who never championed widespread reform was committed to the addition of 100 county members to the Commons. And many subsequent reform Bills contained a similar provision.

Alongside the idea that the shire franchise was relatively uncorrupted was the well-used argument that all interests and all people in Britain were virtually represented in the House of Commons by men whose integrity was undoubted, however they came by their seats. Edmund Burke first expounded the concept of "virtual representation" in his famous speech to his electors in Bristol in 1774. Represented in Parliament, he said, were not individuals but local communities and various ranks and orders. Those who were not directly represented were "virtually represented" which he believed was better than actual representation. Members represented the whole nation, not just the voters who had elected them. Pitt's friend, Lord Camden, cast scorn on the notion and argued that taxpayers should be directly represented.[19]

According to John Derry, in his biography of Charles James Fox,[20] on a motion of Pitt the Younger for reform in 1782 Fox was prepared to go along with the theory of virtual representation despite the existing distortions of the franchise and eccentricities in the distribution of seats. However, he pointed out the exaggerations and misrepresentations that so often disfigured the theory.

---

19. *Parliamentary History.* [16] 747.
20. John W. Derry. *Charles James Fox.* 143/4. 1972.

For instance, some persons had argued that the people of America were as effectively represented in the Commons as the people of Birmingham. But neither was properly represented since the members for the rotten boroughs could alone defeat any motion. The House of Commons, he said, should contain every interest and he believed that those who had a stake in the country ought to be more effectively represented, for their natural anxiety to preserve their interests would add stability.[21] It was an argument to be much canvassed in the nineteenth century by Lord John Russell and others.

Soon after Chatham's earlier speech, in January 1770 he proposed that "one or more members ought to be added to the representation of the counties, in order to operate a balance against the weight of the several corrupt and venal boroughs which perhaps could not be lopped off entirely without the hazard of a convulsion."[22] It would also act as a curb on the "ambition of the Crown." His primary concern was to reduce the extensive influence of the king over Parliament based on royal patronage and strengthening the authority of the electorate would assist this. Nonetheless, as an effort to bring about reform it was a superficial response to a problem he was unable to ignore; made in an effort to ensure that any remedy that was undertaken was on traditional lines.

In any event, with close ties with London mercantile interests, he had been more involved in directing British

---

21. *Parliamentary History.* [22] 1432.
22. *Ibid.* [16] 978/9.

policy in the Seven Years War (1756-63) and destroying French power in Canada on which his fame as a war leader rests. With the American War of Independence (1775-83) he opposed the disastrous policies of Lord North's government[23] and pressed for conciliation with the 13 colonies whom he saw as defending their liberties. He was opposed to independence for the colonists but in the interest of maintaining valuable commercial relations he attacked the taxation and coercion which had fanned the embers of war. To this end he urged that British troops be recalled and negotiations for peace be entered into. After all, America annually paid Britain some two or three million pounds that it would be pitiful to lose for a paltry 50 or 60,000 pounds per annum.[24] He also had the foresight to see that France would actively aid the colonists who would then be difficult to defeat.

Chatham also called for the restoration of triennial Parliaments. As was seen in an earlier section these had been introduced in December 1694 when there was great rejoicing in the country that electors would now have more control over their representatives. It was soon being observed, however, that as elections were more frequent more money had to be spent on them and corruption was spreading. In the event, when the Whigs were in office in 1716 they had wanted a longer life and greater power for the type of Parliaments that followed the Glorious

---

23. Dr Johnson dismissed Lord North with the words "He fills a chair, with a mind as narrow as the neck of a vinegar-cruet." Quoted by Paul Johnson. *A History of the American People.* 116. 1997.
24. Jeremy Black. *Pitt the Elder.* 256. 1992.

Revolution. Accordingly, they replaced three-year Parliaments with the Septennial Act of that year which established the normal life cycle of Parliaments for the next two centuries. The only serious exceptions were a reduced period on the death of the monarch (until 1867) and an extended term in times of abnormal crises such as world war. To the Tories the Act threatened a return to the long Parliaments of the previous century and at the time when the Act was passed Archibald Hutcheson outlined the arguments against it which Pitt and his supporters repeated at frequent intervals. Complaining of a potential for absolute power Hutcheson said:

"I believe it will not be denied that it is very possible for a ministry, by pensions and employments to some, and by the expectations raised in others, and by the corruption of electors and returning officers, to obtain a very great majority, entirely and blindly at their devotion even at the very first meeting of a Parliament, and that by a committee of elections and other proper helps, their party may daily increase and that such a Parliament may ... become themselves the tools of oppression in the hand of such a ministry."[25]

John Wilkes Attempts Reform

A more comprehensive proposal for the reform of the

---

25. *Parliamentary History.* [7] 343. (1716).

franchise than that of Chatham was contained in a motion John Wilkes put to the House of Commons on 21 March 1776. This asked for leave to bring in a Bill for "a just and equal representation of the people of England in Parliament". He told the House that the existing representation was insufficient, partial and unjust. Some decayed boroughs had in the distant past been disenfranchised but "what a happy fate", he said, remained with the boroughs of Gatton and Old Sarum (which had no residents) where "four respectable gentlemen represent their departed greatness as the knights at a coronation represent Aquitaine and Normandy"[26] (which were no longer ruled by the English king). In a foretaste of 1832 he would have disenfranchised the rotten boroughs, allowed their few electors to vote in the counties and given representation to rich, populous trading towns such as Sheffield, Birmingham, Manchester and Leeds.[27]

This went further than Dashwood's proposal some 30 years earlier and was the first time in the eighteenth century that Parliament had heard a detailed plea for a more democratic franchise. But the Commons continued to remain unmoved and the motion was rejected without a division. It was followed in 1780, however, by Major John Cartwright's pamphlet entitled *Take your Choice* which advocated universal male suffrage and annual parliaments. This was proclaimed to be the first written

---

26. *Ibid.* [18] 1288.
27. *Ibid.* 1295.

work since the seventeenth century Commonwealth to be published in support of parliamentary reform and its author came to be regarded as the "Father of the Reform Movement."

In an echo of the Commonwealth pamphleteers he wrote:

"Though a man should have neither lands, nor gold, nor herds, nor flocks; yet he may have parents and kindred, he may possess a wife and an offspring to be solicitous for. He hath also by birthright a property in the English constitution: which, if not unworthy such a blessing, will be more dear to him than would be many acres of the soil without it.

These are all great stakes to have at risk and we must have odd notions of justice if we do not allow that they give him an undoubted right to share in the choice of those trustees into whose keeping and protection they are to be committed."[28]

At this time annual Parliaments were believed to be a means of better controlling MPs and their patrons, all of whom would find the cost of frequent elections prohibitive. For this reason the demand was taken up by a great many county men of property in Yorkshire who felt that their representatives in the Commons were outvoted by nominees of borough patrons.[29] The Yorkshire

---

28. BL. *Add. MSS.* 27,810.
29. The Petition of the County of York. *Annual Register*. 338. (1780).

Association which they formed appealed to freeholders in other parts of the country to support them and in March 1780 twelve other counties joined it with a strong petition to Parliament calling for annual Parliaments and 100 more independent county MPs.

Although these demands were not met they strengthened the opposition to the government of Lord North who, with George III, was being held responsible for the rift with the American colonists and the British military disasters in the War of Independence. This led, on 6 April 1780, to John Dunning's famous resolution in the Commons, "that the influence of the Crown has increased, is increasing, and ought to be diminished" which was carried by 233 votes to 215.[30] Excitement in the country grew with the prospect of North's dismissal but he was saved by the eruption of the Gordon Riots in the summer of that year.

The Gordon Riots

On Friday, 2 June Lord George Gordon who was an ignorant young nobleman with a simple-minded hatred of Roman Catholics took to the House of Commons a petition praying for the repeal of the recently enacted Catholic Relief Act. He was joined by a crowd of some 40,000 people who blockaded the entrances to both Houses of Parliament. No member was allowed to enter until he had

---

30. *Parliamentary History.* [21] 380.

shouted, "No popery! No popery!" Several lords, MPs and bishops who declined to do so were attacked and injured. When the demonstrators were dispersed from the precincts of Parliament the crowds turned to pillaging a number of Roman Catholic churches. Saturday was fairly quiet but on the Sunday violent rioting broke out against which a terrified lord mayor and a fearful government took no action other than confining the troops to barracks. In consequence the district of Moorfields where many Catholics lived saw chapels and private houses looted and set on fire until the locality was gutted. The following day Smithfield suffered the same fate and the City was swiftly devastated.

Readers of Charles Dickens' novel, *Barnaby Rudge,* will recall its vivid description of the riots in which Newgate prison was stormed and destroyed and the houses of Mr Justice Cox, Sir John Fielding and Lord Mansfield burnt down. Much of London was now afire whilst the authorities continued to stand by, petrified. "In the darkness of the night," recalled the *Annual Register,*

"was one of the most dreadful spectacles this country has ever beheld ... at the same instant flames ascending and rolling in clouds from the King's Bench and Fleet prisons, from New Bridewell, from the tollgate on Blackfriars Bridge, from houses in every quarter of the town, and particularly from the bottom and middle of Holborn, where the conflagration was horrible beyond description ... Six-and-thirty fires all blazing at one time, and in different quarters of the city, were to be seen from one spot."[31]

The city lay paralysed at the mercy of "King Mob" for a week and by an ironic turn of fate order was restored only when John Wilkes, now the city chamberlain, ordered the lord mayor to deploy troops. The convulsion was over by 14 June although by then 290 people had been killed and many others injured. Some months later 25 looters were executed but Gordon was found not guilty of treason after being defended by Thomas Erskine. He subsequently converted to Judaism, was imprisoned for a libel on the Queen of France and died of gaol fever after five years in prison. Paradoxically, despite the inactivity of the government during the riots the violence caused opinion to swing back to the view that with Lord North as prime minister the country was in a safe pair of hands. The prospects for reform were not improved.

---

31. 261. (1788).

CHAPTER 3

Pitt the Younger

In the same year of 1780 the playwright Richard Brinsley Sheridan, soon to be MP for Stafford, joined the Westminster committee for electoral reform. This counted among its members John Wilkes and the colourful and brilliant statesman, Charles James Fox, the sitting MP for Westminster and chairman of the committee. Here was a potent mixture that was a foretaste of what was brewing in the country beneath the political surface.

The Westminster Committee

Sheridan drew up the committee's manifesto which called for annual elections, a much wider franchise and equal electoral districts. Indeed, it contained the same six points as would the People's Charter of 1837. It claimed that "nearly twelve hundred thousand" of the five million inhabitants of England and Wales would be entitled to vote if the franchise had remained as it was under Henry VI (1422-61), whereas "no more than two hundred and fourteen thousand are at present admitted to vote", ie, fewer than in the reign of George I. In illustration of the corruption that was prevalent it also pointed out that whereas 92 county members were returned by 130,000 voters, only 84,000 electors were represented by the 421 members who sat for cities, towns and universities.[1] This explosive manifesto was sent to other reform committees around the country where it slowly fermented.

However, when the Duke of Richmond, also in 1780 and amidst the turmoil of the Gordon Riots, introduced a sweeping measure of parliamentary reform in the House of Lords it was defeated without a division.[2]

Perhaps this was not surprising since according to the historian, Lecky, the riots meant "no serious discussion was possible". During their violent course, "Pale, bruised, and agitated, with their wigs torn off, their hair dishevelled, their clothes torn and bespattered with mud, the peers of England sat listening to the frantic yells of the multitude who already thronged the lobbies."[3] Nevertheless, the lack of response by Parliament to calls for reform had been a continuing feature of the period. The riots merely confirmed in the aristocracy their fears of the anarchy that would ensue if the masses, whom Burke had called "the swinish multitude" and "the scum of the earth"[4] could control elections to Parliament.

1. BL. *Add. MSS.* 27,837 and 38,593.
2. *Parliamentary History.* [21] 671/88.
3. W.E.H. Lecky. *A History of England in the Eighteenth Century.* iv. 311. 1883.
4. *Thoughts on the Cause of the Present Discontents.* 1770.

Pitt Proposes Reform

Subsequently, Pitt the Younger was to develop - at least for a time - his father's critique of the royal influence on Parliament which an inadequate and corrupt franchise encouraged. In his maiden speech to the House of Commons in 1781 he advocated an improvement of the electoral system. Then, on 7 May 1782, just after the American colonists who initially had wanted only representation at Westminster finally defeated the British Army and secured their independence, he introduced a motion calling for a select committee on parliamentary reform. According to *The Morning Chronicle* "the avenues" to the House "were crowded; but few were fortunate enough to get admission to the gallery" which had to be closed an hour after it was opened.[5]

Pitt was aware of growing agitation for reform in the country as taxes rose and trade declined. He was also motivated by the belief that the power exercised by the crown, with the connivance of the aristocracy, had unbalanced the settlement of the Glorious Revolution. The solution lay in a moderate reform of Parliament. Speaking of members Pitt said "The representatives have ceased, in a degree, to be connected with the people. It is of the essence of the Constitution that the people should have a share in the government by the means of representation. The representation as it now stands is

---

5. 8 May 1782.

incomplete." Against all expectations built upon the outcome of earlier debates his motion was defeated by only 20 votes (161 to 141).[6]

What should not be overlooked is the profound impact the American demand for "no taxation without representation" had in Britain. Radical demands that all who paid taxes should have the right to vote grew apace and in some cases pointed out that even poor people paid taxes indirectly on many of the goods they bought.

Eleven days later Pitt attended a meeting of reform-minded MPs and representatives of reform societies at the *Thatched House Tavern* in London. Here a resolution in his handwriting was moved which declared: "That the motion of the Honourable William Pitt for the reform of Parliament having been defeated, it has become indispensably necessary that application should be made to Parliament by Petition from the collective body of the people in their respective districts, requesting a substantial reformation of the Commons House of Parliament."[7] The effect was considerable and during the following 12 months numerous petitions were indeed presented to Parliament from many parts of the country.

Encouraged by this, and refusing to accept defeat in the Commons, one year later to the day Pitt became more specific when he set down another motion. In his speech Pitt first eulogised the "glorious fabric" of the Constitution framed by the "wisdom of our renowned

---

6. *Parliamentary History.* [22] 1438.
7. *State Trials.* xxii. 493.

forefathers" and a form of government "so nearly allied to perfect freedom". But despite that "perfect freedom" he rejected utterly the suggestion which had been made that every man in the kingdom should have the vote. That he said, with curious logic, would make half the people slaves since those who voted for an unsuccessful candidate would not be represented in Parliament. He made no mention of the real half of the population who were women and were entirely unrepresented. Nor was he ready to disenfranchise the rotten boroughs since, like his father, he thought such a remedy would be worse than the disease. His brother Thomas did, however, give up his rotten borough of Old Sarum.

He then introduced three resolutions. The first was intended to secure measures for the prevention of bribery in elections - still at the time, and for long after, a public scandal. The second proposed that where the majority of voters in a borough were convicted of gross corruption, that borough should forfeit its right to return members and the non-corrupt minority should become county electors. How this would work in practice is not clear. The third proposal was to give additional members to the counties and the metropolis in order to strengthen the landed and wealthy interests against the patronage of the Hanoverian crown which he believed was also a public scandal.[8]

Despite the mildness of these proposals some discontented members of Pitt's own followers joined the

---

8. *Parliamentary History.* [23] 827/35.

Rockinghamite Whigs who, after losing office in 1766, had come together in opposing the policies of Bute and George III. They wanted to reduce the power of the crown by abolishing some of its offices and disqualifying some of its placemen from the franchise. They claimed to be the heirs of the Glorious Revolution (and were the lineal ancestors of the Whigs of the nineteenth century) but in seeking to return to office, now opposed Pitt and his reforms by abstaining from the vote. Perhaps also because he had moved from the general, which hurt nobody, to the particular, this time the majority against Pitt increased to 144 with Lord North seeing any reform at all as a serious danger to the Constitution.[9]

As far as he went Pitt was in earnest, and in correspondence with an attorney named John Frost he wrote that reform was essential for "the independence of Parliament and the liberty of the people.[10] This is in striking contrast to the special pleading of his Tory successors in 1831. But then they sensed the demise of their privileges as had the 144 who voted against Pitt's resolutions. Regrettably, his actions were also in contrast to his own behaviour in the coming years.

On 1 January 1785 *The Daily Universal Register*, three years later to become *The Times,* was launched by John Walter, a bankrupted Lloyd's underwriter turned printer. Twelve days later it published a letter from

---

9. *Ibid.* 847.
10. Letters to Frost produced by defence counsel, Thomas Erskine, at Frost's trial for treason in 1793. Cf. *State Trials.* xxiv. 472.

"Ignotus" which congratulated Pitt for supporting reform but urged him to declare that he was a *hearty friend* to reform and would not sit in a Cabinet opposed to it, otherwise he ran the risk of being thought to support reform privately whereas as a minister he was labouring to defeat it. Four weeks later a letter from an Andrew Marvel claimed that of the 558 members of the Commons only 131 were from the counties and that 42 of those were from Wales and Scotland.[11] To balance these views a letter from "Antiquus" was against reform. He said that one Bill of parliamentary reform had been consigned to oblivion and he hoped that every succeeding one would be too. Improvement and reform were not synonymous terms.[12] Two days later he wrote another, longer letter expanding his views and addressed it to William Pitt himself.[13]

Pitt's last attempt at moderate reform was in April 1785, by which time he had become first minister of the crown. His long speech was reported in full in *The Daily Universal Register*.[14] He suggested that 36 boroughs with small populations should, with the consent of their electors, have their franchises purchased from public funds and their 72 seats transferred to counties or towns with large populations. A million pounds were to be set aside to compensate the boroughmongers and property rights were to be respected. Hence there would be no

---

11. *The Daily Universal Register*, 3 February, p.1.
12. *Ibid.* 22 February, p.1.
13. 24 February, p.1.
14. 19 April, 1785, p.2.

compulsory disenfranchisement of the rotten boroughs but a voluntary transfer of the privileges of voting for representatives. The motion was opposed by Mr Powis who said that the transfer of franchise was an arbitrary attack on the liberty of the subject. People with property, he said, had an interest in the government of the country by whose laws the person was protected from injury and his life from being destroyed.

Defeat for Pitt this time was by 74 votes[15] which, in the light of his influential office, seems to suggest he made less effort than usual to see his aims achieved, perhaps having become more complacent about abuses which supported him in office. On the other hand the offer of compensation may have stuck in the throats of some MPs. In the country feelings were less squeamish and political fervour spilled out into the streets. Petitions for reform poured into Parliament from such cities as Birmingham, Durham and Sheffield. People were possibly encouraged by the example of the "new democracy" in North America, although in the United States property qualifications for voting were not abolished until 1837 and adult manhood suffrage was not introduced until 1850, in both cases for white males only who alone had the vote.

In 1786, a year after Pitt's latest defeat, Lord Sprey put forward a motion that he modestly suggested "required greater talents than he possessed". He said that representation was in a frail and corrupt situation and

---

15. *Parliamentary History.* [25] 438.

needed restoring to its ancient purity and efficiency. He deplored the fact that gentlemen had bestowed a borough upon another, in other words sold its voting rights, and wished to restore to the people a free choice in representation.[16]

Revolution in France

In March 1790 Henry Flood introduced into the Commons a Bill to strip each rotten borough of one of its MPs, give an additional hundred seats to the counties and extend the vote to resident householders. At the time English boroughs elected almost 73% of the House of Commons. Flood told the House that the revolution in France had made reform more necessary than ever. But there was a caveat. Whilst enfranchising tax-paying householders only would avoid the violent excesses that were occurring across the Channel, he saw the impoverished masses as a rabble who could not be trusted with the vote. Yet even with this concession to conservative thinking a clear majority of MPs were against Flood and he withdrew his motion without putting it to the vote.[17] However, some of the "impoverished rabble" attended a public meeting called by the "Friends to Parliamentary Reform" at the *Crown and Anchor* tavern in the Strand. There it was resolved unanimously that there should be a restoration

---

16. *The Daily Universal Register.* 19 May 1786, p.2.
17. *Parliamentary History.* [28] 452/79.

of the right of adequate representation and that those present would strenuously proceed towards the attainment of this objective.[18]

Then, in 1792, Charles Grey, the future Earl Grey, presented a petition from a newly-formed society called the "Friends of the People" which set out in detail the abuses by patronage they wanted dealt with.[19] The society was composed in the main of aristocratic Whig politicians who distrusted popular enthusiasm and it laid the basis for the Whig ministry of 1830. Its petition pointed out that 71 peers, together with the lords of the treasury, could directly nominate 90 members of the House of Commons and could secure the return of 77 more. Further, that 91 commoners could nominate 82 members and also secure the return of 57. Accordingly, 162 persons, together with the treasury, could effectively select 306 members - a substantial majority of the Commons. Indeed, no ministry lost a general election for over a century after 1714 and the Commons was kept obedient by ministerial placemen.[20] To rescue the franchise from such abuses the society demanded the restoration of the freedom of election, more equal representation of the people and more frequent Parliaments. At the time Parliaments sat for up to seven years, a period changed, as seen earlier, from three years by the Septennial Act of 1716.

18. *The Daily Universal Register.* 19 May 1790, p.1.
19. A full copy is to be found in the Appendix to W.N. Molesworth's *The History of the Reform Bill of 1832.* 1866.
20. Roy Porter. *England in the Eighteen Century.* 111. 1998.

Although the petition received the support in the Commons of the leading Whigs, namely Charles James Fox, Richard Brinsley Sheridan and Thomas Erskine it was opposed by Pitt, who had come to believe that the reformers wanted to subvert the Constitution. In fact, both reformers and their opponents appealed to the Constitution, each claiming that only they could save it from destruction by the other. In the result, the petition was rejected despite the society having pointed to the events in France as an example of what could happen when reform was delayed. The classic eighteenth century theory was put by Robert Jenkinson (afterwards Lord Liverpool and prime minister) when in 1793 he said, "We ought not to begin first by considering who ought to be the electors, and then who ought to be elected; but we ought to begin by considering who ought to be elected, and then constitute such persons electors as would be likely to produce the best elected."[21] Nevertheless, Grey was to return to the question of reform again in 1795 and 1797 although he continued to receive little support. However, he bided his time.

Repression

The interest in reform by both Pitt and many other members of Parliament had come to an abrupt end with the execution of the French king, Louis XVI, in January

---

21. *Parliamentary History.* xxx. 810.

1793 and the outbreak of war the following month. Instead, retrenchment and repression became the order of the day. As Henry Brougham, a future reforming lord chancellor, writing later in the *Edinburgh Review*, saw it, Pitt had "committed in his youth the sin of reform; - now he had his atonement to make for an offence only pardonable on the score of that heedless and tender age - only to be expiated by the most glaring proofs of amendment." To this end, Brougham claimed, he had turned to corruption and power.[22]

The reaction in both England and Scotland was the formation of a number of Corresponding Societies to work for franchise reform, some of which also propagated the radical ideas of Tom Paine whose *Rights of Man*, which advocated political rights and social reform, achieved an enormous popular following and impact. The three most influential of them in England were the Constitutional Society, the Society for Constitutional Information and the London Corresponding Society. That their members were drawn from different circles of society is revealed by their subscription rates. Five guineas a year was the cost of joining the first; one to five guineas to gain admission to the second and one penny a week for the last (4s.4d a year). Among them they enjoyed widespread support which caused the government and the propertied classes to panic in the belief that a violent social upheaval was imminent.

As a consequence, and by way of a rehearsal for what

---

22. p.120 (1810).

was planned in England, trials were successfully prosecuted in Scotland in 1793 before the ferocious Lord Braxfield upon whom Robert Louis Stevenson based his *Weir of Hermiston*. Then, in 1794, the decent and law-abiding shoe-maker Thomas Hardy, who was secretary of the London Corresponding Society, John Horne Tooke, a philologist, and ten other men were charged with high treason, despite their only crime being to call a convention to seek means of securing reform of the franchise. Although they were still awaiting trial, Pitt announced publicly the discovery of an allegedly huge revolutionary plot and he played an active role in preparing the prosecutions. He also took to the House of Commons three large sealed bags of captured documents and a message from the king requiring the enactment of a Special Powers Act. That the lives of the accused were at risk was reinforced when the Whig-turned-Tory Edmund Burke accused the prisoners of being assassins and urged that the disease of the body politic demanded the "critical terrors of the cautery and the knife."[23]

During the trial of Hardy which commenced at the Old Bailey on 28 October[24] his indomitable counsel, Thomas Erskine, pointed out to the jury that the London Corresponding Society was a body of moderate men and had, in fact, merely adopted the doctrines of Pitt the Elder. Not only that but the prime minister had himself once been a reformer like his father before him, and also

23. Thomas Hardy. *Memoir*. 42/3. 1832.
24. 24 *State Trials*. 199. 1818.

like Hardy. After hearing all the evidence, and an electrifying closing address by Erskine, the jury had no hesitation in finding Hardy not guilty.[25] The London crowds went delirious with joy.

When Horne Tooke was next brought to trial on the same charge he enjoyed the irony and pleasure of issuing a subpoena to Pitt requiring him to give evidence. On oath in the witness box, the prime minister at first descended to being what has become known as economical with the truth and denied having attended meetings in the past to press for reform despite knowing that Horne Tooke had been present at some of them. Erskine then invited Sheridan into the witness box where he gave detailed descriptions of such meetings including that at the *Thatched House Tavern* in London on 18 May 1782. Re-called, Pitt reluctantly remembered that he had at times attended meetings composed of delegates to recommend parliamentary reform.

This admission virtually destroyed the prosecution case that delegate meetings to advocate reform were merely a device to cloak the organising of treasonable insurrection. Like Hardy, Horne Tooke was acquitted by the jury and after one more unsuccessful prosecution the government had to scrap 800 warrants of arrest which had been prepared for immediate use following the anticipated convictions.

Historians have described the full picture of this

---

25. For a biography of Erskine see John Hostettler. *Thomas Erskine and Trial by Jury.* 1996.

period of repression as a "reign of terror" and Macaulay wrote, "In Pitt's domestic policy there was at this time assuredly no want of vigour. While he offered to French Jacobins a resistance so feeble that it only encouraged the evil which he wished to suppress, he put down English Jacobinism with a strong hand ... It was hardly safe for a republican to avow his political creed over his beefsteak and his bottle of port at a chophouse ... He [Pitt] was all feebleness and languor in his conflict with the foreign enemy who was really to be dreaded, and reserved all his energy and resolution for the domestic enemy who might safely have been despised."[26]

In spite of the acquittals of the defendants in these trials general repression took on a new intensity with the London Corresponding Society and many other organisations, including trade unions, being declared illegal. Nevertheless, Charles Grey made a fresh endeavour to bring in a Bill "to amend and regulate the election of members to serve in the House of Commons" with every borough householder being given the vote and triennial Parliaments. But in such a repressive climate, with revolt looming in Ireland and with the naval mutinies at the Nore and Spithead, he suffered a decisive defeat when his Bill was rejected by 256 votes to 91 on 26 May 1797.[27] As was intended by the majority of MPs, the demand for reform was largely stifled for decades to come.

---

26. *A History of England in the Eighteenth Century.* Folio Society edn. 198/9. 1980.
27. *Parliamentary History.* [33] 649/50.

CHAPTER 4

A New Century

Wellington's victory at Waterloo and the end of the war against Napoleon in 1815 were hailed with relief throughout a war-weary Britain. Unfortunately the long-awaited fruits of peace soon turned sour.

Post-war Distress

A return to peacetime conditions produced its own problems. To general dismay both exports and prices started to fall rapidly. As a result investment on the land and in industry also fell and there was a catastrophic drop in wages. Unemployment became rife, particularly for thousands of demobilised soldiers and sailors. The corn laws, enacted unexpectedly in a mood of panic following Napoleon's escape from Elba (and with Parliament defended from menacing crowds by troops) exacerbated the situation by assisting the landed proprietors at the expense of other interests in the nation. No wheat at all was to be brought into Great Britain from abroad until the price of local wheat rose above 80 shillings a quarter. In 1812 the price had been 65s.7d. but by 1817 it had risen to 96s.11d. Starvation threatened the poor and food riots were a common sight in many parts of the country. An expected return to the comparative prosperity of the early years of the Industrial Revolution failed to materialise.

Instead of a golden age of prosperity for the victors a large section of the population groaned under the burden of serious distress and a further tightening of the screw of repression aimed at keeping the lid on the consequent despair and growth of class antagonism. There was also a considerable agitation among the growing working class for reform of the franchise as a means of improving their quality of life. For the country's rulers the "enemy" at home came to replace the bogeyman abroad. As long as five years earlier the perceptive *Edinburgh Review* had forewarned of violent class conflicts and its fears were about to be realised.

In 1816, Major John Cartwright, who had campaigned diligently for reform since 1776, began a significant campaign of petitioning for reform organised around both the middle class Hampden Clubs and the radical press. According to William Cobbett in his *Political Register* petitions for reform had been signed by more than half a million men.[1] And, Brougham told the Commons that "the table of this House groans with petitions ... Severe distress is the real cause of this agitation."[2]

The following table taken from *Hansard*[3] shows the dramatic increase in petitions to the House of Commons

---

1. 17 January 1817, p.39.
2. *Hansard.* [35] 366.
3. *Ibid.*, third series. [5] 335.

between 1785 and 1815, that is even before Cartwright's campaign commenced:

			Ann. average
In the five years ended	1789 ...	880 petitions	176
In the five years ended	1805 ...	1,026 petitions	205
In the five years ended	1815 ...	4,498 petitions	900

The aim of the petitioners was reform through annual Parliaments, universal (male) suffrage and the secret ballot (with none of which did Brougham agree)[4] in order to destroy the corruption of boroughmongers and make the House of Commons independent of the aristocracy and landowners. The demand for annual elections, which was to survive into the Chartist movement in the mid-nineteenth century, sounds strange to modern ears. But it made more sense in earlier times when it was believed that MPs would not so readily align themselves with a corrupt Court if they had to seek re-election every year. Cartwright's campaign set alarm bells ringing and the *Quarterly Review* wrote of reform as "this endemic moral malady of this distempered age."[5]

---

4. At this time Brougham was distancing himself from radicals such as Cobbett and "Orator" Hunt, declaring in May 1815 that the English Constitution, despite one or two blemishes which needed removing, had never been in a better state. See Robert Stewart. *Henry Brougham - His Public Career 1778-1868.* 114/5. 1986.
5. 552 (January, 1817).

The Working Class Respond

However, it cannot be denied that the reformers did not have the mass support they sought and the government, faced with a tide of action from the unemployed, refused to adopt conciliatory measures and instead tightened its grip. Yet so serious were the conditions allowed to become that even the ever more severe repression by a blinkered and savage government could only stimulate responses that were sometimes peaceful but at other times violent. The following are three examples of action taken by working men in 1817.

In the first, a group of miners decided to go to Carlton House in London, where the Prince Regent had his home, with two carts of coal. They wanted to impress upon the prince the misery of their situation and ask him to do something for their relief. But the opulent "Prince of Pleasure", although inclined towards the Whigs, was beyond both reach and compassion for working men with whose lives and suffering he had no contact.

Nonetheless, in Manchester a group of starving, unemployed handloom weavers decided they would walk to London with petitions asking the prince and Parliament to introduce a measure of franchise reform. Each man took a blanket and some food with him for their night-time rests in churches at stopping places on the journey where they hoped to gather support. This was the historic "March of the Blanketeers" - a forerunner of the hunger marches of the 1930s. Instead of the march inducing in the prince or the authorities an understanding of their plight, as the men naively expected, their leaders were arrested by soldiers and imprisoned for five months without trial.[6]

An even more tragic incident occurred in Derbyshire. There, a small band of men led by unemployed framework knitter, Jeremiah Brandreth, were incited by Lord Sidmouth, the home secretary's nationally notorious spy and *agent provocateur* W.J. Richards, known to history as "Oliver", to attempt a march on Nottingham from the village of Pentrith as part of an alleged general uprising. En route they met a small party of soldiers sent to intercept them. Far from engaging in fighting they at once fled and most of them were captured. Thirty-five of these hunger-induced marchers were tried for high treason of whom 23 were found guilty. Three of them, including Brandreth, were hanged and *beheaded*, 11 were transported for life and three for 14 years. The remainder were imprisoned for various terms. The executions caused considerable distress among eye-witnesses, including the poet Shelley who wrote indignantly about it.[7] Professor Radzinowicz, after quoting dreadful accounts from those present, says that, "This painful affair - inspired by the machinations of Oliver - constitutes one of the most tragic political trials in the annals of English justice."[8] As if that were not sufficient as an example to other working men of what awaited any attempts at action, *habeas corpus*

---

6. See PRO. HO. 42.172 for lists of the arrested men and their occupations.
7. *We pity the plumage, but forget the dying bird.* Prose Works. ii. 97. 1880.
8. *A History of English Criminal Law.* i. 226/7. 1974.

was suspended and Sidmouth's "Gagging Bills", similar to the repressive legislation of Pitt in the 1790s, were enacted. These restricted the right of public meeting and banned both petitions to Parliament (which was an ancient right) and the election of delegates to reforming clubs. The Bills were extended two years later by the even more ferocious "Six Acts" which will be described shortly.

One fall out from the coercion was that William Cobbett began to voice sentiments similar to those of Thomas Jefferson in America. He wrote that the right to resist oppression by force "is distinctly claimed and established by the law and usages of England. I do not say, that the right ought to be now exercised at all ... I say, therefore, upon this point, what JUDGE BLACKSTONE says: and that is, that the right to resist oppression always exists, but *that those who compose the nation at any given time must be left to judge for themselves when oppression has arrived at a pitch to justify the exercise of such right.*" And what, he asked, "did Brandreth do more than was done by the Whigs at the Revolution?"[9]

It was about this time that a women's suffrage movement began to stir and express itself. At a reform meeting in Yorkshire, addressed by Samuel Bamford, the women present were invited to take part in the vote on the resolution that was proposed. After this the participation of women in not only votes but also

---

9. *Political Register.* 4 April, 6 and 20 June, 26 December 1818.

discussions at such meetings became more general.[10] And, in 1818, as reported by the *Annual Register*, "An entirely novel and truly portentous circumstance was the formation of a Female Reform Society at Blackburn, near Manchester, from which circular letters were issued, inviting the wives and daughters of workmen in different branches of manufacture to form sister societies, for the purpose of co-operating with the men, and of instilling into the minds of their children 'a deep-rooted hatred of our tyrannical rulers'." A deputation from this society attended a Blackburn reform meeting, and, "mounting the scaffold" (ie, platform) "presented a cap of liberty and an address to the assembly. The example of these females was successfully recommended to imitation by the orators of other meetings."[11]

Sir Francis Burdett

It was not until 1819, following a general election in which Lord Liverpool's Tory government was returned to power, that the question of reform was again brought before the House of Commons. Liverpool's Cabinet of 14 contained eight peers and six members of the Commons only one of whom, George Canning, had contested a large constituency (Liverpool with 2,600 voters) that made him responsible to his electors and not a patron. Little wonder

---

10. Julius West. *A History of the Chartist Movement*. 36. 1920.
11. *Annual Register*. 104. 1819.

such a government was hostile to parliamentary reform. So unpopular in the country at large were the victors in the election that Disraeli thought it was at this point that the Whig leaders decided that the existing tiny and largely corrupt electorate could never give them a majority, and so turned their sights towards reform.[12] If this is so their future reforming zeal was scarcely altruistic. But then that is hardly surprising in the world of politics and objectively their response is what matters.

The persistent and consistent people for change were the Radicals and on 1 July of the same year, the long-standing reformer Sir Francis Burdett, a wealthy baronet and the Radical member for Westminster, moved in the Commons "That early in the next session of Parliament, this House will take into its most serious consideration the state of the representation." He said he could fear nothing from pursuing to its utmost extent the ancient and recognised common law maxim - which he called the cornerstone of the edifice of our liberties - "that the people of England have a property in their own goods, which is not to be taken from them without their own consent; in other words, that they are not constitutionally liable to be taxed without their own consent, expressed by a full, free and fair representation in Parliament. This is my principle, upon this I stand as upon a rock, from which I think it impossible to be moved."[13]

---

12. *Coningsby,* book ii. c. i. p.64. 1982 edn.
13. *Hansard.* [40] 1440/67.

The essayist, Charles Lamb, seconded the motion saying that he wished to see the borough franchise purged of its corruption, the elective system extended to populous places where it did not then exist and triennial Parliaments restored.[14] But the Tories continued to insist that Parliament represented the people regardless of whether they had the vote because, they said, members had their interests at heart without slavishly responding to their wishes. This was a repeat of the much vaunted theme of "virtual representation" we have noticed in the past and which was later to be regurgitated again to deny the vote to women. Deep down, Tory opinion agreed with Burke when he declared that, "The sovereignty of the people is the most false, wicked and mischievous doctrine that ever could be preached to them ... The moment that equality and the sovereignty of the people is (*sic*) adopted as the rule of government, property will be at an end and religion, morality and law, which grew out of property will fall with it."[15] The possession of property, it was thought, produced the best voters and the best MPs and kept intact the Constitution. The alternative was anarchy. It is not surprising, therefore, that Burdett's motion was rejected by 153 Ayes to 58 Noes.

Continued frustration of reformers' demands led to some curious responses. For example, in Birmingham, on 12 July 1819, a meeting of 15,000 people resolved that they should no longer wait for representation to be

---

14. *Ibid.* 1467/74.
15. *Parliamentary History.* [30] 554/5.

granted to them. Instead, they there and then elected two members for the town, Major Cartwright and Sir Charles Wolseley, to be "legislatory attorneys for the unrepresented". Sir Charles accepted his election and said he would claim a seat in the Commons![16] He was promptly arrested for his pains.

Peterloo

In Manchester, the seasoned radical campaigner, Henry "Orator" Hunt, persuaded the reformers not to follow the example of Birmingham in an election procedure which had been declared illegal by Lord Sidmouth. Instead it was decided to call a mass meeting to express the strength of public feeling for reform. On 16 August 1819 the meeting was held in St Peter's Field then on the outskirts of the town on the site where the Free-Trade Hall was later built. Huge crowds, estimated at 60,000, flocked to the scene to hear the famous Hunt speak. Flags bore the inscriptions - "Parliaments Annual" and "Suffrage Universal". The carnival atmosphere and the presence of many women and children testify to the peaceful nature of the gathering. There was no disorder. But the magistrates, who had brought in special constables, soldiers and armed yeomen, either panicked or acted to a pre-conceived plan. Whatever the case they ordered the latter to arrest Hunt who was subsequently

---

16. W.N. Molesworth. *The History of the Reform Bill of 1832.* 20. 1866.

sentenced to two years' imprisonment. (In 1830 he was to be elected as MP for Preston.) In the main the yeomen were anti-reform manufacturers, merchants, publicans and shopkeepers. In attempting to reach Hunt through the dense throng they drew their sabres and were joined by a troop of Hussars, although the soldiers remained far more restrained than the yeomen. Violence erupted. The ensuing massacre left 11 dead on the field (including two women) and over 400 injured. Of those wounded, 161 received sabre wounds and the remainder were caught by the crush and the horses' hooves. More than a hundred of them were women and girls.

Eye-witness Samuel Bamford, a Lancashire weaver, painted a vivid picture of the outcome of the charge:

"In 10 minutes ... the field was an open and almost deserted space ... The hustings remained, with a few broken and hewed flag-staves erect, and a torn and gashed banner or two drooping; whilst over the whole field were strewed caps, bonnets, hats shawls, and shoes, and other parts of male and female dress, trampled, torn, and bloody. The yeomanry had dismounted - some were easing their horses' girths, others adjusting their accoutrements, and some were wiping their sabres."[17]

Was the carnage premeditated? Probably we shall never know. But it was at least reckless to use the ill-disciplined

17. *Passages in the Life of a Radical.* 157. 1841.

yeomanry when regular disciplined troops were available. And Sidmouth was quick to congratulate the magistrates and yeomanry "for their prompt, decisive, and efficient measures for the preservation of the public peace", which in reality they destroyed. Why was any force deployed at a carnival-type peaceful meeting? The government refused out of hand to hold a parliamentary inquiry and Eldon, the lord chancellor, declared that the meeting was an overt act of treason. Not to be outdone, two weeks later an outwardly Christian clerical magistrate at Peterloo used his position on the bench to tell an accused, "I believe you are a downright blackguard reformer. Some of you reformers ought to be hanged, and some of you are sure to be hanged - the rope is already round your necks."[18] He was rewarded with the £2,000 living at Rochdale. By contrast, Lord Fitzwilliam, who protested at the massacre, was dismissed from his lord-lieutenancy. Everywhere Sidmouth's spies and *agents provocateurs* were at work and the bloodstained home secretary is remembered today from Shelley's poem, *The Mask of Anarchy:*

Clothed with the Bible, as with light,
And the shadows of the night,
Like Sidmouth, next, Hypocrisy
On a crocodile rode by.[19]

---

18. *The Times,* 27 September 1819.
19. Shelley. *Poetical Works.* 338. 1968 edn. Written on the occasion of the Peterloo Massacre.

One thing is certain. Reports of the bloody scenes remained alive in many memories and kept the torch of reform burning despite the continuing repression exemplified by the "Savage" Parliament's draconian "Six Acts" passed in November 1819. These gave magistrates fresh powers to convict political opponents of the government summarily without the delays involved in prosecutions at assizes. They were authorised to secure searches of private houses as well as places of public resort, to confiscate weapons, to suppress all drilling and training in the use of arms (which was sound policy) and to close any meeting they chose. Penalties against allegedly blasphemous and seditious publications were strengthened and the heavy newspaper tax was extended to all periodical journals. These were measures of alarmed ministers whose resources for maintaining law and order were minimal and who were still concerned by memories of the Terror of the French Revolution. They were not generally seen as directly responsible for the economic plight of the country but as responding to events, not causing them. Accordingly, such measures enjoyed considerable support among the property-owning and middle classes in towns and country districts remote from the large factory and mining areas. Consequently the measures were largely successful for a time although the delay in introducing reforms that these produced only heightened the bitterness and determination that came later.

By suppressing freedom of expression these Acts, alongside the example of Peterloo, dampened action for reform. At all costs the reformers wanted to avoid violence which they knew would hinder their cause. What is surprising therefore, is that the reform-minded Charles Grey wrote to a friend that the popular party, or "the Mob", wanted not reform but revolution, adding that "if a convulsion follows their attempts to work upon the minds of the people, inflamed as they are by distress, for which your Reform would afford a very inadequate remedy, I shall not precede you many months on the scaffold."[20] Ugly memories of the French Terror continued to haunt both the Tory and Whig aristocrats.

In reality, the reformers were anxious to prevent any action that might lead to further violence by the authorities. But the conclusion Grey drew, and which remained with him when he fathered the Reform Bill of 1831, was that, "My line must therefore be a line of moderate and cautious policy and of gradual improvement formed on those Whig principles, which will not allow me to submit to an invasion of popular rights because bad men have abused them, but will not allow me either to give any countenance or support to them or their proceedings."[21]

Whig Pressure

On 30 October 1819 Lord Cloncurry wrote in a letter to

---

20. BL. *Add. MSS.* 30,109. f. 57.
21. *Ibid.*

The Times in which he stated that the people of Ireland were also entitled to full, fair and adequate representation in the House of Commons without religious or other disqualification other than infancy, insanity or criminality.[22] Then, towards the end of the year, on 14 December, Lord John Russell rose in the Commons to present yet another motion for parliamentary reform. At this time he was 27 years old and, although in poor health, he would not be deterred from advocating moderate reform. He charged that opponents of reform were willing that the fabric of the Constitution, "like the temples of the gods of Rome in her last days of empire, should remain covered with cobwebs and falling to ruin." On the other hand, saying he was an enemy of extensive reform, he followed Grey's example when he claimed that the audacious champions of *radical* reform were no better and desired "to apply a firebrand to a magnificent edifice and sanctuary in order to raise their names from obscurity to fame."

On his first point he said that he wished, with moderation, to draw the attention of the House to the unrepresented towns, many of which had risen into places of great commercial wealth and importance whilst others which enjoyed the franchise had sunk into decay and become unfit to enjoy the privilege of sending representatives. Manchester, which in 1778 had only 23,000 inhabitants, now had 110,000. Leeds had 17,117 in 1775, and by 1811, 62,534. In 1700 Birmingham had

---

22. p.2.

15,032; in 1811, 85,753. The result was that in some cases the House did not represent the people. He then moved resolutions similar to those of Pitt in 1783.[23]

Notwithstanding the restraint of his motion he withdrew it on the suggestion of the foreign secretary, Viscount Castlereagh, who said he feared it would cause "discontent out of doors". Fortunately for reform Russell's resolve stiffened later but only under intense pressure from the people, whom Burke, after he defected from the Whigs, described as "the swinish multitude".

The Trial of Queen Caroline

In 1785 the Prince of Wales, whilst living a life of luxury and debauchery, had secretly married the Roman Catholic, Mrs Fitzherbert, contrary to the Act of Settlement of 1701 which disabled Catholics from the succession to the crown and incapacitated any future monarch who married a Roman Catholic. Thereafter the marriage was kept a closely guarded secret. Ten years later his huge debts were paid and his income increased by about £40,000 a year on his promise to the worried king and the government that he would marry Princess Caroline of Brunswick on whom he had never set eyes. In fact she was extremely slovenly and the prince hated her from the first moment he saw her. Indeed, the feeling was mutual but the prince was considered to have behaved

---

23. *Hansard.* [41] 1091/1107.

the worse when a year after his bigamous marriage to her he sent Caroline and their few-months-old baby, Princess Charlotte, to live apart from him. As a result the public began to sympathise with their future queen.

In 1806 the prince forced the government to agree to an inquiry into her conduct, known as "the Delicate Investigation". After the inquiry was completed and published Caroline's reputation was damaged but the serious charges against her of misbehaviour were not proved. When the prince became regent and dropped his Whig friends in 1810 he found that in a tit-for-tat mood they were now more disposed to take Caroline's part when she demanded to have her honour redeemed and take her lawful place beside her husband. Forcefully separated from Princess Charlotte she now became the darling of the people. At this point Henry Brougham was engaged to act as her chief legal adviser. He used the opportunity to play politics and his devious behind-the-scenes manoeuvres caused consternation among his colleagues. These were unknown to the general public, however, and his fame grew apace.

Ultimately, suffering from great indignities at the hands of the prince, Caroline left England for the continent on 14 August 1814. Whilst she was residing in Italy her enemies collected a dossier against her alleging misconduct which in 1819 was handed to the prince who, seizing his opportunity, resolved to divorce her. When he became king, as George IV, on the death of his father on 29 January 1820 he sent the dossier to both Houses of Parliament and ordered the drawing up of a Bill of Pains and Penalties as a means to prosecute the queen for adultery. This contained a clause to deprive Caroline of her title of queen and another to annul her marriage to the king. She, in response, appointed Brougham as her attorney-general.

The trial before the House of Lords was set for 17 August 1820. By then London was in a frenzy of delirious excitement and support for the queen with huge crowds thronging the streets with flaring torches and filling craft on the river Thames. Shouts of "The Queen! The Queen!" rang out everywhere. Here was an opportunity to oppose the king and the government. In ale-houses toasts to the health of the king's enemies were drunk by soldiers and the government began to fear bloody revolution. Viscount Castlereagh, who lived next door to the house in St James's where the queen resided during the trial, moved out all his belongings and had his house shuttered for the duration.

The case was purely a political act and there was no necessity to prove guilt beyond reasonable doubt as in a criminal trial. Brougham made a brilliant opening speech and his peroration pleading for mercy and justice for the queen had peers in tears. At one point he audaciously took the initiative by obliquely suggesting that he held in reserve the secret of the king's secret marriage to Mrs Fitzherbert, the disclosure of which would have resulted in his abdication. He also proceeded to tear to shreds the flimsy evidence of many prosecution witnesses.

The nation rocked with laughter when witnesses from Italy, and in particular a formerly trusted servant of the queen named Theodore Majocchi, constantly replied to Brougham's penetrating questions with the words, *Querto non mi ricordo* (I don't remember). Referred to by *The Times* as "Signor Non Ricordo", Majocchi, and other witnesses who joined in the refrain, lost all credibility. Reluctantly, the government recognised that it was defeated and announced that it would not send the Bill to the Commons.

After her acquittal the queen travelled in triumph to her home on the banks of the Thames near Hammersmith amidst tumultuous throngs of excited people. Many houses on the route were illuminated with candles, glimmering gaslights, huge initials "CR", stars and imperial crowns. Such scenes of intense rejoicing lasted several days with an estimated one million people expressing spontaneous joy. An unrepentant king refused to allow the queen to attend his coronation in Westminster Abbey where she was rudely turned back at the door. Then Caroline died unexpectedly on 7 August 1821. Accompanied by Brougham her body was conveyed to Germany where she was buried in the family vault in her native Brunswick.

CHAPTER 5

Approaching Reform

Henry Brougham

Brougham, who was born in Edinburgh in 1778, was a fearless and energetic advocate, although not entirely effective before a jury. He was a great orator, debater and organiser. His interest in, and knowledge of, law, literature and science were deep and he had boundless energy. On the other hand, he was often impulsive, excitable, wayward and capricious. But, despite his failings he was always a wholehearted supporter of the causes of education, law reform, anti-slavery, Catholic emancipation, a free press and, not least, moderate parliamentary reform. As we shall see, he was to play a vital role in bringing about and securing the passage of the Reform Act of 1832.

In one of his last public appearances, at a dinner in the Middle Temple in 1864 when he was 86 years of age, he referred to his speech on behalf of Queen Caroline and said that it was the duty of an advocate "to reckon everything subordinate to the interests of his client". This earned him a rebuke from the younger but less memorable lord chief justice, Lord Cockburn, who replied that the arms which the advocate wielded were those of a warrior not of the assassin. The incident led the biographer of Victorian Chancellors, J.B. Atlay, to comment, "Poor Old Brougham! That was the light in which [was] regarded the man who rescued a Queen of England from the very jaws of destruction, who struck the fetters from the slave, who carried the Reform Bill in the teeth of King and Peers."[1]

Moderate Reform

Shortly before the death of Queen Caroline a new proposal for franchise reform had been made on 17 April 1821. John George Lambton (son-in-law of Earl Grey and afterwards Lord Durham) moved that the balance of the Constitution be restored with triennial Parliaments and the extension of the franchise to all persons possessing property, however small in value, who contributed to taxation. He also included the abolition of rotten boroughs.[2] This was reform with a vengeance but it failed to stir those MPs who were indifferent to the issues. Nevertheless, in spite of a thin attendance the debate continued for two days at the end of which the proposal was defeated by 55 votes to 43.

A few days later, on 9 May, Lord John Russell, by now the leading Whig advocate of moderate reform, concerned, he said, at the growing threat to the Constitution,

---

1. J.B. Atlay. *The Victorian Chancellors.* i. 339. 1906.
2. *Hansard*, new series [5] 359/85.

returned to the fray with a more specific plan.[3] First, however, as proof of the effect a corrupt system of bribery produced, he related an anecdote told to him by the playwright and MP Richard Brinsley Sheridan who had died in 1816. During an election, he said, Sheridan fell into conversation with one of the voters. "I am," he told him, "a friend to reform.". "I am glad you are for reform," observed the voter; "so am I - but some gentlemen behave so ill, they will not give their poor voters a single guinea" (ie, a bribe) "and I think *that* should be reformed." Having got this off his chest Russell then put forward four resolutions:

"First, that there was gross and illegal bribery and corruption in elections which might lead to the destruction of the constitution of Parliament.

Secondly, to strengthen the connection between the people and MPs, those places that had greatly increased in wealth and population but were not adequately represented should be granted the franchise.

Thirdly, a select committee should be appointed to consider which additional constituencies should be created and the best means of doing so.

Fourthly, the committee should also decide how to proceed against boroughs charged with notorious bribery and corruption in order to disable those found guilty."

---

3.   *Ibid.* 604/22.

It is noteworthy that whilst Russell's proposals were desirable in themselves he was not advocating a lowering of the property qualification which would have considerably extended the franchise. Still oblivious to the rising tide of feeling in the country, not one leading Whig or Tory took part in the debate and the first resolution was defeated by 155 votes to 124. The other resolutions were then negatived without a division. Yet the substantial minority voting figures on the first resolution themselves exposed both the extent and the awareness of the corruption.

"Nightingale Notes"

It is not surprising, therefore, that the following year saw petitions for reform flowing into Parliament from a number of towns and from the counties of Middlesex, Cornwall, Surrey, Devon, Cambridge, Bedford, Norfolk and Suffolk. In response, Russell once more raised the issue in the Commons, having by now served, he said, an apprenticeship in the cause of reform. He urged that although the condition of the people had altered materially over time the House had not adapted to meet their needs. On the contrary, it had followed the opposite tendency. The wealth, manufactures and resources of the country and of the people had increased considerably as, in consequence, had the importance of the middle classes of society. Knowledge had also advanced substantially. One publisher alone had sold five million volumes in one year and given constant employment to 250 printers and bookbinders. Furthermore, there were over 2,000 circulating libraries and book clubs in the country. The interest in political matters was shown by the sale in the country of 23,600,000 copies of newspapers in the previous year.

Any government, he continued, which ignored such advances must soon come to final ruin. Yet a majority of the members of the Commons were returned by fewer than 8,000 electors. In England, 140 boroughs which each had fewer than 5,000 inhabitants returned 280 members - a majority of the House. Forty boroughs contained from 3-5,000 persons and 100 fewer than 3,000 each. Moreover, even in larger boroughs there were often few voters. In Plymouth, for instance, which in the reign of Charles II had 7,000 inhabitants of whom 300 had the vote, there were now 60,000 persons of whom only 200 had the vote. And of the 44 members returned for Cornwall only five were natives of that county. It was time for each of the smaller boroughs to return one member only instead of two. He then outlined in detail the abuses of the franchise in the boroughs and the widespread use of bribery and corruption which, he said, were well-known. The return of many members was procured only by direct bribery with money.

"We cannot," Russell exclaimed, "confine liberty in this country to one class of men: we cannot erect here a senate of Venice, by which a small part of the community is enabled to lord it over the majority; we cannot in this land, and at this time make liberty the inheritance of a *caste.* It is the nature of English liberty, that her nightingale notes should never be heard from within the bars and gratings of a cage; to preserve anything of the grace and sweetness, they must have something of the wildness of freedom."[4]

The Tory spokesman and future short-term premier, George Canning was highly regarded as a liberal but not in regard to the franchise where he was a strong opponent of any change. Dismissing the strength and appeal of Russell's case he complained that, "the plan is little more than to make an addition of 100 members to this House, to be returned by the counties and larger towns; and to open the way for this augmentation by depriving each of the smaller boroughs of one half of the elective franchise which they now enjoy."

Failing to see the wood for the trees, he said he could not accept Russell's suggestion that Pitt would have approved of the plan since, although Pitt would have added 100 members to the House, there would have been no forcible abolitions. Where a decayed borough was *willing to sell* its right of franchise it would have been *purchased* from the fund of £1,000,000 Pitt had proposed to establish for the purpose. Pitt, he added, would have avoided coercion and protected vested interests - which was no doubt true. Russell's plan was "dangerous and violent" and would never satisfy genuine reformers. He denied that there was any defect in the Constitution of the House that required the adoption of "so fearful an

---

4.   *Ibid.* [7[51/88.

experiment". Canning spoke at considerable length and his influence on members was immense, although it is noteworthy that he never again spoke on reform. His efforts on this occasion were rewarded, however, when the Commons voted against Russell by a decisive 269 votes to 164.[5] Nevertheless, the minority was the highest Commons vote in favour of reform since Pitt's last attempt in 1785.

The question was not raised again in Parliament for another four years when, with the country's banking system in deep crisis and following a succession of bad harvests, civil unrest became widespread and the demand for electoral reform intensified. On 27 April 1826, it was Lord John Russell who once more made the running. A new motion from him claimed in general terms that the state of representation of the people in Parliament required the most serious consideration of the House.[6] Although he again spoke at length his arguments were largely the same as on earlier occasions and once more he was defeated. This time it was by an even more commanding majority of 247 votes to 123.

Troubled Tories

But changes were coming. Lord Liverpool's Tory government had lasted from June 1812 to April 1827,

---

5. *Ibid.* 106/36.
6. *Ibid.* [15] 663.

buttressed by the unreformed electoral system. It was succeeded by that of George Canning, once a devoted Whig[7] and now a Pittite Tory, who was to die five months later. With his "liberal" government there came a dramatic upset when the old guard Tories led by Wellington, Peel and Eldon refused to join his Cabinet and were replaced by three Whigs. Yet, despite this favourable turn of events for the Whigs, it was also during Canning's short term of office that Grey dismayed the Whig reformers by announcing in the House of Lords on 11 May 1827 that reform should not be made a key issue in forming an administration.[8] As if to reinforce Grey, the *Birmingham Journal* claimed that its unrepresented city did not need MPs as, "The advantage of sending representatives is merely theoretical and is surely attended with disorder."[9]

The weak Viscount Goderich followed Canning as prime minister and was himself succeeded, after his resignation four months later, by the more formidable Duke of Wellington. Yet soon afterwards the Tories suffered another debilitating blow when Palmerston and Melbourne left to join the now reviving Whig Party. Then, in 1829, the Tory government reluctantly granted Catholic Emancipation in order to avoid impending rebellion and civil war in Ireland. This meant that Roman Catholics would no longer be barred from sitting in the

---

7. See Dorothy Marshall. *The Rise of George Canning*. xiii and 26. 1938.
8. *Hansard*. [17] 732.
9. October 1829.

Westminster Parliament. As a consequence, Wellington in turn now lost more of his old guard as the worn fabric of the Tory Party was rent even further.

With the Tories reeling, another critical change came a year later when the movement for reform was stimulated by the peaceful French Revolution of 1830. This resulted in the flight of Charles X to England and his replacement by Louis Philippe of Orleans, the "Citizen-King" who was accepted on condition he ruled as a constitutional monarch. Charles had sparked off the revolution by issuing decrees abolishing the freedom of the press and incredibly reducing the franchise by three-quarters. "This is a revolution made by the industrious classes, and by the working part of those classes," proclaimed William Cobbett, "and will any man now be so impudent as to assert that these people are unworthy of being permitted to vote for representatives?[10] The response among the citizens of England was the widespread formation of strong political unions dedicated to the presentation of more petitions to Parliament for reform.

In both 1829 and 1830 the Marquis of Blandford moved for reform in the House of Commons. On the first occasion, on 2 June 1829, he proposed in two resolutions that since in decayed boroughs bribery was notorious the existence of such boroughs was prejudicial to the best interests of the country.[11] These resolutions were defeated

---

10. *Political Register.* 14. (7 August 1829).
11. *Hansard.* [21] 1672/9.

by a majority of 74. Then on 18 February 1830 he called for an extension of the right to vote to all taxed householders and a general franchise reform to restore to the people their rightful share in the legislation of the country.[12] However, largely because of suspicions of the personal motives of the marquis in attempting merely to discomfort the government, the motion secured little attention and was defeated by a majority of 113. One of his supporters in 1830 was Sir Francis Burdett who related to the House a personal electoral experience:

"I have gone, he said, through the whole process under the present system of representation, and a most ruinous one it has been. Early in my life I came into this House in order to defend the constitution of England. I purchased my seat of a borough-monger. I purchased it of the Duke of Newcastle. He was no patron of mine. He took my money, and by purchase I obtained a right to speak in the most public place in England.

With my views, and my love of the liberty of my country, I did not grudge the sacrifice I made for that commanding consideration. If I had abused the right I had purchased, and passed through corruption to the honours of the peerage, I should not enjoy the satisfaction I now feel - to be one of the people of England."[13]

---

12. *Ibid.* [22] 678/98.
13. *Ibid.*

This diverting confession did nothing to prevent the defeat of the motion.

A few days later, on 23 February 1830, Lord John Russell attempted to bring in a measure to confer the franchise on Birmingham, Leeds and Manchester whose populations, he repeated, had more than doubled since the turn of the century. But this attempt was also defeated - by a smaller majority of 188 votes to 140.[14] Yet when Daniel O'Connell, who had recently become the member for County Clare in an electrifying election in the wake of Catholic Emancipation, moved on 28 May for leave to bring in a Bill to establish triennial Parliaments, universal suffrage and vote by secret ballot, he was opposed not only by Tory Peel but also by Whigs such as Russell, Henry Brougham and Lord Althorp on the suffrage issue. Not surprisingly, the motion was lost, by 319 votes to 13.[15]

Naturally, at the time the Whig champions of reform were not democrats and universal suffrage was not within their sights any more than it was for the Tories. For both parties the idea of the vote being divorced from the ownership of property was unthinkable. But the clamour for reform was growing rapidly and John Wilson Croker, secretary of the admiralty from 1809 to 1830, claimed that the "appellations of whig and tory" should be dropped since the struggle was no longer "between two political parties for the ministry, but between the mob

---

14. *Ibid.* 915.
15. *Ibid.* [24] 1204/54.

and the government."[16] Men like Wellington and Grey, on both sides of the political divide, also sensed an ominous threat of revolution. But whereas Wellington was prepared to use force to put down any disturbances, Grey and the Whigs were wiser in proposing moderate reform as a means to prevent pressure for change that would threaten the rule of the aristocracy. It was a theme Grey was to return to frequently.

Political Union in Birmingham

However, a significant event had occurred at Birmingham on 25 January 1830. Thomas Attwood, a distinguished banker and friend of the industrial workers of the city, called a meeting to form a Political Union. This pronounced its aim to be "to obtain by every just and legal means such a reform in the Commons' House of Parliament as may ensure a real and effectual representation of the lower and middle classes of the people in that House". The meeting was attended by some 15,000 persons and lasted for nearly seven hours.

This endeavour to bring together in action the working and middle classes, but also to seek agreement with employers, was destined to have important repercussions. Attwood's example was widely followed throughout the country, despite *The Times* claiming in an editorial that the meeting and its resolutions were "a

---

16. *Quarterly Review.* (January 1831).

nonsense" and would probably die away quickly. The newspaper's reporter was more perceptive and described the meeting as "the largest ever assembled in this kingdom within the walls of a building" and concluded that "such an exhibition of public feeling, nor one which has excited so intense an interest throughout the whole neighbourhood, is not in the recollection of man". Despite the "nonsense" *The Times* gave his report four-and-a-half columns of its four pages, one of which was the front page of advertisements.[17]

The ultra-Tory *Standard*, under the editorship of Stanley Lees Giffard the father of the first Lord Halsbury, decided it was time for a Tory attempt at reform in order to ditch the Whigs. Properly encouraged, the paper mused, the country districts would return at least a three-quarters majority of good "Church and King" men to the Commons. No large towns should be enfranchised, however, as that would multiply workhouse and alehouse votes. "If," it said, "the Tory nobility and gentry imitate Mr Attwood by early taking a lead in the popular cause, there will be no 'crisis' whatever."[18] Dr Giffard was to be deeply disappointed.

Wellington's Defeat

Things looked distinctly brighter for the Whigs' kind of

---

17. 27 January 1830.
18. 27/9 January 1830.

reform when on 26 June 1830 the Tory-supporting King George IV died and was succeeded by the vaguely Whig Duke of Clarence as William IV, popularly known as the "sailor King" and an "honest tar". By statute this necessitated a general election which took place in August and September accompanied by a great deal of excitement and, in some places, disorder. Of course the franchise was still unreformed. Only nine of the 40 English counties were contested and the government gained seats in Ireland where the 40 shillings freeholders had been disenfranchised by the raising of the property qualification as the price of Roman Catholic relief.

Nevertheless, the movement of public opinion was clearly towards the Whigs particularly in the boroughs but also to some extent in the counties and not a single member of the Duke of Wellington's Cabinet was returned for any seat where there was a free and open election. Furthermore, of the 28 elected members who represented the largest cities only three supported the duke. And a mere 28 out of the 82 members who were elected for the 40 English counties did so. But although the Tories were estimated to have lost some 30 seats overall they retained a majority. Wellington again formed a government which it was generally expected would produce a moderate measure of reform since most sections of society, including many Tories, had by now concluded that the existing franchise was looking increasingly unsatisfactory. Wellington himself had admitted that, "there was scarcely an election, even in a corrupt borough, in which the candidates were not called upon to give pledges, and did not pledge themselves to vote for Reform."[19]

Yet despite this, and great successes by the reform-minded opposition in the more than usually hard-fought election, Wellington was content to proclaim in the House of Lords that he had, "never read or heard of any measure up to the present moment which can in any degree satisfy me that the state of the representation can be improved or rendered more satisfactory to the country at large than it is at the present moment."[20] Amidst loud murmurs of disbelief, when he sat down he is reported to have whispered to a colleague, "What can I have said which seems to make so great a disturbance?" "You have announced the fall of your government: that is all," was the reply.[21] This blindingly insensitive assertion when discontent with the electoral system was growing transformed the situation. Wellington, who had successfully trimmed on Catholic Emancipation a year before, was beset by fear of revolution if the fences of the franchise were breached and being primarily a soldier and not a statesman simply failed to understand the significance of parties and the fluidity of the situation.

Edward Stanley (afterwards Lord Derby) and Sir James Graham immediately deserted him and entered into a temporary alliance with the Whigs, in order to help secure reform. Both were to join Lord Grey's Cabinet

---

19. J.R.M. Butler. *The Passing of the Great Reform Bill*. 97/8. 1914.
20. *Hansard,* third series. [1] 52.
21. Lord John Russell. *Recollections and Suggestions*. 62. 1875.

which he formed later in the year when other Tories were to join them. Such defections, and those of Palmerston and Melbourne earlier, revealed that the nature of the franchise was increasingly unsatisfactory even as far as the ruling élites were concerned and they mirrored feeling in the country generally as shown in the results of the election. As if by magic, caricatures now appeared in many shop windows with the once-feted duke represented as an old hackney coachman and his lieutenant Sir Robert Peel as a ratcatcher.

One contemporary observer wrote, rather picturesquely, "When mariners observe the sea to heave and roll in swelling waves while scarcely an air is stirring, they lay their account with a coming gale, take in their lofty canvas, reduce their top-hamper, and make all snug for what may happen ... There is a force in the country beginning to act, which is not seen on the surface. There is a power in operation which is not suspected in its individual component parts, but which speaks broadly in the aggregate type. The swell of opinion is rolling in before the tempest; of drops, separately of insignificance it is composed, but how mighty is the united mass!"[22] Nevertheless, a massive effort was to be required to shift entrenched positions in the unreformed Parliament.

At this point London was in turmoil and the authorities began to fear for the safety of the king and queen on their visit to the Guildhall on lord mayor's day, Tuesday, 9 November. The Duke of Wellington had

---

22. *The Examiner*, 22 August 1830.

already been stoned in Hyde Park. Accordingly, a hundred Foot Guards were assembled in the grounds of Buckingham Palace and Wellington's home. Then, on 8 November, the royal visit was suddenly cancelled. Sir Robert Peel, who was home secretary and whose Police Act of 1829 had recently introduced the police, impolitely known as "Raw Lobsters", explained to the House of Commons that the quiet of the City could not be guaranteed if a royal procession took place.[23] He produced handbills which had been distributed, one of which read:

"Liberty or Death! Englishmen! Britons!! and honest Men!!! The time has at length arrived - all London meets on Tuesday - come armed - we assure you from ocular demonstration, that 6,000 cutlasses have been removed from the Tower for the immediate use of Peel's Bloody Gang - remember the cursed Speech from the Throne. These damned Police are now to be armed. Englishmen, will you put up with this"?

The opposition were unimpressed and the stock of a government which appeared to be incapable of governing fell dramatically.

"Captain Swing"

The Summer of 1830 also saw the commencement of a

---

23. *Hansard*, third series. [1] 267/74.

serious rising of agricultural labourers whose servitude and starvation are well documented by J. L. and Barbara Hammond in *The Village Labourer*.[24] As part of a campaign for a rise in wages and the abandonment of threshing machines which were perceived to destroy jobs, threatening letters were sent to landowners and wealthy farmers in many parts of England over the signature, "Captain Swing". These resulted in farmworkers marching from village to village breaking threshing machines and on some occasions burning ricks and barns. Like "King Ludd" of the Luddite Riots there was no "Captain Swing" and there is a good deal of evidence to show that on the whole the rioters were respectable men.

In this case also the government proved incapable of dealing swiftly and effectively with the outbreaks, in part because of sympathy with the labourers which even extended to magistrates. By the end of December 1830 however, some 2,000 alleged rioters had been arrested and, with many magistrates considered to be unreliable to deal with the prosecutions, a special commission was appointed to try them. With echoes of Judge Jeffreys and the "Bloody Assizes" of 1685, a total of 1,976 defendants were tried by 90 courts sitting in 34 counties. Two hundred and fifty two were sentenced to death of whom 19 were executed; 481 were transported; 644 sent to prison; seven fined; one whipped and 800 bound over or acquitted. These sentences and the privations of the families of those executed, transported or imprisoned

---

24. J.L. and Barbara Hammond. *The Village Labourer*. 1911.

were intended to strike terror and were unparalleled for a protest movement of this kind.[25]

Brougham Sidelined

Henry Brougham was now at the peak of his fame in the country, and having publicly disapproved of the commander-in-chief of the army being placed at the head of the civil government, chose this moment to give notice of his intention to propose to the Commons two weeks later a motion for a considerable degree of reform which included enfranchisement of large towns, household suffrage for borough residents and the creation of new boroughs. As Wellington's wobbling government clearly faced defeat from Brougham's onslaught the duke resigned on 16 November and was replaced by Lord Grey and a coalition, including Canning's followers, under Whig leadership, the "party" of reform. As Asa Briggs expresses it in *The Age of Improvement*, "It was this ministry, which was far from being a coherent 'party' ministry - the Whigs themselves were divided - that re-awakened English politics."[26]

Unlike Brougham, Grey was in no way inclined to move towards household suffrage but, as we have seen, he had long considered that a measure of reform was necessary, particularly as he believed it would act as a

---

25. See E.J. Hobsbawm and George Rude. *Captain Swing*. 262/3. 1969.
26. *The Age of Improvement*. 235. 1969.

bar to further, or more radical, change. He distanced himself from deep-rooted reform and described the reforming radicals as men who had "degraded themselves from the character of gentlemen."[27] One obstacle to Grey's plans was the popular standing of Brougham, the member for Yorkshire which was the largest constituency in the country with 20,000 voters. Brougham was widely perceived to have brought down Wellington and was in effect, although not in name, the leader of the Whigs in the House of Commons. His reputation at the Bar and his crusades on behalf of educational reform and an end to slavery were formidable assets.

He was also an ardent advocate of franchise reform who wished to retain his position of strength and influence in the House and the country. If he were not offered a suitable position in the new government, such as master of the rolls which would enable him to continue to represent Yorkshire in the Commons, he was expected to refuse to take office; in that case such was his popularity in the country that it was likely that a Whig government could not be formed. However, both William IV and Grey really wanted him out of the Commons and the prime minister declined to appoint him master of the rolls. Instead, he was offered the post of attorney-general but instantly refused it and tore the offer into pieces. Grey even asked the king how he could carry on the government if Brougham had to be a part of it.

To avoid the dilemma Grey offered Brougham the lord

---

27. BL. *Add. MSS.* 30,109. f. 9.

chancellorship which, although it would mean he would remain in the government, would also take him to the House of Lords and largely neutralise him. Lord Althorp, the nominal leader of the Whigs in the Commons who had made it clear that he would refuse to serve with Brougham, accepted the role of Judas and pleaded with him that their party, which had been out of office for 25 years, would be in the wilderness for another quarter of a century if Brougham did not join the government.

Faced with this appeal to his loyalty Brougham, against his own judgment and inclinations, finally yielded - to his everlasting regret - and took the Great Seal as Lord Brougham and Vaux. In doing so he ignored the advice of his mother who wrote to him: "Do not be tempted to leave the House of Commons. As member for Yorkshire, backed by all you have done for the country, you are more powerful than any official that ever existed, however high in station or rank. Throw not away the great position you have raised yourself to - a position greater than any that could be bestowed by King or minister."[28] Thomas Creevey, who was given to parodying people he knew, mischievously nicknamed Brougham, "Guy Vaux". Taking the credit for his removal to the Lords the king told Lord Holland, "You are all under a great obligation to me. I have settled Brougham. He will not be dangerous any more" - as was indeed to prove the case.

Lord John Russell, whom Creevey called, "Widow's

---

28. Brougham. *The Life and Times of Henry, Lord Brougham*. iii. 80. 1871.

Mite", was not yet a member of the new Cabinet but for his previous efforts he was to be rewarded with the opportunity of introducing the Reform Bill on 1 March 1831. This signalled the start of a battle that was to be fought over the following 14 long, wearying and often violent months. Before that, however, the state of the franchise that led to introduction of the Bill must now be considered.

CHAPTER 6

Need for Reform

Before the Great Reform Act of 1832 there were 658
members of the House of Commons of whom 513 were
from England and Wales, 45 from Scotland and 100 from
Ireland. Of the 513 nearly one half had no constituents to
whom they had any accountability. The number of
members from England and Wales had remained static
for 66 years; even when the corrupt borough of
Grampound in Cornwall was deprived of its franchise by
Parliament in 1821 its right to elect two members was
transferred to Yorkshire in an act of electoral justice.[1]

Battle Lines Drawn

The cause of Parliament's ire against Grampound was
that the franchise had been sold by the corporation at
public auction. But this was not uncommon elsewhere
and other boroughs that were indicted survived - for the
time being at least. Bribery was so extensive in the
following general election of 1826 that Parliament felt it
necessary to take action in at least two other cases. In the
boroughs of Penryn in Cornwall and East Retford in

---

1.   1 and 2 Geo. IV, c. 47.

Nottinghamshire votes were sold; for 20 guineas a vote in the latter (equal to an annual income for some people). As a consequence, in 1827, two Bills were introduced which resulted in a declaration that these two boroughs would be disenfranchised. However, both Bills were subsequently dropped after an open quarrel in the Cabinet.

Then, a year later, they were reintroduced with a proposal to give the Penryn seat to Manchester and that of East Retford to Birmingham. The new Bills met the same fate with the House of Lords refusing to create a new seat for Manchester. Apart from Grampound and Yorkshire, therefore, the franchise remained as unrelated to the distribution of population as it was in the reign of Charles II (1660-85). Indeed, not since Edward I had any real measure of reform been enacted except during the Commonwealth, and that had proved to be extremely temporary.

However, with the transfer of the franchise from a corrupt borough to a large county, Grampound signalled a turning point for a number of Whigs. At last something might be accomplished. But not at the time for Lord Grey or the mercurial Lord John Russell, both of whom were ever-fearful of the latent power of the people, and now declined to support a thoroughgoing inquiry into representation generally since it would "throw a slur upon the representation of the country, and fill the minds of the people with vague and infinite alarms."[2] As for the Tories, we have seen that the blinkered and complacent Duke of Wellington went out of his way to say that the system of representation was so perfect that it could not be improved upon.

In some constituencies party political in-fighting was often present with unrestrained and partisan press involvement and tumultuous scenes of rioting and sometimes mayhem. This was certainly the case in the 1830 general election soon after which a Whig-dominated coalition secured power on a pledge of reform. Despite that promise, however, the domination of the landed interests in Parliament and the virtual submission to them on vital issues for the commercial, manufacturing and trading concerns were still widely expected to continue - as indeed they did for a considerable time after 1832. Nevertheless, the battle lines for the future had been drawn and, as will be seen, under pressure Earl Grey and Lord John Russell were to stand firm in Parliament for their own proposals. This augured well for limited reform but it was to be an uphill struggle.

In 1831, of the 513 members of the House of Commons from England and Wales 82 represented counties and in the main were still elected by 40 shilling freeholders (that is between 3,000 and 4,000 men in most counties); four were from the universities and 427 represented cities and towns. Of the 203 English boroughs, 59 continued with a

---

2. Porritt. *The Unreformed House of Commons. Parliamentary Representation before 1832.* i. 89. 1903.

"scot and lot" franchise in some of which all payers of certain small municipal rates could vote and in others the apparent heads of families known, as noticed earlier, as "potwallopers" were electors. Elsewhere there had been some changes since earlier times. In 39 boroughs alleged burgageholders alone might vote; in 43 the corporation and in 62 the freemen, although again, as already seen, this was more theory than fact. In any event, the number of voters in all of them was often small and many of the nomination boroughs were still "owned" by wealthy landed proprietors.

Rotten Boroughs

It was notorious, for instance, that in the rotten borough of Old Sarum, the "accursed hill near Salisbury", there were no houses, merely a thornbush. At election times, in a scene of pure farce, a tent had to be erected in a field to house the returning officer. Nevertheless, this "borough" sent two members to the Commons - elected it was said by "the landowner, an old woman and a pig". In fact, a solicitor handed title deeds to local properties to seven voters just before they voted and immediately took them back again after the votes had been recorded.[3] For many years the seat was in the hands of the Pitt family who also commanded a seat at Okehampton, two in Dorset and others in Buckinghamshire and Worcestershire.

---

3.   Asa Briggs. *The Age of Improvement*. 102. 1969.

Almost as infamous as Old Sarum was Gatton which had its members nominated by a "patron" since although it had a "scot and lot" franchise it boasted only six houses and one resident elector. After attending a public sale of the borough, the dramatist Thomas Holcroft wrote that, "the celebrated auctioneer scarcely noticed the value of the estate. The rental, the houses, the views, the woods and water were unworthy of regard compared to what he called *'an elegant contingency'*." There were "no tempestuous passions to allay", the auctioneer told a prospective purchaser, "no tormenting claims of insolent electors to evade, no tinkers' wives to kiss, no impossible promises to make, no canvassing to drudge through; but his mind at ease and his conscience clear with this elegant contingency in his pocket, the honours of the State await his plucking and with its emoluments his purse will overflow."[4] Many boroughs could be bought and sold like any other piece of property and "Borough for Sale" was a familiar advertisement in the newspapers of the time.

We know that at Haslemere in rural Surrey, Lord Lonsdale settled a colony of Cumberland miners to occupy the burgage houses and vote according to his instructions at elections. And the Cinque Port of New Romsey had eight voters but two members. In fact, five of the eight Cinque Ports had fewer than 40 voters each and were heavily influenced by the government through the

---

4.   Quoted by G.D.H. Cole and Raymond Postgate. *The Common People: 1746-1938*. 88. 1938.

admiralty. All these were nomination, or pocket, boroughs in which elections were controlled by a single individual through the votes of his friends or dependants. Yet large towns like Manchester had no representation at all.

The practice of selling seats had been referred to in the Commons by Mr Curwen on 4 May 1809. "Seats are bought and sold in this House," he said, "like the stalls in Smithfield ... But, sir," (to the Speaker) "if I needed any proof of the existence of these abuses, besides their notoriety, I might refer to the conduct of the chancellor of the exchequer (Spencer Perceval) witnessed by the whole House. In a Bill he has introduced to stop the sale of places he consented to accept a clause inflicting penalties 'on the traffic of seats in this House'. Here, sir, is an avowal of the existence of the abuse."[5] Later in the debate the Speaker of the House added his own confirmation of the practice. "The question now before us," he said, "is no less than this - whether the seats in this House shall be henceforth publicly saleable? A proposition at the sound of which our ancestors would have startled with indignation; but a practice, which in these days and within these walls, in utter oblivion of every former maxim and feeling of Parliament, has been avowed and justified."[6] He should not, however, be forgiven his ignorance about past abuses.

Where there were voters they were often treated as property as much as the boroughs were. For example, in

5. *Parliamentary History.* [19] 357.
6. *Ibid.* 837.

September 1829 the Duke of Newcastle evicted tenants who had voted against his candidate. When reproached, he said "Is it to be presumed that I am not to do what I will with my own?" The matter was then raised again in the House of Commons on 1 March 1830.[7] Undeterred, the duke evicted more tenants for the same reason after the November 1830 general election as did Lord Exeter. Did they not see, asked *The Times*, "what it was that brought about this mighty French Revolution of July 1830? ... When they expel honest men from their habitations for exercising a constitutional right they have perpetrated a *coup d'état* against the people of England which they, the people, may be apt to repay ... A better case for parliamentary reform could never be imagined."[8]

Borough seats in the main were also unfairly distributed. The Duchy of Cornwall, which was subject to considerable crown influence, returned 44 borough members, which was only one fewer than for the whole of Scotland. None of the Cornish boroughs had an electorate of more than 200 but the situation was worse in Scotland where the total electorate was only between 2,500 and 3,000, all in corrupt counties or corrupt boroughs. On the other hand, English counties such as Derbyshire and Durham, whatever their size, had to make do with a mere two members each. Daniel Defoe complained that:

---

7. *Hansard*, new series. [22] 1077/1122.
8. 29 September 1830.

"We think it no small misfortune to the English constitution, that so great a number of members are chosen by the corporations of England, and according to our weak opinions, it seems not equal, that all the freeholders of a county should be represented only by two men, and the towns in the same county be represented by above 40, as it is in Cornwall, and near the like in other counties."[9]

John Wilkes, in introducing his Reform Bill in 1776, had shown that on recorded figures the command of 254 seats in the House of Commons was sufficient to secure a majority and that this number was elected by no more than 5,723 persons, whom he said were "generally the inhabitants of Cornish and other very insignificant boroughs, perhaps by not the most respectable part of the community."[10] Earlier, the formidable Lady Mary Wortley Montagu, a relative of Sir James Lowther who collected parliamentary boroughs as a hobby, suggested to her husband that the most expeditious way of entering the House of Commons would be for him "to deposit a certain sum of money in some friend's hands and buy some little Cornish borough."[11]

---

9. Daniel Defoe. *The Freeholder's Plea against Stock-jobbing Elections of Parliament Men.* 16/17. 1701.
10. *Parliamentary History*: [18] 1288.
11. Porritt. *Op. cit.* 354.

Patronage

It is clear that some boroughs were owned by a single peer or wealthy man as an almost hereditary form of property. Members of the Grosvenor family "represented" Chester without a break from 1715 to 1874 and during 42 of these 159 years held both seats. The large constituency of Preston was in the grip of a local family, the Stanleys, although it had no real residential qualification at all until 1786. It was remarked that there was nothing to hinder a regiment of soldiers from marching into the town one night and voting at an election the next morning.[12] Until the Restoration the franchise at Preston had been exercised by the corporation. Then, in 1661, an election was challenged and it was determined that all the male inhabitants had the right to vote even if resident for one night only and not paying local rates. This was ignored by the Stanleys, however, and the situation endured until 1786 when statute required a six months residential qualification for all householder boroughs.[13]

In fact, in the early nineteenth century three-quarters of the members of the Commons were drawn from the landed gentry.[14] Where there were two owners who quarrelled, an election might ensue with bribery on both sides and with money and beer being dispensed on a considerable scale. In 1817 Lord Cochrane unashamedly

---

12. Asa Briggs. *Op. cit.* 102.
13. Porritt. *Op. cit.* 49.
14. Linda Colley. *Britons.* 61 and 155. 1994.

told the Commons that in the election in which he was returned for the borough of Honiton, "the bellman was sent through the town to order the voters to come to Mr Townsend's, the head man in the place and a banker, to receive 10 guineas each for their vote" for Cochrane. "How," he asked, "could I in that situation be called a representative of the people?" He knew he had done wrong, he added, but that was how things were arranged.[15]

As we have seen, nearly one half of the members of the Commons had no constituents to whom they had any responsibilities. These men owed their seats not to constituents who were politically in agreement with them, and who nominally chose them, but to patrons. Just before the flight to the continent of James II on 23 December 1688 the Duke of Newcastle could influence the election of 16 MPs; the Earl of Aylesbury, eight; Lord Teynham, eight; the Earl of Huntingdon, six; Lord Preston, six; and Sir Robert Homes, six.[16] By 1793 parliamentary reformers, including Charles Grey and Sir James Mackintosh, calculated that 307 members of the Commons were returned by patrons.[17]

In 1795 the penetrating Charles James Fox spoke in the House of Commons about such patronage. There was, he said,

---

15. *Hansard*. [35] 92.
16. BM. *Add. MSS*. 34,516. Folios 50-54.
17. Society of Friends of the People. *House of Commons Journals*. xlviii. 740.

"one class of constituents whose instructions it is considered the implicit duty of members to obey. When gentlemen represent populous towns and cities, then it is a disputed point whether they ought to obey their voice, or follow the dictates of their own conscience. But if they represent a noble lord or a noble duke, then it becomes no longer a question of doubt, and he is not considered a man of honour who does not implicitly obey the orders of a single constituent.

He is to have no conscience, no liberty, no discretion of his own. He is sent here by my Lord This, or the Duke of That; and if he does not obey the instructions he receives, he is not to be considered as a man of honour and a gentleman. Such is the mode of reasoning which prevails in the House. If he dares to disagree with the duke or lord or baronet whose representative he is, then he must be considered as unfit for the society of men of honour."[18]

Often boroughs controlled by their corporations would sell their seats to the highest bidder. During the seventeenth century it was recorded by Sir Matthew Hale, chief justice of the king's bench, that on occasion members of corporations, such as mayors, were fined for accepting bribes from people whom the corporation then returned

---

18. *Parliamentary History.* [33] 728/9.

to the House of Commons.[19] A century or so later, in Dundee the inhabitants petitioned Peel, as home secretary, for a change in the town's constitution since, they said, they were at the mercy of the magistrates and the borough's council. "In that body," continued the petition, "likewise is vested the exercise of the political privileges of the Burgh. Since 1818 the Town Council has consisted of 21 members - 18 self-elected; two returned by the suffrages of the guildry and one by the nine incorporated trades."[20]

Finally, there were boroughs that were owned by, or sought by, the crown whose members were expected to support the government of the day. In 1749 the Prince of Wales agreed to pay £3,000 down to Thomas Pitt and "to put Mr Pitt in the receipt of his allowance and salary of £1,500 a year," in return for conceding to the prince "the nomination of each and every member of Parliament that shall be elected at the borough of Old Sarum for the term of .... years." And in the general election of 1774, George III's prime minister, Lord North, wrote on behalf of the king to Sir Grey Cooper that, "Lord Falmouth must be told in as polite terms as possible that I hope he will permit me to recommend to three of his six seats in Cornwall. The terms he expects are two thousand five hundred pounds a seat, to which I readily agree." As it happens Falmouth insisted on guineas not pounds to

---

19. *The Original Institution, Power and Jurisdiction of Parliaments.* Posthumously published in London in 1707.
20. PRO. HO. 102. 40.

which North responded, "My noble friend is rather shabby in desiring guineas instead of pounds. If he persists I would not have the bargain go off upon so slight a difference."[21]

Nevertheless, there were also "scot and lot" constituencies without patrons such as Westminster where up to 12,000 adult male inhabitants could exercise the vote and where radicals could stand with some chance of being elected. But such constituencies were few and far between.

The absurdities and corruption were accompanied by hypocrisy. The *Black Book* of 1820, by which time 100 members had been added to the size of the House of Commons by the Act of Union with Ireland in 1801, claimed that 144 peers nominated 300 MPs, and the government and 123 persons together nominated 187 more, making a certain majority when required. If those figures are not very reliable, in 1827 John Wilson Croker, an influential Tory and the secretary of the admiralty, himself put the number of members returned by wealthy men at 276. Of these, he said, 203 were "in the hands of what may be called the Tory aristocracy" and 73 in the hands of territorial families or patrons politically allied with the Whigs.[22] Such patronage did not prevent the House of Commons from solemnly passing at the commencement of each session a resolution that for a peer to involve himself in elections was "a high infringement

---

21. Quote d by Porritt. *Op. cit.* 340/41 and 356.
22. *Croker Papers.* i. 372. 1884.

of the liberties of the Commons."[23]

Bribery

In the eighteenth century two statutes were in force which were directed against bribery and corrupt practices. One was an Act of 1695[24] and the other an Act of 1729.[25] By the first Act, after the issue of writs of election, no person, by himself or an agent, was to directly or indirectly give to electors money, meat, drink, entertainment or provision; or make any present, gift, reward or entertainment; or promise to give any of these things either to an elector or to any county or borough. The second Act required electors, before admission to the poll, to take an oath that they had not received any money or other reward for their votes. False oaths were punishable as for perjury and, on conviction voting rights were taken away for ever. Neither Act was able to stem the tide of corruption, however, and both remained largely unenforced. And, in 1754 the town of Tewkesbury made it known that "no persons could be elected unless they would advance £1,500 each for the repair of the roads," and many other towns effected improvements in their public buildings in this way.[26]

It was well known that the crown and governments

---

23. Cole and Postgate. *Op. cit.* 91.
24. 7, 8 William III. c. 4.
25. 2 George II. c. 24.
26. Porritt. *Op. cit.* 161/4.

themselves frequently bribed both patrons and members with sinecures, distinctions and, sometimes, cash. In turn the recipients flagrantly bribed the voters at elections with drink, food and money. In 1830, £6,000 was considered to be the lowest reasonable price for a seat - the same price as the Duke of Bedford was paid for a seat at Camelford in Cornwall in 1812.[27] And, according to the *Morning Chronicle* of 26 July 1830, one member paid upwards of £30,000 for an uncontested seat. In fact the 1830 general election was said to be the most corrupt for a generation and it was during its course that Cobbett started his *Twopenny Trash*, as a monthly both to avoid the government stamp duty imposed on newspapers to restrict their number, and in order to send the message of reform across the country.

Even the exemplary Samuel Romilly was prepared to buy his way into the Commons rather than accept a seat from the Prince of Wales. He wrote to Creevey, that he wished to enter Parliament as a supporter of Charles James Fox but "I formed to myself the unalterable resolution never, unless I held a public office, to come into Parliament but by a popular election, or by paying the common price for my seat."[28] His letter was written from Little Ealing, to the west of London, on 23 September 1805, a year before he was appointed solicitor-general in the "Ministry of All the Talents" without being in Parliament. Subsequently he was elected member for

---

27. T.H.B. Oldfield. *Representative History*. ii. 236. 1816.
28. *Creevey Papers*. 41. 1905 edn.

Queensborough, a burgage borough in Kent in which less than a third of the population could vote.

In similar vein, when Sir Robert Peel was approached in October 1830 to stand for Liverpool he declined to give up his pocket seat at Westbury in Wiltshire where he was "elected" by the owner of the borough, Sir Manasseh Lopes, and his nephew who was mayor. "I think," explained Peel with special pleading, "that a Minister of the Crown has an advantage in being free from the double, occasionally perhaps the conflicting, obligations which are imposed by high responsible office and by such a trust as the representation of Liverpool."[29] He did not say whether he would have stood for election if he were out of office.

As for aspiring members who needed to woo electors, when Richard Brinsley Sheridan stood for Stafford in 1780 he kept open accounts of the expenses of his campaign - an unusual course at the time. The total expenditure amounted to some £2,000 from which 250 burgesses were paid £5 each, other voters were treated to beer and meals and subscriptions were made to various charities.[30]

When William Cobbett stood for Honiton in 1806 he wrote that after he had addressed the crowds, "telling them how wicked and detestable it was to take bribes, most of the corrupt villains laughed in my face; but some

---

29. *Peel Papers. Add MSS.* 40391, 40392.
30. Fintan O'Toole. *A Traitor's Kiss. The Life of Richard Brinsley Sheridan.* 158. 1997.

of the women actually cried out against me as I went along the streets, as a man that had come to rob them of their *blessing*. The whole of the inhabitants of this borough, the whole of the persons who return two members to Parliament, are bound together in an indissoluble chain of venality".[31]

Despite all the examples of abuse and corruption, during 30 years of almost uninterrupted power before 1830 the Tories refused to budge an inch towards reform on the ground that by "virtual representation" the people were represented by those who knew what was best for them. Many of the abuses were centuries old and this seemed only to give them legitimacy in the eyes of those who benefited from them. However, in the country at large they were seen as overdue for sweeping away and again Parliament was deluged with petitions for reform. In his important speech to the House of Commons in 1822[32] Lord John Russell complained of an MP who had said that corruption reminded him of the man who said he had all the symptoms of gout except the pain. On the contrary, exclaimed Russell in annoyance at what he thought was an unnecessarily jocular and insensitive remark, with corruption they had all the pain.[33]

If it were necessary the need for reform was later confirmed by the preamble to the 1831 Reform Bill which declared: "It is expedient to take effectual measures for

---

31. *Weekly Political Register.* October 1806.
32. See *ante*, chapter 5.
33. *Hansard.* [7] 51/88.

correcting divers abuses that have long prevailed in the choice of members to serve in the Commons' House of Parliament; to deprive many inconsiderable places of the right of returning members; to grant such privilege to large, populous and wealthy towns; to increase the number of knights of the shire; to extend the elective franchise to many of His Majesty's subjects who have not hitherto enjoyed the same; and to diminish the expense of elections."[34]

The time had arrived for the Whigs to come out of the political wilderness and respond to the torrent of demand for popular representation. It will be seen in the next chapter how they met the challenge.

---

34. 2 Will. IV. c. 25.

CHAPTER 7

The Great Reform Bill

Towards the end of 1830 Lord Grey, the new prime minister following Wellington's resignation, asked his son-in-law, Lord Durham, to prepare a Reform Bill in collaboration with Lord John Russell, who was not yet a member of the Cabinet. Durham, a committed reformer known as "Radical Jack", was an inspired choice and Sir James Graham and J.W. Ponsonby, afterwards Lord Duncannon, were co-opted to what was quickly dubbed "the Durham Committee". During the winter of 1830/31 they set to work with a will at Durham House. The times were also propitious for reform because Catholic Emancipation had shattered the Tory Party, and with the accession of William IV the crown had ceased to be an obstacle. From his youth the new king had associated mainly with the Whigs.

Reform Considered

A *Times* leader at the end of January discussed a pamphlet entitled *A Question of Reform Considered*. The paper stated that:

"The proposal of parliamentary reform which

Ministers are pledged to introduce after the recess is one of the most important measures ever submitted to the deliberative assembly; and whether it shall obtain the sanction of the whole legislature, or be defeated by the weight of interest, prejudice and opinion arrayed against it, the consequences cannot be indifferent to the public welfare and tranquillity.

It must be acknowledged that Ministers have undertaken a task of prodigious difficulty. They have to encounter the active, zealous, and disciplined hostility of the whole host of the late disbanded administration ... who have grown up in the employment of government; they have further to combat the interest of many powerful and respectable individuals, and of the class to which they belong, who have long enjoyed the personal benefit of engrossing the actual nomination of a large proportion of the members of the House of Commons."

The Times believed that the pamphlet writer's anticipation of hostility was an accurate assessment of the plans for thwarting the measure of reform at every stage of its progress through the Commons. The Tories had made it clear that they would oppose parliamentary reform to the utmost. Curiously, the leader-writer believed that there would be no direct resistance to the principle of reform but in this he was proved wrong. Nonetheless, he also, more correctly, forecast that the "plotters" would oppose, clause by clause, syllable by syllable, every detail of the measure that was laid before the House. The item closed with an appeal to the people: "Unless the people ... come forward and petition ... for the reform it is they who abandon an honest Minister - it is not the Minister who betrays the people. But in that case reform, and Minister, and people too are lost."[1]

Reform meetings were being held all over the country. At the beginning of the month there was one at Lostwithiel in Cornwall to state the necessity of a general measure of reform to redress public grievances and to procure the adoption of such measures as were calculated to remove distress and restore national prosperity. It was said to be the firm conviction of the petitioners that only by doing away with the borough system would reform be effective or satisfactory. A resolution in favour of vote by ballot was adopted with only three voting against. In fact, the ballot was demanded in 280 of the 645 petitions for reform that reached the Commons between 5 November 1830 and 4 March 1831.[2]

At the time voting was not secret but open and recorded in poll-books with people in dependent positions rarely able to exercise a free choice. That landlords should exert political influence over their tenants was accepted as normal. For instance, barrister Daniel Coke in his nomination speech at Nottingham in 1803 had declared that the practice was quite fair and he would be "sorry to see the day when men of property would not use such

---

1. 29 January 1831, p.1.
2. *Hansard*. [3] 421.

influence."[3] And as late as 1841, in the Flintshire election one of the Grosvenor family complained of Gladstone violating the sacred canons of electioneering etiquette by canvassing Lord Westminster's tenants. "I did think," he said, "that interference between a landlord with whose opinions you were acquainted and his tenants was not justifiable according to those laws of delicacy and propriety which I considered binding in such cases."[4]

In Abingdon a resolution to consider reforming Parliament was unanimously adopted. A similar resolution was passed in Banbury, a borough in which there were only 18 electors some of whom were non-resident friends of the patrons, their tenants and clergymen who held livings in their gift. It is clear that the remainder could be easily outnumbered since from time immemorial the electors had returned members nominated by the patrons. It was hoped, said the petitioners, that never in the future would it be possible for a peer to send a member to the Commons. In Inverness, 100 signatories, some nine-tenths of the adult male population, voted for reform.[5]

The Times, quoting the *Lincoln Times,* commented that meetings for reform had become so general that "scarcely a week passes over but we read of some county, borough or parish petitioning Parliament, and their necessity is evident." And the *Glasgow Scots Times* had

---

3. *Dictionary of National Biography.*
4. Lewis Namier. *The Structure of Politics at the Accession of George III.* 69. London 1957.
5. *The Times,* 1 February 1831, p.5.

declared that a petition of 25,000 men, virtually all the male householders of the city and suburbs, called for reform.[6]

There were further reports of meetings at Oldham which called for immediate, though moderate, reform which would enable sending members from towns which had a population of at least 30,000, equal, it was said, to the inhabitants of 150 of the English boroughs; and at Halifax where there was a demand for reform and vote by ballot. Here the call for reform was passed but voting by ballot was not, the majority wishing "that the votes be taken as heretofore."[7] Other petitions were also passed in Cripplegate in London and in Calne in Wiltshire.[8]

Yet another *Times* leader commented that the subject of parliamentary reform had grown in such great interest that the ministers would be compelled, by virtue of a solemn pledge already given to the people of England, to come forward and submit a specific plan for remedying those abuses which "time and public profligacy had engrafted on the national representation." The writer, kept in the dark by the Cabinet as much as everyone else, doubted whether the Bill had yet received much of a definite shape and highlighted what he saw as two conflicting difficulties. One was to make reform so temperate "as to insinuate its own way through that assembly whose vices it severely rebukes while it

---

6.   *Ibid.* 8 February p. 3.
7.   *Ibid.* 14 February, p. 5.
8.   *Ibid.*, quoting the *Devizes Gazette.*

purifies," and the other was, at the same time, to ensure that it was "so vigorous and extensive as to ensure a good reception from the people."

A pamphlet which *The Times* considered contained "much solid and useful discussion," was extensively quoted. The pamphlet first criticised the existing situation by pointing out that a majority of members were placed in the House of Commons by the aristocracy and that 350 members were returned directly or indirectly by fewer than 200 individuals. The wishes of the people, it said, were not being taken into account and in most cases bribery, cajolery and intimidation were prevalent. In order to make the representatives responsible the remedy was that the election must be in the hands of the people; representatives must be removable at stated and not distant periods by those who elected them; and the votes must be taken in such a way as would collect the real senses of the electors.[9]

When Charles Buller, MP for West Looe in Cornwall, published a short statement on reform it was immediately criticised by the newspaper for not supporting either annual Parliaments or universal suffrage. Although admiring his "vivacity and spirit" the leader disagreed with the limited objectives of his reform. Buller thought the proposed Bill would abolish boroughs with populations of less than 1,000 and grant representation to towns containing more than 10,000 inhabitants which at that time sent no members to Parliament. He

9. *Ibid.*

considered that the plan was open to objections because it would be difficult, he wrote, to decide which towns were to be placed on the list. For instance, London was already represented, but what of the towns of Marylebone, Islington, Lambeth, Greenwich and others? Were they to have franchises? What of the Plymouth Dock area lately called Devonport which had 40,000 inhabitants; was that to be enfranchised separately from Plymouth? He also cited Cornwall which was well inhabited but which had no towns of more than 10,000; were they to be disenfranchised? "This will be a species of reform," he concluded, "which will not conciliate those who are deprived of their present privileges: it will disgust all who are disappointed at the electoral franchise, the dereliction of the very principle on which the change is professed to be made; it will please only those who value their vote more for its being withheld from their neighbours."[10]

The next day *The Times* attacked the 300 or so members of the House of Commons who it claimed were in agreement to oppose or hinder reform. They would nearly all lose their seats if there were disenfranchisement but they habitually repeated to each other, *There will be no disenfranchisement.* This was the last hope of the borough-proprietors but they ought to be clearly shown that it was a perfectly vain hope. Ministers were so irrevocably pledged to reform that their very existence depended on it. They would, therefore, have to propose a dissolution of Parliament in the event of their

---

10. *Ibid.* 28 February, p. 5.

being out-voted on the reform question. Although the leader-writer considered there was no ground for believing that such a danger existed he nonetheless thought it advisable that ministers, having first made sure of the ground on which they stood, should give the opposing portion of the House a notion of their intentions. They should say that the country required and demanded it and that if they thought otherwise they should appeal to their constituents. If such a point were put it would reverse the votes of some who intended to vote against reform.[11]

Lord John Russell

Because of his many speeches advocating reform in the House of Commons in the past Russell was entrusted with the task of preparing the final draft of the Bill. His terms of reference from the still cautious Lord Grey[12] were that the draft should be sufficient to satisfy public opinion whilst maintaining the essential character of the Constitution; and at the same time provide a basis for avoiding any further change in the future. But no details were to be made public in advance of its presentation in the Commons to avoid arming the opposition with arguments in advance. This explains some of the public

---

11. *Ibid.* 1 March, p. 3.
12. In Grey's Cabinet of 13 only three were commoners. The remainder were members of the aristocracy.

confusion being reported in *The Times*.

What proved to be the opening shot in a long, hard-fought and bitter campaign commenced at six o'clock on 1 March 1831 when, on behalf of the Cabinet, Russell rose in a crowded, dark and gloomy House of Commons in St Stephen's Chapel to introduce the Bill.[13] The principle on which a unanimous Cabinet was agreed, he said, was that the "question of right" was in favour of reform since the ancient Constitution of the country declared that no man should be taxed for the support of the state who had not consented by himself or his representative to the imposition of the taxes. This, perhaps unwittingly, reflected the proclamation of the American colonists when they set up the cry: "no taxation without representation".

Although it had done so in the past, Russell continued, the House of Commons no longer represented the people of England. In the most free, wealthy and civilised country in the history of the world it was not right that the representatives of the people, the guardians of their liberty, were chosen only every six years. Further, would not a stranger from another country be astonished, he asked, if he were taken to a green mound and told that it sent two members to Parliament; if he were shown a stone wall and told that it also sent two members; or if he walked into a park without a vestige of a dwelling and learned that this too sent two members?

The stranger would be still more astounded, he declared, if he were to go to the north of England and see

---

13. *Hansard*, third series. [2] 1061/1089.

flourishing towns with immense manufacturing industries and populations which sent no representatives at all to the assembly which was said to represent the people. And what would he think of, say, a great trading port like Liverpool, where in general elections bribery was rampant and men were paid openly for their votes? In reality, he said, the confidence of the country in the constitution of the House had long ceased. Right, reason and expediency all called loudly for reform.

Details

The Bill provided that 60 listed boroughs with fewer than 2,000 inhabitants each would be disenfranchised, creating 119 vacancies. At one stroke most of the rotten boroughs were to be obliterated. When Russell announced this, "It was a ludicrous spectacle," wrote J.R.M. Butler, "to see members lying back in disgust, not knowing whether to be amused or enraged, while a little fellow, not weighing above eight stone, solemnly pronounced the doom of the ancient boroughs for which they sat. As each venerable name was read, a long shout of ironical laughter rang from the benches opposite. 'More yet,' smiled Russell unperturbed, at the end of the fateful roll."[14]

Whig John Cam Hobhouse, afterwards Lord Broughton, described the same scene: "There was a sort

---

14. *Op. cit.* 194/5.

of wild, ironical laughter, mixed with expressions of delight from the ex-ministers, who seemed to think themselves sure of recovering their places again immediately. Our own friends were not so well pleased. Baring Wall turning to me said, 'They are mad! They are mad!' and others made use of similar exclamations ... Lord John seemed rather to play with the fears of his audience; and after detailing some more clauses which seemed to complete the scheme smiled and paused and said, 'More yet'."[15]

Russell then turned to the 47 boroughs with between 2,000 and 4,000 inhabitants which were to be deprived of the right of sending more than one member to Parliament; and the borough of Weymouth which sent four and would in future send only two. Thus the total reduction in borough members was to be 168.

The government, said Russell, was also determined that boroughs retaining the franchise should not be in the hands of a small number of persons to the exclusion of the large proportion who owned property in them. Fifteen different voting qualifications for boroughs would be replaced by giving the vote to all adult male householders who had been resident for 12 months in a property having an annual value of at least £10. (Grey had wanted the amount to be £20 but was overruled in Cabinet on the insistence of Russell.) This did not produce uniformity however. For instance, in Leeds most working men lived in houses of £5 to £8 in value and were debarred from the

---

15. Quoted by Michael Brock in *The Great Reform Act.* 161. 1973.

franchise. In London, on the other hand, rents were so high that the £10 clause enfranchised most genuine householders.[16] In the main the Bill regularised the nature of the borough franchise rather than broadening it by using the £10 householder who had recently been identified for tax purposes. So far as the counties were concerned the 40 shillings freeholder was to retain his rights and the franchise was to be extended to include copyholders to the value of £10 a year and leaseholders with a term of 21 years or more and an annual rent of not less than £50.

Not all the disenfranchised boroughs were to be replaced. But in the place of those that were, seven large towns, including Birmingham, Leeds and Manchester, would in future send two members each and 20 others, including Halifax, Cheltenham and Wolverhampton, would each send one member.

Although London had a population approaching one million, large districts of the city had no representation at all and eight new members were to be divided among Tower Hamlets, Holborn, Finsbury and Lambeth. In addition, in the counties two members would be given to each of the three ridings of Yorkshire and two additional members each to 26 counties in which the number of inhabitants exceeded 150,000 including Cheshire, Derbyshire, Gloucestershire, Essex and Sussex.

The Bill also provided that all electors should be registered in order that the poll might take place over two

---

16. Asa Briggs. *Op. cit.* 263.

days instead of the prevailing eight days or more. Russell hoped that at some time in the future polling might take only one day. Polling districts would be reduced in size to avoid voters travelling long distances to the poll particularly in the counties, each of which, however large, until then had only one polling place. The expense of bringing voters to the poll in Yorkshire, he said, was nearly £150,000 - even when there was no contest.

Turning to Scotland, he claimed that it needed reform even more than England and Wales since, "no such thing as a popular election was known in that country." Indeed, the total number of electors in the whole of Scotland, all in corrupt counties or corrupt boroughs, was less than 3,000. The government intended, therefore, to give the suffrage to copyholders and leaseholders as in England and 22 counties would return one member each. Peebles and Selkirk were to be joined together to send one member, as would Dumbarton and Bute, Elgin and Nairn, Ross and Cromarty, Orkney and Shetland, Clackmannan and Kinross. Edinburgh and Glasgow would each have two members, Aberdeen, Paisley, Dundee, Greenock and an extended Leith would return one each as would 13 district boroughs. The result would be five new members for Scotland, taking the total from 45 to 50.

In Ireland the vote was to be given to all holders of houses or land with a rental value of £10 or more a year. As Belfast, Limerick and Waterford were under-represented they would be given one new member each which would increase Irish representation by three.

In sum, the effect of the Bill, Russell declared, would be to set the future number of MPs at 596 - a decrease of 62. The number of *new voters* would be:

In the counties	-	100,000
In the towns	-	160,000
In London	-	95,000
In Scotland	-	60,000
In Ireland	-	40,000

In relation to the population of 22 million, fewer than half a million voters was still an unimpressive total. However, Russell was more concerned with what he described as the "quality" of the voters. He pointed out that these numbers made an addition to the constituency of the Commons of about half a million persons, "all connected with the property of the country, having a valuable stake amongst us, and deeply interested in our institutions." They would support Parliament and the throne and have an incentive to industry and good conduct. Hence his peroration appealed to the gentry and the aristocracy to show their generosity - to convince the people of their public spirit - and to identify themselves for the future with the people and join those who were seeking only "the glory and welfare of England."

Two Camps

Both Whig and Tory members were surprised at the

far-reaching nature of the proposals and Russell sat down to cheering only from Radical members. The reforms, and Russell's words, were mistakenly perceived by most to involve a transfer of power to the middle class although this was not the intention of either Grey or Russell as they had repeatedly made clear. Nonetheless, at this point the case for reform might have seemed irresistible but that would have been to under-estimate the aristocracy and their representatives who felt that their interests were being threatened and the Constitution undermined. As they saw it the "wisdom of the centuries" was safer than the "frothings" of the Radicals or Russell. The *Standard*, expressing the indignation of the ultra-Tories, wrote that "The Bedlam scheme can never be put into execution."[17]

Letters to the editor of *The Times*, although often long and flowery, were almost without exception in support of the Bill. Beneath a list of the 60 boroughs proposed to be disenfranchised a letter from "A Radical Reformer" urged people who were friends to reform to call on both Houses of Parliament to back not just reform in general but the details of the Bill. He wanted there to be no cavil concerning whether there should be voting by ballot, universal suffrage or annual or triennial Parliaments. There should be no disunity among reformers; what the people wanted was a reform in Parliament.[18]

Two days after the Bill was introduced *The Times*,

17. 1 March 1831.
18. *The Times,* 3 March, p. 6.

under the heading "Reform", listed papers that were in favour or against. Of the London dailies, *The Times, Morning Herald, Morning Chronicle, Public Ledger, Morning Advertiser, Globe, Courier, British Traveller, Star* and *Sun* (10) were for, whereas the *Morning Post,* the *Standard* and *Albion* (3) were against. Of the once, twice and thrice weekly papers, 20 were in favour and three against: the *London Packet, The St James' Chronicle* and *John Bull.* Of the county and provincial papers examined and listed by name, 54 were in favour and seven were against.[19] One of those supporting the Bill was the *Manchester Guardian* and also in favour, although not mentioned by *The Times*, were the *Prompter* and William Cobbett's *Political Register.*

On 7 March a huge meeting took place in Birmingham attended by more than 15,000 people. After a long but rousing address by the chairman, Thomas Attwood, Dr Joshua Scholefield, later to be mayor of the city, moved "that this meeting feels deep and sincere gratitude to the King's most excellent Majesty, for the great comprehensive planned parliamentary reform which His Majesty has graciously authorised his Ministers to bring forward; and this meeting is perfectly convinced that the success of the great measure proposed is absolutely indispensable for the prosperity, peace and security of the country." The corollary of the last sentence implied that if the measure were *not* passed prosperity, peace and security would be in jeopardy. Scholefield's motion was

---

19. *Ibid,* 5 March.

passed unanimously as was, to cheering and singing of the national anthem, a further motion pledging support to the king.[20]

On the same day there were meetings in Cambridge and Bedford confirming support for reform. The people attending the meeting at Cambridge were particularly pleased that their patron "the Duke" would be annihilated by the proposed Bill as he had "not a single guineasworth of property in the town." Further, a host of non-resident voters, "men who have no more interest in the town than their master" would be swept away.[21]

Further meetings in favour of reform were reported from Suffolk, Horsham, Hastings and Lewes. In Newport, Isle of Wight, "Friends of Reform" resolved to hold a public meeting in support and in Sheffield a meeting was held in the town hall where a petition in favour was carried unanimously.[22] Other reform meetings were held in Dublin, Leicester, Chester, Newcastle upon Tyne, Wolverhampton, Cheltenham, Lincoln and St Mary Whitechapel. Enthusiastic petitions were also passed at reform gatherings in Manchester, Southampton and Battle in Sussex.[23]

20. *Ibid.* 9 March, p. 4.
21. *Ibid.*
22. *Ibid.* 10 March, p. 6.
23. *Ibid.* 12 March, p. 3.

The Debate

In the Commons on 1 March, once the motion for leave to bring in the Bill had been briefly seconded, the opposition immediately reared its head in the shape of Sir Robert Inglis who had defeated Peel to become the member for the University of Oxford. He was well-known as a strong supporter of the landed interests and an uncompromising opponent of reform. Population and taxation, he claimed in a lengthy speech that was published as a pamphlet, were not the criteria for representation. Furthermore, in the past clamours for reform had been silenced without concessions being made.

"The noble lord," he said, "has pointed, with the confidence of triumph, to the green mound of Old Sarum, as if the shame and ridicule of it ought to silence us." Yet, in the reign of Edward I, he continued, it had been given the franchise by the king and when it was purchased by Mr Pitt he gave his posterity an hereditary right to sit in the House of Commons as owners of it. Equally unhelpful to his case he then added that, "it was probably invested with the elective franchise, in order that its then holder, the Earl of Salisbury of that day, might place his Representatives in this House." All the alleged abuses that were spoken of had existed in the past and what was being proposed was not therefore a restoration of ancient rights or reform. On the contrary, in one single word it was revolution - a revolution that would overturn all the existing influence of rank and property and lead to the destruction of the other orders of the state.

Having commenced his speech by saying that MPs did not represent their constituents but sat to consider the affairs of the country and the good of the empire, Inglis now said that when, as in his own county, a person came to the House by only a casting vote, the minority, which was all but equal to the majority, were left with no representation. Accordingly, on Russell's principle, they should pay no taxes. Unable to keep a steady grip on his mind he then claimed that the unreformed Commons represented all interests and admitted all talents - something that the Bill would destroy by admitting mob oratory.[24]

Not surprisingly Horace Twiss, a nephew of the famous actress Mrs Siddons and a persistent opponent of reform over many years, found Russell's speech "painful". Increasing the number of electors, he said without any qualms, would heighten the expense of elections by the necessity of carrying a greater number to the poll and having a greater number to bribe. He could not countenance the doctrine that Parliament should wait upon the will of the people which would only teach them that their will was higher than the Constitution.[25]

In line with the thinking of his elders in the Cabinet, the young Thomas Babington Macaulay, who represented Lord Lansdowne's pocket borough of Calne in Wiltshire, said he supported the Bill because he was opposed to universal (male) suffrage which would produce a

---

24. *Hansard. Op. cit.* 1090/1128.
25. *Ibid.* 1129/39.

destructive revolution. In some countries, he declared, including the United States, the labouring classes could be trusted with the right to vote, but not the labourers of England who did not enjoy plentiful employment, high wages and cheap food, although from his soul he wished they did. Great distress inflamed the passions of the lower orders and made them distrust those who would serve them. The middle classes, on the other hand, were entitled to the vote.

As to the argument that many great and eminent men had been brought into Parliament through rotten boroughs he thought that equally if one hundred of the tallest men in the kingdom were to be elected members some among them would be eminent.

He appealed to members to join in the salvation of their country. "Save property, divided against itself", he cried. "Save the multitude, endangered by its own ungovernable passions. Save the aristocracy, endangered by its own unpopular power. Save the greatest, and fairest, and most highly civilised community that ever existed, from calamities which may in a few days sweep away all the rich heritage of so many ages of wisdom and glory. The danger is terrible. The time is short."[26]

Lukewarm support for the Bill came from "Orator" Hunt, now MP for Preston. He would give it his support, he declared, since it did not touch the rights of his constituents. In this he was mistaken since the artisan vote in Preston and elsewhere was under attack.

---

26. *Ibid.* 1190/1205.

Although it has been seen that Preston had for long been in the grip of the local Stanley family there was now a substantial "scot and lot" vote and many of them would be lost with the £10 test which was a property test designed to keep out a large part of the population.[27] But Hunt was sorry the questions of a secret ballot and the duration of Parliaments were not included.

"Those who said the ballot would make men greater hypocrites seemed to know little of human nature or society. They did not seem to recollect that at the clubs of the highest classes in England the secret ballot was constantly resorted to as a means of avoiding the odium of an open vote; but if any man was to say in these clubs that the ballot made its members hypocrites he would have his heart made a very cullender of bullets.". He deplored that the lower orders - "whom I call the useful classes of society" - were denied their right to vote when in fact they paid taxes on almost every article of human subsistence.[28]

The ballot had been included in the original draft by Durham but was deleted by Grey in Cabinet where Russell's proposal for five-year Parliaments had also been defeated. The dropping of the ballot meant that votes would continue to be given orally and in public, surrounded by the crowd. Although not needing much encouragement, Grey had been strongly influenced by the king's desire to avoid both the ballot and any hint of

---

27. Asa Briggs. *Op. cit.* 263.
28 *Hansard.* 1208/17.

universal suffrage. Grey told the House of Lords quite frankly that, "If any person supposes that this reform will lead to ulterior measures they are mistaken; for there is no one more decided against annual Parliaments, universal suffrage, and the ballot, than I am. My object is not to favour, but to put an end to such hopes and projects."[29] William IV had expressed a fear that the Bill might lead to "a democracy in its worst form."[30]

The member for Calne, Hunt continued in the same speech and taking liberties with Macaulay's words, had talked of the rabble who should not be given the vote and had said that if the Bill was not conceded to the middle classes there would be revolution and massacre. What sort of massacre, he asked? When the people of Manchester assembled legally and peacefully in 1819 to petition for constitutional reform there was a real massacre. A drunken and infuriated yeomanry, with swords newly sharpened, slaughtered 14 and maimed and wounded 648. (Cries of, No!, Question!) It was not the Radicals who would threaten massacre since the proposed reform was only what had been asked for twenty years ago by the weavers of Lancashire.

In a speech full of invective Sir Charles Wetherell, MP for Boroughbridge in Yorkshire which was to be extinguished, said the Bill meant that he was making his last, dying speech. He opposed it for being "corporation

---

29. *Ibid.*
30. See Grey's *Correspondence with King William IV and Sir Herbert Taylor* (the King's Secretary). i. 96. 1867.

robbery." Had there not existed in Cromwell's time, he asked, a purge of the House of Commons called "Colonel Pride's Purge?" Now they were being promised "Russell's purge" which would expose the House again to the nauseous experiment of a repetition of that earlier purge (which he failed to mention had reduced the Commons to a rump of some 50 MPs - a far cry from Russell's aim). The principle of the Bill, he said, was republican, destructive of all property, all right, of all privilege.[31] The attorney-general, Sir Thomas Denman, responded that his learned friend was confusing a military usurpation with Cromwell's plan for elections which was a well-digested scheme of civil polity.[32]

Lord Palmerston supported the Bill but Sir Robert Peel opposed it. Ironically, Tory leader Peel claimed that whereas the Bill would give power to the middle class it would drown the voice of the humble "scot and lot" and "potwalloper" voters who then voted in elections - as indeed in some cases it did. Limited alterations in the system of representation he would have assented to. But not the monstrous evil of perpetual change in the executive government of the country. They should never be tempted "to resign the well-tempered freedom which we enjoy, in the ridiculous pursuit of the wild liberty which France has established". The institutions of England had stood uninjured amid foreign wars, disputed successions, rebellions, extreme distress and the bitter

---

31. *Hansard. Op. cit.* 1220/40.
32. *Ibid.* 1241/2.

contentions of parties.

The rotten boroughs, he declared, afforded the means of access to the House to men who had no claims beyond their ability. He was including himself, presumably, since after being rejected by Oxford University he had turned to the pocket borough of Westbury. Ignoring Macaulay's analogy of tall men, he said, "I wrote down this morning the names of those distinguished men who have appeared in this House during the last 40 or 50 years, as brilliant lights above the horizon, and whose memory has had buoyancy enough to float down to posterity on the stream of time." They were 22 in number and 16 of them were returned for boroughs which the Bill would wholly exclude from the franchise. They included Burke, Pitt, Fox, Canning, Brougham, Romilly and Lord Grey.[33] Whatever the talents of such people, perceptively retorted Edward Stanley, the future Lord Derby, they were not looked upon by the people as representatives.

Altogether seventy-one members joined in the debate of whom 34 spoke in favour of the Bill and 37 against. Of those against, 13 came from boroughs to be disenfranchised and seven from those due to have their representation reduced. After Lord John Russell made a brief reply to the debate, leave to bring in the Bill was accepted without a division. This had earlier been agreed by the leaders on both sides of the House although both Peel and the House had been kept in ignorance of the sweeping nature of the Bill. It surprised many that Peel

---

33. *Ibid.* 1330/56.

honoured what they saw as a deviously-induced agreement without which the Bill might well have been strangled at birth. In the event the Bill was read for the first time on 14 March without opposition. The next stage would be the more crucial, although much shorter, second reading.

Inconsistencies

In the meantime, the lord mayor of Dublin presided over a meeting held in that city and a resolution in favour of the Reform Bill was moved by the Duke of Leinster. It was considered by a Mr O'Connell that under the Bill the representation of England would be increased but not that of Ireland. However, as has been shown, before the Bill England had 513 representatives and Ireland 100, giving England an excess of 413 whereas after the Bill England would have 436 and Ireland 103, giving England an excess of only 333. This, said *The Times*, meant that Ireland would gain from the Bill in the proportion of 413 to 333, demonstrating that even in those days anything could be "proved" by statistics.[34] More importantly the 40 shilling freeholder in Ireland had previously been disenfranchised and a £10 franchise introduced in the boroughs. In reality, the franchise in Ireland was restricted in order to limit the consequences of Catholic Emancipation in 1829 which had produced more Radical MPs.

---

34. *The Times*, 18 March 1831, p. 2.

A correspondent of *The Times* who signed himself "A Lawyer" pointed out an inconsistency of the Bill. The writer was a leasehold owner of a house held for 99 years at a peppercorn rent. He had rented out a smaller house to his neighbour for 21 years at an annual rent of £60. Under the terms of the Bill, his neighbour would have a vote but "A Lawyer" would have none. Not surprisingly, he could not imagine that anything so unfair and absurd as this could be the intention of the framers of the Bill.[35] Another correspondent agreed with "A Lawyer" concerning the inconsistencies with regard to leaseholds and the right of voting in the counties given to leaseholders occupying property for 21 years at a rent of not less than £50 a year. He wrote, "The objection to this is that it removes from the franchise owners who occupy their own property ... the votes of leaseholders like those of copyholders should be made independent of the annual value of the estate and not on the reserved rent; and that the condition of the lease should be excluded."[36]

Meanwhile, in the City of London, on the day of the second reading of the Bill, a canvass was in progress to secure signatures to an address *against* reform, the authors of which were the directors of the East India Company and Bank of England. Two responses were quoted. One was from the head of a wealthy house who was invited to sign, but when he expressed a wish to read the document was told it was unnecessary because it

---

35. *Ibid.*
36. *Ibid.* 19 March, p. 5.

contained those sentiments he had always had and that it contained many good things that would be lost. The man, declining to sign, replied that the good things should be given up as the times had wholly altered. Another individual, who did sign, said, "This is a petition in favour of corruption; I have lived by corruption all my life: give me the paper."[37]

---

37. *Ibid.* 21 March, p.4.

CHAPTER 8

The Lords Intervene

It is useful to consider the political and social conditions under which the Reform Bill was conceived. Among other things, the Industrial Revolution produced a growing working class, centred in the main in the large industrial towns, whose members were without representation in Parliament. At the same time it also brought about a great expansion in the numbers of the middle class who, although also largely denied representation, were experiencing a new sense of power which was voiced by their champion James Mill, the philosophical radical and close friend of Jeremy Bentham.

Middle-class Support

Mill liked to think that the "middling classes", as he often called them, had guided the majority of the people throughout history and were the highest product of civilisation. In the *Westminster Review* of January 1824 he wrote of the contemporary middle class:

"It contains beyond all comparison, the greater proportion of the intelligence, industry, and wealth of the state. In it are the heads that invent, and the hands that execute; the enterprise that projects, and the capital by which those projects are carried into operation ... The people of the class below are the instruments with which they work; and those of the class above, though they may be called their governors, and may really sometimes seem to rule them, are much more often, more truly, and more completely under their control. In this country at least, it is this class which gives to the nation its character."

In similar vein but more brazenly Macaulay, in the *Edinburgh Review* of March 1829, claimed that, "the higher and middling orders are the natural representatives of the human race. Their interest may be opposed, in some things, to that of their poorer contemporaries, but it is identical with that of the innumerable generations which are to follow."

With more political acumen Mill generalised the experience of the people who made up the middle class, contributed to their understanding of their place in society and pointed the way forward for them. They had to destroy aristocratic rule if they were to command their inheritance and he called for an open attempt to replace aristocratic with middle class leadership of society. In his *Essay on Government*, written for the *Encyclopaedia Britannica* in 1818 and republished in 1820 for a wider audience, he made a ferocious attack on government by aristocracy and called on the middle class to see themselves as the leaders of society and guardians of the people against tyranny. This was exactly what large numbers of the expanding middle class wanted to hear. As Lord John Russell illustrated in the House of Commons on 25 April 1822,[1] they had become politically literate. Times and thinking had changed and, not surprisingly, their demand for reforms which had been so long delayed burst upon the scene with a fresh energy and a new sense of urgency.

Unmoved by, and perhaps unaware of, this sea-change the Tories remained adamantly hostile to reform. As a consequence the large number of Political Unions which had been formed in many parts of the country continued to spread the gospel of reform. By 1831 the resultant agitation was particularly successful in Birmingham where for a time 25 Political Union debating clubs were meeting weekly and, under Attwood's inspiration, encouraging members of the middle and working classes to join forces in support of the Bill.

On the other hand some radical working class elements, particularly in London, wanted no alliance with the middle class and saw the awakening struggle as a means to press for an even more democratic and universal solution. On 2 April 1831 they formed the National Union of the Working Classes led, among others, by William Lovett who gave it a strong Owenite bias. The NUWC soon had a number of local branches outside London which were in contact with radical members of the Political Unions. It was to counter their influence that in

---

1. *Hansard*, new series. [7] 51/88. See *ante*, chapter 5.

October 1831 Francis Place, who was at the heart of the reform agitation, decided to found a National Political Union to unite all the middle class Political Unions and keep the NUWC at bay. What resulted after the troubled course of the Reform Bill in Parliament will be considered later.

Second Reading - A Majority of One

The second reading of the Bill was moved in the House of Commons by Lord John Russell on 21 March 1831[2] and lasted two days. It was opposed by Sir Richard Vyvyan, a member for Cornwall, who contended that it would lead to a pure democracy because it would not stop short at what it had gained but would work to make Parliament the mere speaking-trumpet of the multitude.[3] This was also the tenor of other opposition speeches - the fear of democracy being paramount - and when the dramatic division took place in the dark hours of the night of 23 March the government Bill was passed by 302 votes to 301 - a majority of only one.[4]

Macaulay's vivid pen sketched a picture of the ensuing memorable scene:

"It was like seeing Caesar stabbed in the Senate

---

2. *Ibid.*, third series. [3] 629.
3. *Ibid.* 629/45.
4. *Ibid.* 804.

House, or seeing Oliver taking the mace from the table; a sight to be seen only once, and never to be forgotten. The crowd overflowed the House in every part. The Ayes and Noes were like two volleys of cannon from opposite sides of a field of battle. After the count, and amid great excitement, the tellers scarcely got through the crowd; for the House was thronged up to the table, and all the floor was fluctuating with heads like the pit of a theatre. But you might have heard a pin drop as Duncannon read the numbers.

Then again the shouts broke out, and many of us shed tears. I could scarcely refrain. And the jaw of Peel fell; and the face of Twiss was as the face of a damned soul; and Herries looked like Judas taking his necktie off for the last operation. We shook hands, and clapped each other on the back, and went out laughing, crying, and huzzaing into the lobby.

And no sooner were the outer doors opened than another shout answered that within the House. All the passages, and the stairs into the waiting-rooms, were thronged by people who had waited till four in the morning to know the issue. We passed through a narrow lane between two thick masses of them; and all the way down they were shouting and waving their hats, till we got into the open air.

I called a cabriolet, and the first thing the driver asked was, 'Is the Bill carried?' 'Yes, by one.' 'Thank

God for it, Sir'."[5]

The driver's sentiment was echoed in illuminated celebrations and public demonstrations throughout the length and breadth of the country. The king accepted the verdict and even Thomas Hardy the shoemaker declared himself "now for the first time a ministerial man" and a supporter of the government that was doing what Pitt had declared to be treason in 1794.[6] Fresh meetings in favour of reform were held at Chester, Pontefract and York, and at Aylesbury the vote was taken at 3 am and the result celebrated by the hoisting of the flag on the church tower. The bells there rang out for most of the day, the ringers "being regaled with large quantities of good ale" bestowed by the local brewers.[7]

A letter taking up more than an entire column of *The Times* from "Philo-Radical" celebrated the success on the second reading of the Bill. The anti-reformers, he said, had become a lawless band. Answering their cry that a victory by a margin of one was no majority, he pointed to the succession of Queen Anne which had also been decided by a single vote. He ended his letter by saying that the king had expressed his feelings by dismissing from his household the cousin and nominees of the Marquis of Hertford as well as "the old hack of office" Mr

---

5.   Letter to Thomas Ellis reproduced in G.O. Trevelyan's *The Life and Letters of Lord Macaulay*. i. 201/4. 1876.
6.   Hardy to Hobhouse. 2 April 1831. BL. *Add. MSS.* 36,466. For Hardy's treason trial see *ante*, chapter 3.
7.   *The Times*, 28 March 1831, p. 2.

J. Calvert, the nominee of the house of Montague. The king, he concluded, feared nothing and dared do anything of benefit to the people,[8] thereby overlooking the fact that the king, who was far from daring, had acted on the advice of the Cabinet.

Despite the wild enthusiasm for the Bill in the country generally, those in favour were not unanimous about precisely what changes they wanted and petitions against reform, though by no means common, were published. Some indication of the language used by those against reform may be gleaned from a petition from Blandford Forum in Dorset which read, "The petitioners view with horror and dismay the Bill introduced into the House for the purpose of reforming the representation of the people ... its direct tendency to overthrow the equilibrium now so happily established in King and Lords and Commons appears to the petitioners to be equally dangerous and unconstitutional." In Edinburgh also petitioners said they contemplated the reform with the most serious alarm and believed that the whole system of political representation under which the country had risen to a condition of prosperity unexampled in the history of the world was to be suddenly and violently overturned.[9] But *The Times* carried details of the far greater number of petitions still flowing into Parliament urging reform. The total number at this time calling for universal suffrage *and* the ballot was 34, and for the

---

8.   *Ibid.*, p. 5.
9.   *Ibid.* 1 April 1831, p. 4.

ballot alone 133. There were also 314 other reform petitions giving a total of 481 presented to Parliament between 16 November 1830 and 21 March 1831.

Defeat

After Easter the House went into committee on the measure but it was clear that with such a small majority the Bill would not pass in the Lords. However, in a misguided effort to save the situation Russell told the members of the committee on April 18,[10] that several boroughs would no longer be disenfranchised, certain new towns would be given the vote and eight counties would receive an extra member. This would bring the total of the House to 627 instead of 596. Using a minor issue of what the appropriate number of members of the House from each part of the kingdom should be the Tories, on an amendment in committee by General Gascoyne, a determined ultra-Tory, proceeded to defeat the government by eight votes.[11] It was a pyrrhic victory, however since, in response, the government decided upon a dissolution of Parliament and an opportunity to appeal to the people. As in the prevailing mood of the country a general election would undoubtedly see the Whigs return with an increased majority, the Tories proposed in the Lords an Address to the Crown against dissolution. They

---

10. *Hansard*, third series. [3] 1510/30.
11. *Ibid.* 1688.

preferred to see the government stumble on in ignominy. This brought forth, on 23 April another thundering *Times* leader, quoted here in full:

"We now call upon the people of England to unite as one man. The crisis has arrived! It is clear to demonstration that no Reform Bill will be passed by the present House of Commons! It is an enemy to reform. At first we were sorry that a majority should have been obtained against ministers upon a point which seemed, though coming from the friends of the boroughmongerage, to propose an addition to the popular representations; but it is obvious that this was all a trick, and nothing else. It is clear, therefore, that Parliament meant to resist reform, and must be dissolved, or there is an end to all hope of reform!

The cup is dashed from our parched lips; and the sale of seats in the Commons, like the bullock stands in Smithfield; and the nomination of members to act as our representatives; and the aggrandisement of great families for their parliamentary influence, at the expense of the people, and in defiance of modest merit, all, all must continue, till the state, and its noblest institutions, is akin to one common ruin. A dissolution only can stay the evil, and a dissolution is now called for and determined on unanimously by Ministers. The House is an enemy to reform! It is worse than a rancorous enemy - it is a subtle one. It has shuffled off the question of reform by a stratagem. What, then, are the people of England to do to retain a glimpse of their beloved reform, otherwise lost - lost perhaps for ever? Let them now prepare themselves to petition for a dissolution, unless, indeed, which is most probable, dissolution shall be immediate. The King, it is certain, will not hesitate to take this decisive step: still the people, till they know that dissolution is decided on, should call meetings and combine in resolutions and petitions to the throne for a dissolution of Parliament. In fact, we should see England in motion at this moment, and everything that we have hitherto observed in county, borough, and parish meetings, for reform, is the stillness of private life when compared with the fervid bustle now excited for the dissolution of that House of Commons which has put its veto on reform.

'If,' we say to our countrymen, 'you have ever grieved over the scandal of a mock representation, - if you have ever sighed for your just rights, and a voice in your own House of Parliament, - if you have ever met and resolved, and re-resolved, and screwed up your courage to the sticking point, that your noblest and wealthiest towns *should* have representatives, and the mere nominees of peers be banished from the Commons House of Parliament, - that Gatton and St Mawes, and Boroughbridge and Old Sarum, and scores of other depopulated ruins should be erased from the list of parliamentary boroughs, - now is the time to follow up the blow and call for the immediate dissolution of that body which says, in more than words, that these abominations shall exist in spite of you. If a new Parliament sanctions them, then we will become anti-reformers too'."

The only recourse left open for the Whigs in face of the Tory attempt to prevent dissolution, was to persuade the king to prorogue Parliament as soon as possible and in person. Grey and Brougham attended upon the king whom they found furious at actions the government had taken without his consent, including calling out troops to prevent any possible disturbances. Brougham proved both strong-willed and conciliatory and, considering that by their Address the Lords were infringing his prerogative, William finally agreed to a prorogation. This now provoked the Tories to endeavour to pass their motion for an Address before the king in person reached the Upper House. As a result there were scenes of violent uproar in the Lord's chamber as the king approached in his coach. So disorderly were the usually sedate members that frequently peers endeavouring to speak could not be heard. Similar scenes were taking place in the Commons.[12] Finally the Tories' move was foiled by the filibustering of Brougham as lord chancellor. The king, whose coronation had not yet taken place, duly appeared with his crown awry and prorogued Parliament which was thereby dissolved. Nevertheless, the struggle was by no means over although without that one-vote majority on 23 March, the Bill would have been lost altogether.

The government, *The Times* said in another leading

---

12. *Ibid.* 1806/24.

article, had now transferred the defence of their cause to the people at large. The paper wanted nothing unreasonable, not revolution but reform to prevent revolution. It concluded that, "the people will never sit down tranquilly under the atrocious wrong of having block representatives presented to impose taxes on them in Parliament."[13]

With a fervour in the country not previously witnessed, the consequent general election, with the rallying cry of "freedom versus privilege", saw the defeat at the polls of Tory placemen in the most unlikely constituencies and a far stronger Whig government was swept into power with popular support and a majority of between 130 and 140. A typical example of an election came from Cockermouth in Cumberland. *The Times* headed its report from the constituency, "The defeat of the Great Northern Boroughmonger". Sir James Graham with 942 votes and William Blamire with 915, both reformers, heavily defeated Lord Lowther who received 452 votes. Beneath this result the newspaper exclaimed, *"Lord Lowther has resigned"*. It pointed out that Cumberland, "which has now so nobly emancipated itself" had been 72 years under the influence of the Lowthers.[14] As, indeed, had other places. In 1780 Lord Lowther had secured the nomination of Appleby for Pitt who was expected to do what he was told but he quickly exchanged his seat for that of Cambridge University. Nevertheless,

---

13. 25 April, p. 2.
14. 11 May, p. 2.

Lowther frequently returned nine of his nominees to the House of Commons where they were known derisively as his "ninepins".[15]

At this point the king conferred the Order of the Garter on the prime minister, and Lord John Russell introduced a second Reform Bill on 24 June.[16] After speeches in the Commons similar to those which had been made earlier, the second reading was passed on 6 July, this time by 367 votes to 231 - a much increased majority of 136.[17] But subsequently in committee the government made a surprising concession. Among a host of Tory amendments, one, known as the Chandos clause after its sponsor the Marquess of Chandos, which was intended to enfranchise in the counties £50 tenants-at-will who had no security of tenure, was accepted by the Cabinet, although only following a vote of 232 to 148 in its favour. It was disliked by reformers since its effect would be to enable landlords to control more votes on their estates - the so-called "faggot votes". After 40 nights of debate the committee stage ended on 7 September and the report stage took a further three nights. The remaining stages of the Bill were soon agreed and it was finally passed by the Commons on 21 September by a majority of 109.[18] It was then sent on its fateful journey to the Lords where petitions in its support again flooded in. Brougham alone tabled eighty and Grey more than 40.

---

15. Porritt. *Op. cit.*, 313.
16. *Hansard*. [4] 322.
17. *Ibid.* 906.
18. *Ibid.* [7] 464.

The City Moves

Anticipating what might happen in the Upper House, *The Times* was relentless in its attack on the peers. A further leader feared that the majority could be so ill-informed or reckless as to think they were passing an ordinary vote when they threw out the Reform Bill. "Can the Tory leaders govern England by means of the army and the House of Lords?" it asked. "Would the troops be made the instruments of such a base dominion? Never!" The Lords, it continued, were poorly qualified to carry out an internecine war with the nation. If they mutilated or rejected the Bill they would be "guilty of throwing the empire into confusion and endangering their own existence."[19]

Two days later an approach was made to the lord mayor of London with a requisition to call what was known as a Common Hall for the purpose of petitioning, on behalf of the Livery of London, the House of Lords to pass the Bill. The lord mayor responded positively and said he would appoint a deputation for the assembly of the Livery for the occasion. Placards were ordered to be paraded through the City saying that the Common Hall would take place on the following Monday and calling upon the Livery to attend to the petition.[20] The merchants and bankers of the city duly presented their requisition and the lord mayor expressed his utmost gratification on

---

19. *The Times*, 12 September, p. 4.
20. *Ibid.* 16 September, p. 3.

receiving it. Other requisitions, from Farringdon Within, Mile End Old Town, Westminster, Kent, Boston, Edinburgh, Sheffield and Dumfries all aimed to petition the Lords.[21]

The pressure on the Lords continued. A special court of the Common Council waited on the lord chancellor, Lord Brougham, to request that he present their petitions praying that the Lords would not reject the Bill. As was to be expected Brougham assured the lord mayor that he accepted with pleasure the office of presenting the petitions and would support them by every means in his power.[22]

The Lords' Decision

The second reading in the House of Lords was moved on 3 October, 1831 by Lord Grey who still believed, correctly, that it was no threat to the aristocracy. It could be adopted, he said, "with perfect safety to the rights and privileges of all orders of the state, and particularly of that order to which your Lordships belong." The Bill was a measure of justice, sound policy, peace and conciliation. The right to send representatives to Parliament, he said, was a trust and not a form of property as was being argued by the Tories. And it was a great mistake to confuse the obligations of a trust with the rights of

---

21. *Ibid.* 19 September, p. 5.
22. *Ibid.* 28 September, p. 5.

property.

In a final attempt at reassurance he told the Lords, "The respect due to your rank, and the influence which, from property, you necessarily possess, will belong to you after the passing of the Bill, as fully and in as great a degree as they do now. The odious power which is possessed by some of you does not help to increase that legitimate influence ... but if you resolve to maintain the nomination [ie, rotten] boroughs the whole voice of the United Kingdom will be raised against you." If they did not adopt the Bill they would have a call for something infinitely stronger and more extensive in its stead![23]

According to *The Times* Grey had made "a grave and dignified speech, a model of luminous statement and calm reasoning, the product of a whole life's observation of the most momentous subject that could agitate the British state." He had said, it continued, that he would stand or fall by the Bill and that he would never attempt such a fraud upon the nation as to offer it a less complete reform. The meaning of that, said the paper, was that should the Bill be lost he would propose to the king that a sufficient number of new peers be created to carry the Bill in a speedily ensuing session and if that request were denied he would then be bound in conscience to retire.[24]

Lord Wharncliffe, however, remained unimpressed by the speech. He defended nomination boroughs, he said, because they acted as a check in the House of Commons

---

23. *Hansard. Op. cit.* 928/69.
24. 4 October, p. 4.

on those members who were more popularly elected.[25] Popular feelings should not have too great an influence. The Duke of Wellington agreed and thought the Bill if carried would make the government of the country impossible and force would be required. He foresaw the "horrors of a democratic revolution" which would probably end in the establishment of a military despotism. The country's prosperity would be lost if there came about a wild democracy, a complete democratic assembly, under the name of a House of Commons.[26] He was afraid of what today is termed an "elective dictatorship".

In the words of J.R.M. Butler, the Tories believed that after the duke had resigned as prime minister the Whigs abused an unparalleled opportunity of restoring quiet by a grant of moderate reform. Instead, "Mere wreckers, without a single constructive idea, they were thoughtlessly demolishing the subtle product of ages of political wisdom, or rather of unplanned organic growth ... They were smashing the entire fabric."[27] As was seen earlier, in the days before there was a widespread suffrage little attempt was made to sweeten blatantly anti-democratic sentiments in favour of privilege

Brougham, the lord chancellor, now sidelined in government but remaining resolute in his support of the Bill, told the Lords that it was complained that in future members would be delegates. But already, he said, a

---

25. *Hansard. Op. cit.* 969/87.
26. *Ibid.* 1186/1205.
27. Butler. *Op. cit.* 248/9.

member was a delegate even if he was returned by only one delegator. Surely, he contended, there could be no more mischief in a person being delegated by 4,000 persons than by one or fourteen. A member returned by a real constituency was still honest, whereas the nominee of an individual was returned under false and hypocritical pretences for he was called the representative of the people when he was only a guardian of the interests of the individual who had delegated him.

In a lengthy speech lasting over three hours delivered in a temperature of 85 degrees, Brougham eulogised the middle class as the guardians of wealth and knowledge. He declared that:

"Opponents have protested against yielding to the clamour of the mob. If there is a mob there is the people also. I speak now of the middle classes - of those hundreds of thousands of respectable persons - the most numerous and by far the most wealthy order in the community; for if all your Lordships' castles, manors, rights of warren and rights of chase, with all your broad acres, were brought to the hammer, and sold at 50 years' purchase, the price would fly up and kick the beam when counterpoised by the vast and solid riches of those middle classes, who are also the genuine depositories of sober, rational, intelligent, and honest English feeling ...

They will neither be led astray by false reasoning, nor deluded by impudent flattery: but so neither will they be scared by classical quotations, or brow-beaten by fine sentences; and as for an epigram, they care as little for it as they do for a cannon-ball ... They had weighed the matter well, and they looked to the government and to the Parliament for an effectual Reform ...

Rouse not, I beseech you" [he cried raising his arms] "a peace-loving, but a resolute people; ... I pray and I exhort you not to reject this measure. By all you hold most dear - by all the ties that bind every one of us to our common order and our common country, I solemnly adjure you - I warn you - - I implore you - yea, on my bended knees, I supplicate you - Reject not this Bill!"[28]

After that *tour de force* a number of fairly mundane speeches followed (except those of Lord Lyndhurst who feared the aristocracy in the Commons would lose 135 members and of Lord Grey who emphasised that he was honestly serving king and country) and eventually the House of Lords divided at 6 o'clock on the morning of Saturday, 8 October. The voting was: Contents (including 30 proxies), 158; Non-Contents (including 49 proxies), 199. Thus the majority against the Bill was 41, with 21 out of 23 bishops having voted against.[29] As E.L. Woodward has pointed out, it is an interesting fact that 108 out of the 112 peers whose creation went back before 1790 voted in favour of the Bill and that if the 21 bishops

---

28. *Hansard,* third series. [8] 220/75.
29. *Ibid.* 340.

had voted in favour it would have had a majority of one.[30] Grey was now forced to consider the question of creating new peers but the king vetoed the idea. Two days later the Commons responded to the Lords by passing a motion of confidence in the government by a majority of 131.[31]

---

30. *The Age of Reform: 1815-1870. Op. cit.* 79.
31. *Hansard. Op. cit.* 460.

CHAPTER 9

Reform or Revolution

The rejection of the Reform Bill by the House of Lords was received in London as a national calamity. *The Times* could barely get over the enormity of what had happened. It asked, "What have the Lords done?" and answered, "They have done what they can never undo ... the four hundred or so Lords have drawn a line between them and 22 million people."[1]

Rioting

On 9 October 1831 the Whig *Morning Chronicle*, the *Sun* and the radical *Ballot* each appeared with black borders and there were many disorderly meetings. The house of the Duke of Newcastle was attacked and the Marquis of Londonderry was nearly murdered in his coach. The police had great difficulty in controlling a large body of NUWC supporters who marched on Westminster.[2]

In Derby there were riots during the night of 9 October. "The banking house of Messrs Crompton suffered dreadfully, every window being forced in. The

---

1. 10 October, p. 4.
2. Public Record Office. Home Office. 52. 14.

house of Mr Hayden, a surgeon, shared the same fate and his son Henry was killed by the mob. Every [street] lamp was broken and although soldiers paraded the whole of the night, owing to the darkness they were of little use." Shots were fired and a man hit in King Street was not expected to live. The next day business was at a standstill and all shops were shut. The Riot Act was read and soldiers fired on the people; two more men were shot, one dead and the other seriously wounded. In Nottingham every house was closed up and all business was at a standstill.[3] The castle was burned down, for which, in the following year, three men were hanged. In Birmingham the bells were tolled all night when the news reached the city and Thomas Attwood quickly called a meeting to protest which was attended by 100,000 people. In London demonstrations culminated in the windows of Apsley House, the home of the Duke of Wellington, being smashed for the second time that year.

The *Poor Man's Guardian* called upon the people to establish an armed Popular Guard as a counter-force against a middle class National Guard which had been proposed to protect property from either the military or mob violence.[4] For its part *The Times* demanded a force of "Conservative Guards" formed from householders who should "be drilled and taught the use of the firelock."

Lord Brougham attempted to calm the situation. After denouncing the outrages as the work of the enemies of

---

3. *The Times*. 12 October, p. 5.
4. 8 October 1831.

reform he called upon the people not to give way to any unfounded disappointment and told them that reform was delayed for only a short period. "I tell you," he declared, "the Bill will pass."[5]

A meeting of merchant bankers and traders in the City of London was held and expressed "grief, surprise and dismay at the rejection of the Reform Bill". Further meetings were held in Manchester, Bolton, Chatham, Bristol and Portsmouth. *The Times* said it had received brief accounts of meetings from so many parts of the country that it could find no room to report them in detail.[6] But there was room for one other report, taken from the *Derby and Chesterfield Reporter*, that the rioting in Derby had lasted for three days during which a great deal of property had been destroyed.[7]

A leader two days later declared that the king, Commons, nation and some of the peers themselves had said that they must be emancipated from a hundred boroughs. The law did not pass only "because 41 individuals in the Lords declared that the voice of the King and Commons and nation did not deserve to be listened to". Was it not utterly unheard of, it asked with a Churchillian ring, "that so much intrinsic power should suffer itself to be paralysed by such small means?"[8]

The next day a letter from Lord Grey assured readers

---

5. William Nassau Molesworth. *The History of England from the Year 1830-1874.* 181. 1875.
6. *The Times.* 14 October, p. 4.
7. *Ibid.* 15 October, p.4.
8. *Ibid.* 17 October, p. 2.

that another Reform Bill would be offered to Parliament immediately on the opening of the following session. All measures would be taken with a view to "the most effectual means of ensuring the success of this important object."[9] But the paper claimed yet again that the only way to achieve this was to "create or call up more peers and thus present a majority who would support the Bill."[10] A month later, it warned Lord Grey's Cabinet "not to knock its own brains out against another wall of its own building ... Make peers, Lord Grey, and prove the King's confidence in you; or resign tomorrow and prove at least you have not been the fabricator of your own bad fortune. The nation will then know what part to take."[11]

In the meantime Bristol had exploded.

Bristol in Flames

The Tory corporation of Bristol was self-elected and weak-willed. The die-hard anti-reformer Sir Charles Wetherell, who had been attorney-general in Wellington's government and was recorder of Bristol, went to the city on 29 October for the ordinary gaol delivery. As angry crowds had already fired Nottingham castle, the property of the highly unpopular Duke of Newcastle, and sacked the gaol at Derby, he made his entry in a carriage drawn

---

9. *Ibid.* 18 October, p. 3
10. *Ibid.* 19 October, p. 3.
11. *Ibid.* 15 November, p. 2.

by four grey horses many hours before he was due. It was an attempt to avoid any hostile reception that might be waiting for him. Even so, he was also escorted by a body of special constables and three troops of horse were sent to assist in keeping order, the soldiers being seen by the Bristol Political Union, and even some members of the city council, as a serious provocation.

In the event, the precautions were not entirely successful and large numbers of men and women who lined the route early yelled, hissed and groaned when they saw the recorder and threw stones at his carriage. Then, soon afterwards, when Wetherell was in the courtroom and the town clerk said reform was not relevant to the proceedings, uproar broke out. Wetherell told the members of the public present that if anyone caused a disturbance he would be sent to prison. This only provoked the spectators to further fury and the court was quickly adjourned. The recorder managed, with difficulty, to get to the Mansion House outside of which a man was killed by a blow on the head from a constable.

Something approaching a riot ensued and indeed the Riot Act was read. At this the crowds, instead of being cowed, rushed the constables who fled and also took refuge in the Mansion House. This building was soon itself attacked and Wetherell escaped in disguise by clambering over the roofs of adjoining houses. He then left the city. More troops now appeared on the scene and order was restored overnight. However, early the next morning of Sunday, 30 October, several hundred people assembled in the city square. They managed to occupy the

Mansion House and then attacked the gaol, to which several arrested men had been taken, and sent it up in flames after releasing all the prisoners. The troops returned but under the weak command of Colonel Brereton, who was said to support the reformers, they took no action despite the colonel having been authorised by the city's mayor, Charles Pinney, to take such steps to restore order as he thought fit once the Riot Act had been read. Encouraged by the immobility of the soldiers, the crowds set the Mansion House on fire followed by the Bishop's Palace, the Excise Office, the Custom House, two more prisons, four toll houses and 42 private dwellings and warehouses. *The Times* reported that altogether eight people were killed,[12] although in reality the total number of casualties ran into several hundreds. After all this the troops received cavalry reinforcements from Gloucester and Colonel Brereton belatedly found the will to restore order.

Aftermath

In early January 1832, just over two months after the riots had broken out, a number of men prominent in the disturbances were tried for various forms of riot by a special commission sitting at Bristol Guildhall with Sir Nicholas Tyndal, lord chief justice of the court of common pleas, as the presiding judge. Most pleaded their

---

12. 1 November 1831.

innocence but were found guilty amidst scenes of distress of both the defendants and the spectators in court. Of 127 prisoners, 81 were convicted and 21 acquitted; against 12 no bills were found by the grand jury; and on 13 indictments no evidence was offered. Of the prisoners convicted, 31 were sentenced to death, one was transported for fourteen years, six for seven years, and 43 were sentenced to various terms of imprisonment with hard labour.[13]

On 9 January 1832 Colonel Brereton was brought before a court-martial charged with conducting himself so feebly during the riots as to encourage the violence. He pleaded not guilty but after four days of the hearing, and facing disgrace, he took his own life by shooting himself through the heart.

Whilst Bristol was burning riots had also occurred at Bath, Coventry, Warwick and Worcester and in London angry crowds manhandled the king's carriage. On Guy Fawkes night effigies of bishops were hanged and burnt on many bonfires in place of the usual guy.

In point of fact these extreme outbreaks were an expression of the revival of spiritual and political life taking place among the middle and working classes after decades of repression. They transformed the battle for

---

13. A Citizen (John Eagles). *The Bristol Riots, their Cause, Progress and Consequences*. 258. 1832. It is perhaps not surprising that the author should have wished to remain anonymous as the book is seriously flawed by anti-reform bias. But it does contain useful appendices about the trials which followed the riots and statements by participants and observers including Sir Charles Wetherell.

reform. There was now to be a fight to the finish with either reform or revolution triumphant. A third way was no longer possible.

Propaganda

Talk of revolution was widespread and home office files bear witness to numerous disturbances occurring up and down the country. MPs and peers who opposed the Bill were mobbed and had their houses broken into, indeed often burned down. Pamphlets, leaflets and posters tumbled off the presses in profusion and many are still to be seen in the public record office. Examples of propaganda abound. One poster headed, "Reform! or Revolution!!" asked, "The House of Lords have presumed to *reject the Bill* ... Will you submit that 200 individuals shall make slaves of millions?" After calling for the creation of new peers its main message was: "Pay no more Taxes - Pay no more Tithes."[14] Another poster, under a heading "BLACKLIST", set out in full the names of the Lords who had voted against the Bill with figures of their wealth - described as "Pickings".[15] All were backed by argument in an era when posters put a case in words rather than by a visual image. More succinct was a handbill which simply called for the right to vote and

---

14. Public Record Office. Home Office Files. 40/29.
15. *Ibid.*

179

"war to the knife".[16]

The issue of Richard Carlile's *The Republican* journal for November 1831, dated merely "November - Year of the People", cried "Down with the Lords" and after referring to their lordships as "indescribable animals" called for the abolition of the House of Lords as a public nuisance. In the same month an unstamped issue of the *Poor Man's Guardian* told members of the working class that the Bill was "tyrannical, abominable, infamous and hellish." It urged, "You will be starved to death by thousands if this Bill passes, and thrown on the dunghill or on to the ground naked like dogs." On 10 December 1831 this paper published a statement by a Macclesfield radical that "it mattered not to him whether he was governed by a boroughmonger, or a whoremonger, or a cheesemonger, if the system of monopoly and corruption was still to be upheld."

On the other side were posters giving details of arrangements for the enrolment of special constables and a pamphlet by Joseph Sparrow entitled "Reform not Revolution". Edward Gibbon Wakefield published an undated but eagerly read pamphlet entitled: *Householders in Danger from the Populace.* In it he classed Rotunda radicals (of whom more below) and London thieves together as special objects of menace to all householders. "These," he wrote, "will be the fighting men of our revolution, if we must have one." Not to be outdone, both Whig and Tory newspapers denounced the

---

16. *Ibid.* 44/24.

Rotundists as revolutionaries, pickpockets and incendiaries contemplating an attack on every possessor of property and the uprooting of all law and order. Thus did the inflammatory war of words rage around the Bill.

The Rotundists

Most middle class reformers considered the Whigs' Bill to be a crucial step forward despite not meeting all their demands, in particular manhood suffrage and the ballot. Accordingly, they endorsed the famous slogan on the hustings: "The Bill, the whole Bill and nothing but the Bill." This was not the view however of the National Union of the Working Classes whose members were soon dubbed "Rotundists" by those who considered its full title, and its activities, distasteful. The Rotunda, as its name implies, was a large round building, situated in Blackfriars Bridge Road south of the Thames. Built originally as a riding school it was by this time owned by Richard Carlile, a frequently imprisoned radical printer, who issued from it the *Prompter* at 3 pence weekly. His politics may be summed up by his avowal that if moral resistance was not effective, physical resistance was to be recommended whenever there was a prospect of its success. Nevertheless, he supported the Bill, seeing it as a stepping stone to universal suffrage.

Lectures were given at the Rotunda most evenings and on one occasion when William Cobbett spoke not only was the hall filled but 3,000 people assembled outside.

This then, called by Carlile "the real House of Commons", came to house the meetings of the NUWC. Francis Place wrote that in 1831 the NUWC had some 500 members who each paid one halfpenny a week for their card. There were also about 1,000 who paid only occasionally at times of great excitement, but who reckoned themselves to be members.[17]

Some dozen branches were formed in various districts of London but the Rotunda was the important centre. Weekly public meetings were held there by the NUWC which, said Place, in confirmation of other reports, "would probably contain a thousand persons, and I have seen hundreds outside the doors for whom there was no room within." Other meeting places included the *Argyle Arms* in Argyle Street, the chapel in Finsbury Square, the *Blind Beggar* in Bethnal Green, the *Duke of York* at Hammersmith, the *Yorkshire Grey* in Hampstead, *The Compasses* in Bermondsey and the lecture room in Theobald's Road, Holborn; a clear indication of the extent to which the NUWC's activities in the capital stretched.

According to Place, the programme of the NUWC called for an end to the system of exploitation of wage slaves by masters and proclaimed that everything produced belonged to those whose labour produced it and should be shared among them. There should be no

---

17. The various statements by Place are taken from his journals in the *Place Papers*. BL. *Add. MSS*. 27,790/1, 27,796, 27,828, 35,149. This extract is from 27,790. fol.22. Place was, of course, partisan and the journals, written some years after the events they describe, whilst remaining an extensive and invaluable source are not always reliable.

accumulation of capital permitted to enable a few to employ others as labourers. And they considered, Place said, that anyone who differed from them was a "political economist" and a bitter foe of the working class. As a consequence, he claimed, they were not interested in a general election or in support for the middle class to secure reform. To Place this was an approach that could lead only to violent revolution and was a clear threat to the future of the middle class. Afraid of losing his prestige with the middle class Political Unions, he declared, with outraged feelings, that the Rotundists were "perfectly atrocious, resolute, reckless rascals" who desired nothing less than insurrection.[18] Yet, at least in Nottingham his own Political Union was itself reported to be arming rapidly.

In fact, the official declaration issued by the NUWC, and bearing some resemblance to both the United States' Declaration of Independence and the programme of Gerard Wynstanley's "Diggers" in seventeenth century England, proclaimed that all men were born equally free and had certain natural and inalienable rights. It demanded manhood suffrage and the ballot, as did a number of Radical MPs. As was usual at the time little thought was given to women having the vote. The natural and inalienable rights that all men were entitled to enjoy, it continued, were the same as those on which all governments should be founded. All property, honestly acquired, was sacred but all laws should be for the

---

18. *Ibid. Place Papers.* 27,791, fol. 48.

common benefit, protection and security of all the people. Notwithstanding the views of Place, in October 1831, after the rejection of the Bill by the House of Lords, a huge procession of 70,000 people marched on Westminster. Here a deputation of the NUWC waited upon Lord Melbourne, the home secretary, with an address praying his Majesty not to create any new peers but to abolish the House of Lords and introduce universal suffrage with vote by ballot. Melbourne responded that he could not present the address to the king because of its strong language. Furthermore, he said, his Majesty might as well hang a man without trial as attempt to suppress the House of Lords. The deputation replied that the Lords had already been tried and were convicted as traitors to their king and country and ought to be abolished,[19] which appears to have left Melbourne speechless. Meanwhile outside, all the nearby shops were closed - although whether in support of the deputation or out of fear of damage is not known - and white scarves of the Rotundists were to be seen everywhere. The NUWC appeared to be about to assume the leadership of the working class in London and it had close ties with Unions in other parts of the country.

However, the working class was divided and a great many of its members failed to support the Bill when they saw it would not be amended to offer them visible benefits. The new £10 voters supported the Bill but were mainly members of the middle class and it is significant

---

19. *Ibid.* fol. 306.

that "Orator" Hunt had found no enthusiasm for it among his industrial constituents. Many of them, along with a good many farmers, whom the Bill also left voteless, looked for leadership to Cobbett who wanted the ballot and an enlargement of the franchise in the Bill. Another group, made up mainly of better off artisans, followed Place and Henry Hunt and joined the Political Unions. But many trade unionists believed Parliament would never reform itself in a meaningful sense and supported the NUWC in its demand for direct action to establish universal (manhood) suffrage and redress economic grievances.

Francis Place

Alive to the threat posed by the NUWC, Place called a meeting at the famous *Crown & Anchor* tavern in the Strand for 31 October in order to inaugurate a *National Political Union*. The purpose was to recruit members, which was in accord with the tradition of the time that new political organisations should be formed at public meetings. According to the *Morning Chronicle* the next day, some 2,000 people attended. The tavern was crowded to suffocation with a strong contingent of Rotundists present. Place complained of their "fluent but remarkably ignorant" speeches filled with bitter notions of animosity against everybody who did not concur in their absurdities.[20] Because of the overcrowding the chairman, Sir Francis Burdett, adjourned the meeting to nearby Lincoln's Inn Fields where the crowd swelled to 20,000.

A resolution was duly proposed that the NPU be formed and a council elected. There were to be two objectives. The first was to secure effective representation of the middle and working classes in the House of Commons. The second, to preserve peace and order and guard against any disorder that enemies of the people might endeavour to incite. A bitter discussion followed with a great deal of disorder in the meeting. Ultimately, Dr Thomas Wakley,[21] a supporter of the NUWC, successfully moved an amendment to the resolution which provided that 50 per cent of those to be elected to the council of the NPU be drawn from the working class and 50 per cent from the middle class. Place was aghast. He had visions of middle class support for his new NPU vanishing into thin air. Although he wanted the two classes to present a common front he firmly believed leadership must be, and must be seen to be, in the hands of the middle class led by himself, with the artisans in a purely supportive role.

Accordingly, Place called another meeting, for 10 November, at which the council would be elected. Wakley said he would stand for the council provided 50 per cent of its members were drawn from the working class. This,

---

20. *Ibid.* fol. 47.
21. For more about this remarkable man see John Hostettler. *Thomas Wakley - An Improbable Radical.* 1993.

said Place, would increase animosities and he described Wakley as particularly obnoxious, whilst admitting that it was impossible to proceed without him. He was less than pleased when Wakley was elected on to the committee formed to devise the procedure for the election of the council.

Thomas Wakley

In the meantime the NUWC called their own meeting to be held outside *White Conduit House* in White Conduit Street to the east of King's Cross at 1 pm on 7 November to press for manhood suffrage and the ballot. In fact, during this time Wakley, who had already founded *The Lancet*, was producing his own weekly newspaper called *The Ballot*. Remarkably like *The Times* of the day both in size and appearance, and with front-page advertisements, the first number had rolled off the presses on Sunday, 2 January 1831. Also like *The Times* its price was seven pence of which four pence went to the government in stamp duty. Typically, from its second issue it bore beneath its name the legend: "Edited by Thomas Wakley - to avoid the charge of 'secret' writing." Its first leader proudly claimed that the paper's title declared in one word its political creed - "We are Reformers in the fullest acceptance of the term." Accordingly, it campaigned not only for the ballot but also for universal suffrage and an end to all political abuses and corruption.[22]

Large numbers of handbills advertising the 7 November meeting were distributed and many were placed in the windows of small shopkeepers. They proclaimed the aims of the meeting and indicated that Wakley would take the chair. Place commented bitterly that Wakley and the Rotunda men had called the meeting to see how far they could rely on the mob for mischief. He maintained that at a meeting in a coffee-house in Fleet Street, held to organise the White Conduit meeting, it was proposed that everyone who attended should take a 20-inch stave as a weapon.

In response Wakley said he had accepted the chair of the forthcoming meeting to ensure its peaceful nature and he called upon members not to attend with staves. But the possession not of staves but of arms was being encouraged by *The Times*. After giving a full report of the Lincoln's Inn Fields' meeting, it editorially thundered; "We say to our fellow subjects, organise and arm."[23] "Fellow subjects" meant the middle class. This was, of course, the time when the preoccupation with the Reform Bill of its editor, Thomas Barnes, earned the newspaper the title of "The Thunderer". However, the Rotundists saw a middle class "National Guard" of the kind *The Times* wanted to see support the police and troops as a threat to themselves and, as we have seen, in consequence the *Poor Man's Guardian* (the weekly paper

---

22. For issues of *The Ballot* see BL Newspaper Library at Colindale.
23. 1 November 1831.

of the champion of a free press, Henry Hetherington) proposed an alternative "Popular Guard for England". "Keep yourselves prepared," it told its readers, "abstain from gin drinking, and lay by as much as possible out of your scanty earnings for the purchase of a musket." The *Guardian* bore the emblem of a hand-press, the motto "Knowledge is Power" and the heading: "Published contrary to 'Law' to try the power of 'Might' against 'Right'."[24]

In the event the NUWC meeting was cancelled when Melbourne declared its aims to be illegal, seditious and treason. According to the *Poor Man's Guardian* the members of the committee were to be seized as traitors. What is certain is that in the wake of the Bristol riots the government saturated the capital with troops and special constables. To avoid a probably bloody confrontation, Wakley lost no time in publishing on the day before the meeting was due to be held a huge poster bearing his name. Addressed from "Bedford Square, Sunday Morning" it called for prudence and postponement of the meeting on the ground that the "sanguinary Boroughmongers intended to make the working class victims of a fake plot for the forcible overthrow of the government and the entire destruction of peace and the social order." And for good measure he added, "Remember the KING himself is on your side and has declared unequivocally for REFORM."[25]

---

24. BL. Newspaper Library.
25. PRO. HO. 40/29.

And indeed the king had declared for reform, although not quite unequivocally, despite his dislike of the Unions working for it which he desired to have banned. Indeed, on 4 November the king's secretary, Sir Herbert Taylor, had written to Grey of the forthcoming demonstration, "His Majesty is by no means displeased that the measures contemplated by the meeting in question are so violent, and in other respects so objectionable, as he trusts that the manifestation of such intentions and such purposes may afford the opportunity and the facility of checking the progress of the Political Unions in general, the introduction and establishment of which, the King orders me to say, he cannot too often describe as being, in his opinion, far more mischievous and dangerous than any proceedings of a more avowed and violent character, palpably illegal and treasonable."[26] However, the government was not prepared to risk allowing the meeting to take place.

Wakley was heeded and the meeting did not materialise but on the following day a meeting at the Rotunda was attended by over 1,000 people, many armed with wooden truncheons and wearing tricolour cockades.[27] Nevertheless, by careful and unscrupulous selection of members for the NPU at the 10 November meeting, Place managed to sideline Wakley and the Rotundists, at least for the time being.

---

26. *Correspondence of King William IV and Earl Grey.* I. 401. 1875.
27. *Morning Chronicle.* 9 November 1831.

Cholera Alarm

The influence of the NUWC was also to be felt in 1832 when an epidemic of cholera had spread across the country killing several hundred people and provoking widespread alarm. Home Office files are full of reports of the terror it was causing. The response of the government was to call for a National Fast Day on 21 March 1832 when the people would be asked to atone for their sins and beseech God to dispel the epidemic. In the House of Commons "Orator" Hunt had earlier asked if the government were not aware that "one-third of the people of this kingdom fast almost every day in the week?"[28] And a lampoon distributed in London read:

Found lately dead, a bishop (quite aghast),-
Verdict - The prospect of a general fast.

The Rotundists, for their part, promptly ridiculed the government's "solution" , which they said lay in its own hands not the Almighty's, and called it a National Farce Day. To establish their point, and exhibit their strength, they called a demonstration in London for the same day. At 11 am their supporters assembled and some 100,000 people paraded the streets in a procession carrying at its head a loaf of bread and a round of beef bearing the inscription, "The True Cure for the Cholera". This

---

28. *Hansard,* third series. [2] 205.

continued until 4 pm when the protesters were asked to go home to feast.

As leaders of the procession, William Lovett, James Watson and William Benbow were arrested but were acquitted at their trial on 16 May. Their jury was no doubt aware that poverty and the lack of even the most elementary sanitation in towns and cities caused the cholera. As the medical officers of the Holborn Poor Law Union reported, if the cesspools of London were joined together they would have formed a channel 10 miles long, 50 feet wide and six feet deep. Together they polluted the Thames daily with 7,000 loads of poisonous filth. Not surprisingly disease, as well as hunger, was rife in many districts of London and it was many years before the scourge of cholera was defeated by improvements in sewage disposal and sanitation. The London sewerage system was not to be constructed until the 1860s and 1870s and the last great cholera outbreak was in 1866.

The revival of the Bill will now be considered.

CHAPTER 10

Victory

On 6 December 1831 Parliament was recalled and six days later Lord John Russell moved for leave to reintroduce the Reform Bill. It was now slightly amended to reduce to 30 the number of boroughs to be partially disenfranchised.[1] This meant that the existing number of MPs would not be reduced.

The Third Reform Bill

Sir Robert Peel claimed that the amendments justified the earlier rejection of the Bill by the Lords and added that some more might make it acceptable. Why then, asked Lord Althorp, were none of the amendments, which had been made, raised earlier by the opposition? In any event, he said, the main principle of the Bill remained precisely the same as it had been, as did all its material provisions.[2]

During the second reading debate on 16 December, Macaulay said there were two [hostile] parties in the country, a narrow oligarchy above, with all the vices that

---

1.   *Ibid.* [9] 156.
2.   *Ibid.* 178/81.

came from abuse of power, and an infuriated multitude below with all the vices that came from distress and destitution. However, he did not fear a collision since he found between them a third party infinitely more powerful than either, which was the party that supported the Bill - the middle class of England.[3]

In other respects the debate, with some interminable speeches, followed the lines of the earlier ones with a great deal of repetition and on 17 December the second reading was carried by a majority of 324 votes to 162. Despite the size of the majority the creation of more peers was believed by many to be the only means by which the passage of the Bill could be ensured in the Lords. Following a visit to Brighton by Lord Grey to see the king it was said in the press that William would create as many peers as were necessary to ensure the "restoration of the privileges of England". Some would be created immediately and others a little later.[4] But the king refused to agree to stages and whilst accepting that he might have to create some new peers he was prepared to do so only as a last resort if it was necessary to save the Bill and provided the number was not too large. When publicly nothing appeared to be happening, "Liberal" wrote to *The Times* warning that the Lords would throw out the Bill unless more peers were created.[5]

A hoax report, which was put down to a trick of

---

3. *Ibid.* 386/7.
4. For example, *The Times*, 9 January 1832, p. 2.
5. *Ibid.* 26 January, p. 3.

anti-reformers, appeared in the French newspaper *Le Temps* which assured its readers that the Reform Bill had been withdrawn at a late hour on the previous Saturday.[6]

In mid-January 1832 the House went into committee[7] and, although many amendments were proposed, none raised the issues of the ballot, universal suffrage or annual Parliaments. When "Orator" Hunt suggested that all householders and everyone paying taxes and rates should have the vote he received support from only 11 members against 290.[8] A damaging, and outrageous, motion by Lord Chandos to get rid of the metropolitan members drew a warning that reformers should not absent themselves from the chamber[9] and in the division an amendment to retain the metropolitan members was passed by 236 to 116.[10]

By this time *The Times* was also becoming irritated at the lack of action regarding the Lords. An editorial actually attacked Lord Grey, asking for proof of what he would do about the creation of more peers. He should, it said, react to Lord Harrowby's ultimatum that he would support the Bill only if it were a different Bill. A list of new peers was necessary, "sufficient to guarantee the peace of the kingdom from immeasurable ruin."[11] On 22 March 1832 the third reading of the Bill in the Commons

---

6. *Ibid.* 4 February, p. 3.
7. *Hansard. Op. cit.* 651.
8. *Ibid.* 1223.
9. *The Times*, 27 February 1832, p. 3.
10. *Ibid.* 29 February, p. 3.
11. 7 March, p. 3.

received a majority of 116 votes. However, a further letter from "Philo-Radical" warned Grey that he could place no reliance on waverers in the Lords and only the creation of peers before the second reading in that place would suffice.[12] But in a letter in the same issue "An Alarmist" wrote that notwithstanding the powerful appeals to Grey it appeared certain that the king would not create peers and there was therefore a risk of the Bill being rejected. In fact, unknown to "An Alarmist" or the newspaper, the vacillating William IV had by now actually agreed with Grey, on certain conditions, to create new peers if necessary, a suggestion first put to Grey by Brougham some time before.

Truculent Lords

The Bill was duly sent to the Lords again and the second reading, proposed by Lord Grey, commenced on 9 April[13] with the debate lasting four days. Not all change was revolution, said Grey in opening the debate, least of all what would be achieved by the Bill. Lord Ellenborough, with some unusual prescience, still wanted the measure to be rejected since otherwise it would be impossible to resist demands for further concessions until universal suffrage was established - which, of course, is precisely what eventually happened. What was needed instead,

---

12. 23 March, p. 3.
13. *Hansard*, third series. [12]. 1.

Ellenborough declared, was firm government.

Most speakers in both Houses, and on both sides, spoke of the prosperity and international prestige of Great Britain. Not so the Catholic peer Lord Shrewsbury who on the second day of the Lords' debate struck a very different note. He accepted what he called "the irresistible demands of the people" and said he for one believed the Constitution had never been anything but a "beautiful theory". He saw it as having involved the country in unjust and expensive wars, debt of £800m, civil strife, rebellion, revolution and commercial disasters. They were surrounded by a crowded population, poor, unemployed and starving in the midst of plenty. Crime had increased both in atrocity and in frequency and the reins of government were stained by the most profligate corruption in every department of state. As a consequence the people, driven to desperation by their sufferings, had risen to emancipate themselves from a state of oppression they could no longer endure. "The Bill," he went on to predict, "will give the constitution fair play ... producing a freedom and activity and energy which have hitherto been unknown." The Lords, he continued, now stood for judgment before the people. Their only hope of pardon was to sue for it in "this act of justice". "Pass this Bill my Lords," he pleaded, "and all your power will be restored - not the power which you have hitherto possessed of doing mischief - but the power of doing good."[14]

The influential Earl of Harrowby confirmed that he

---

14. *Ibid.* 122/6.

had changed his mind since the previous Lords' debate despite being denounced as a "deserter" to his party and a "treacherous friend". He was clearly influenced by the activities of the public and also asked how the peers could say otherwise when the House of Commons, by large and increased majorities, had declared of itself that it was unworthy of the confidence of the people it professed to represent.[15] Clearly the situation was changing and his view was accepted by Lord Wharncliffe who had moved the amendment which threw out the former Bill.[16] The Bishop of London also said he would support the Bill. The mood of the country was penetrating the House of Lords although characteristically the Duke of Wellington remained unmoved by it all, still firmly believing that the Bill would lead to revolution.[17]

Dr Phillpotts, the Bishop of Exeter, in a long and virulent speech, took a novel stance in opposing the Bill. First, he believed that the nomination boroughs involved no usurpation of the rights of the people since their existence was justified because they had been created precisely for the benefit of great proprietors. He also thought that whilst democracy was glorious and valuable it had to be restrained. Thirdly, although he said he approved of having the debates of Parliament published the public had most seriously usurped the rights of their Lordships by doing so![18]

---

15. *Ibid.* 148/59.
16. *Ibid.* 177.
17. *Ibid.* 166.
18. *Ibid.* 271/87.

Lord Durham, who was absent from much of the debate through illness, on this occasion enjoyed attacking the bishop's speech for its "coarse and virulent invective, malignant and false insinuations, the grossest perversions of historical fact, decked out with all the choicest flowers of his well-known pamphleteering slang," and went on to make a vigorous speech extolling the middle class. He suggested that the gentry, living apart in the country, followed the amusements and enjoyments of their class and left the support of the liberal arts to the inhabitants of the towns whose political maturity was now apparent. Accordingly, the middle class had become entitled to a share in the government and were fit to exercise it.[19]

When the House finally divided on 13 April, the voting was as follows: Contents (including 56 proxies) 184; Non-Contents (including 49 proxies) 175 - a majority of nine for the second reading. This was treated in an anxious country as a glorious victory but the Duke of Wellington and 73 other peers immediately entered a protest against the decision in the journals of the House.[20] The Lords then went into committee on 7 May when a motion by Lord Lyndhurst to delete the disenfranchising clauses of the Bill was carried by 151 votes to 116.[21]

---

19. *Ibid.* 353/65.
20. *Ibid.* 459/63 for the full text and the names of the signatories.
21. *Ibid.* 724.

The Government Resigns

The government, decided to treat this vote as fatal to the Bill and Lord Grey asked the king to create 50 new peers, without which he warned him the ministers would resign. When the king claimed that the number desired was too large and refused Grey's request the ministers carried out the threat and William accepted their resignations. Such was the popularity of William that many people blamed the queen and the king's advisers for his decision. "Radical" wrote that the refusal on the part of the king arose from a deep-laid intrigue of which he had become the victim. Grey had done his duty and observed his integrity.[22]

In the meantime the ministers were to remain in office until their successors could be appointed. In fact, the king had earlier agreed to create forty new peers if that proved necessary to get the Bill through - so the number at issue was only 10.

For the moment the Bill was lost and dismay and indignation were again felt throughout the country at the Lords' action. The king asked Lord Lyndhurst, a former lord chancellor, to test the water in order to find if it would be possible for a new administration to be formed which could introduce what he called "moderate but extensive" reform. Lyndhurst approached Wellington who supported the idea but Peel threw the Tories into disarray when he opposed it and refused to serve in such a

---

22. *The Times,* 10 May 1832, p. 4.

government either as prime minister or as a member of the Cabinet. The king nevertheless gave an audience to the duke who was asked to endeavour to form an administration even if he were not its head.

Wellington had already expressed in the strongest terms how unconstitutionally he believed the Commons were acting[23] but with the defection of the more astute and far-seeing Peel it was likely that he would find his task impossible to perform. He began attempts to form a ministry but the Commons lost no time in debating the situation on 10 May on a motion of confidence moved by Viscount Ebrington in order to press the king to change his mind. Peel objected strongly on the ground that it amounted to a claim by the Commons to override both the amending powers of the Lords and the right of the crown to select its ministers.[24]

Joseph Hume alleged that the Bill's opponents in the Lords were acting from inside knowledge - "whispered by some little bird" - of the stand the king would take.[25] Macaulay, for his part, contended that under the constitution there was no doubt that the king could dissolve Parliament as a means of dealing with the House of Commons. In turn, however, the House was a check upon the king for it could refuse supplies. But there was no check at all upon the House of Lords. In any event, it was necessary to ensure a proper balance of peers by

---

23. *Hansard.* 998/9.
24. *Ibid.* 839.
25. *Ibid.* 822.

creating peers from the Whig party. Fifty such would help, he thought, and could hardly be denied when the Tories had created 200 from their own party when they held power.[26] In the end the Commons voted by a majority of 80 not to support any other ministry but that of Grey.[27]

Nevertheless, it was widely assumed, without any solid basis, that the duke would succeed and *The Spectator* speculatively published details of the "new ministry" with the duke appearing as premier. Equally premature, *The Times* dryly commented that the popularity of the "new administration" could be estimated from the fact that the troops from Windsor were marching towards London and the marines had been ordered from Portsmouth.[28]

Whilst behind-the-scenes manoeuvres by Wellington were taking place Francis Place and the Political Unions were also active; hatching plans to defeat the duke. On 11 May delegates from Birmingham and other parts of the country began to arrive in London for a council of war. An enthusiastic meeting at the *Crown and Anchor* in the Strand petitioned the House of Commons to grant supplies only to a Whig government. Similar meetings were held in towns as far apart as Preston and Portsmouth and carried over 290 petitions against supplies.[29]

---

26. *Ibid.* 851/2.
27. *Ibid.* 864.
28. *The Times*, 14 May 1832, p. 4.
29. Place Papers. BL. *Add. MSS.* 27,793. fol. 100 and 27,794, fols. 58, 344 and 347.

A Tactical Risk

It had taken the House of Lords' final attempt to torpedo the Bill in May to bring the NPU and the Rotundists into joint action for the first time. Political tension was rapidly mounting to ever greater heights. According to the *Morning Chronicle* of 12 May 3,000 new members joined the National Political Union in the three preceding days. *The Times*, in one issue alone on 16 May, gave lengthy reports of meetings in Birmingham, Leeds, Manchester, Liverpool, London, Norwich and other cities, all held the previous day and all giving vent to lively feelings of anger at the Lords' manoeuvring. Francis Place, encouraged, but with desperation, now played a high-risk tactical game.

He had long been known as the back-room mastermind behind all the great agitations of the early nineteenth century. The son of a debtors' lodging house keeper he had left school at 14 and by his own efforts had become the master tailor of Charing Cross Road known to every history book dealing with the period. It was, of course, the room behind his shop that was so important and the passage to it so well trodden. From it Place had directed the campaigns of Sir Francis Burdett to become the long-sitting member for the turbulent constituency of Westminster. Here too, with Joseph Hume, he had plotted and secured the repeal of the Combination Acts that had made trade unions illegal. He was also a close adviser to royalty and a friend of Jeremy Bentham whose utilitarian philosophy was to give birth to so many reforms of the

Victorian age. Bentham advocated near universal suffrage, annual Parliaments, the ballot and equal electoral districts. But he was a thinker not an organiser like Place, who was a masterly tactician and was now to use his skills to gamble with the future of the Constitution.

Many of the Lords, aided and abetted by Queen Adelaide, whose name was consequently removed from the signs of many public-houses, set out to persuade the king to act at once by making the Duke of Wellington prime minister and thus enabling him to wreck the Bill. Although the army was only 11,000 strong Wellington had said in October 1831 that, "the people of England are very quiet if they are let alone, but if they won't be quiet, there is a way to make them." Now, by May 1832, insurrection was expected. The NPU held meetings every evening and began to prepare for armed resistance to the duke. Place recorded in his journals later that if Wellington had been appointed prime minister there would have been an open civil and military response. He wrote that soldiers of all ranks, as well as military and naval men of wide experience were in contact with him and were ready to organise and conduct the operations of the people. Even generals and colonels were involved. And by this time many people were armed with swords, pike-heads and muskets. The clouds of revolution threatened.

Success

On 12 May Place and delegates from many parts of the country held a secret meeting at a tavern in Covent Garden at which they hit upon the cry: "To stop the Duke, Go for Gold." Apparently sufficient cash was raised on the spot to have bill-stickers at work posting bills raising this call in less than four hours. Shortly afterwards the delegates were on their way throughout the land taking the message to their supporters. Place wrote to the government warning that if it allowed the duke to take office as premier there would be civil war with the money from the banks "at our command". In fact, in two days the Bank of England had already had to pay out large sums of money.[30] "When we obtain the money," Place claimed, "he cannot get it ... we shall then have power to feed and lead the people and in less than five days we shall have the soldiers with us."[31]

Behind the message, which Place hoped would be enough to forestall the appointment, plans went ahead to have all large towns such as Birmingham barricaded, to have families of Tory Lords seized and held as hostages for the conduct of the duke towards reformers and for a call to be issued to soldiers to join the people. On 16 May, *The Times*, in a leading article, strongly attacked the duke for preparing coercive laws. Such "oppressive and revolting laws" it said, "*must* be enforced by violence -

---

30. *Ibid.* 27,793. fol. 148.
31. *Ibid.* 27,794. fol. 278.

there is no other method. It is not then the people's Bill, but the people's butchery!" Claiming that there would be reform or revolution the paper asserted, "The Tories do not dread the mob: the mob is their natural ally." But it considered that an armed people embraced the nation itself and would not make war on itself or its representatives.

Despite the rhetoric, after his failure to form a ministry by 15 May there is no evidence that the duke was any longer interested in attempting to destroy the Bill and yet, in such a critical situation, for the first time the Whigs pledged to support a Tory Reform Bill if one should be forthcoming. When the Commons met on 14 May there were unprecedented scenes of excitement and violence. On the House receiving a petition from the Livery of the City of London, Viscount Ebrington declared that he would give cordial and zealous support to a Tory Reform Bill if it were similar to the Whigs' own. However, he would be surprised if the duke were capable of adopting such a course after previously calling down the vengeance of heaven on the principle of the Bill.[32]

Thomas Duncombe, MP for Finchley, said that he did not deny the duke's learning or talents, "but his whole life had been one scene of political prostitution and apostasy."

He continued that if a new administration was to be composed of the opponents of the Reform Bill, "their principles must be like certain vehicles, like crane-necked carriages, the advantage of which is, that they turn round

---

32. *Hansard*, third series. [12] 908.

in the smallest possible space. In such a vehicle must the Duke of Wellington go down to the House of Lords. What will be the beasts that draw him, who the charioteer that drives him, or who the pensioned lackeys that stand behind him, I know not; but this I know, that, under the circumstances I would rather be the tailor that turns his coat than the Duke of Wellington with all his glories."[33]

Macaulay declared that the duke, who had said the Reform Bill was shocking to all notions of justice and destructive of the monarchy, was guilty of public immorality and faced the possible degradation of what was perhaps the most illustrious name in British history.[34] Lord John Russell spoke in similar terms. From a different position Wellington's staunch supporter, Sir Robert Inglis, viewed any possible new Bill with the "greatest pain, as one of the most fatal violations of public confidence which could be inflicted."[35]

Not that there *was* a Tory Bill however, as the very men the duke needed to form a government wilted under the assault and on 15 May he was forced to tell the king that he was unable to go ahead. William was now reduced to hoping that Grey, who was still in office, would find the Bill no longer opposed by the Lords, although many peers continued to express their contempt for the "evil" Whig Bill with great vehemence.

Tory newspapers were less than enthusiastic about

---

33. *Ibid.* 971/8.
34. *Ibid.* 921/2.
35. *Ibid.* 947.

the situation in the country being allowed to continue, reflecting on the panic afflicting the City at the prospect of the threatened run on gold. And behind the scenes the bankers themselves were as busy as Place. The king now appealed to the Lords to end their opposition to the Bill and avoid his having to create sufficient new peers, which he let it be known he was at last prepared to do. They accordingly voted in favour of the Bill by 106 to 22 and the Reform Act became law on 7 June - one day after the death of the apostle of reform, Jeremy Bentham. But Thomas Hardy, the secretary of the London Corresponding Society, lived to see the Act carried although he died four months afterwards, aged 80.

However, the royal assent was not given by the king in person, since he declined to attend, but by commissioners of the lord chancellor. Lord Grey with several others and a few peers were in attendance. When the Speaker made the usual announcement in the Commons that the royal assent had been given it was reported that there was no sign of "joyful animation" by the members; perhaps they were exhausted. *The Times*, commenting on the fact that the king did not give the royal assent in person, denied that he was against reform as he had three times recommended it to Parliament in speeches from the throne[36] although, of course, the King's Speech was prepared by ministers. Nonetheless, the widespread popular belief that the king was wholehearted for reform did a great deal to ensure that

---

36.   8 June 1832, p. 3.

the Bill was supported and passed. Despite the lack of "joyful animation" in the Commons, wild rejoicing took place throughout the country with illuminations, the ringing of church bells and public banquets. Not least, Thomas Attwood was presented with the freedom of the City of London - the first private person to be so honoured.

In *The Ballot*, Thomas Wakley jubilantly poured bitter scorn on Wellington, the defeated hero. "Discomforted old man" he wrote, "go thy ways ... what a pitiful picture does this conqueror of armies and of states present of fallen greatness! - not of *real* greatness, but of that species of 'glory' arising from the hue reflected by sacrifices of human blood. Wellington fought not for freedom, risked not his life for the liberties and happiness of his countrymen, but for the success of the hellish designs of the Holy Alliance - for perpetuating the misrule of the boroughmongers."[37]

Place's desperate gamble had paid off but in part because the temper of the times gave him the will to threaten to use arms and cause a run on the pound. Unlikely as it may seem today the threat of revolution was real. "We were within a moment of general rebellion," wrote Place.[38] It is significant that the Duke of Wellington himself saw the essence of the reform struggle as a contest between the establishment and the Rotunda, which he described as two engaged armies. He regretted

37. 10 June 1832, p. 3.
38. *Add. MSS.* 27,795. fol. 27.

he could place no river between them with adequate sentinels and posts on the bridges because the enemy was installed at sensitive points within his own camp.[39] And John Croker, the influential secretary to the admiralty, claimed that the struggle was no longer between two political parties for the ministry but between the mob and the government.

The More Things Change ...

Apart from averting rebellion what then did the Act achieve? The electorate increased from a nominal figure to 931,735 immediately. The number of MPs remained at 658 as before. However, the distribution of seats changed with those in England reduced from 513 to 500 whilst Scotland's rose from 45 to 53 and Ireland's from 100 to 105. The changes in Scotland and Ireland were those referred to by Lord John Russell in the House of Commons earlier. In England 56 boroughs each returning one member lost the franchise. Thirty-six other boroughs lost one member each. Twenty-two large towns were enfranchised with two members each and 20 with one member each. Certain counties were re-arranged with some of them returning two members for the first time and the number of county MPs rose from 94 to 159.

However, equal electoral districts were not introduced and small boroughs often exercised the same influence as

39. PRO. HO. *Wellington Despatches.* 2nd ser. vii. 353. 1878.

larger ones. As the *Westminster Review* was to ask later, why should Honiton with a population of 3,300 have the same number of members as Liverpool or Glasgow with half a million people and incalculable wealth of commerce?[40] Without the ballot, bribery and violence in elections continued and even increased as the number of voters grew. And although the worst of the rotten boroughs disappeared more than 70 nomination boroughs still remained in the gift of landlords.[41]

Far fewer people secured the vote than had been hoped for, or feared, by different parties. As the Bill's champions had foreseen, and Grey and Russell had ensured, members of the working class were not given the vote. The franchise in the new boroughs was confined to "male persons" thus excluding women in explicit terms for the first time in British history. By way of contrast, the new House of Commons contained 217 sons of peers or baronets and that had changed little by as late as 1865.[42] Even by then it was still seen as a "comfortable rich man's club."[43] In *The Making of Victorian England*, G. Kitson Clark refers to "the old governing class of the country, still in control 27 years after the Reform Bill."[44] As late as 1900 it was calculated that a quarter of the members of the House of Commons had been educated at Eton or

40. *Westminster Review*. 512. (April, 1865).
41. C.S. Seymour. *Electoral Reform in England and Wales*. 92. 1915.
42. E.L. Woodward. *The Age of Reform, 1815-1870*. 87. 1954.
43. *Westminster Review*. 185. (January, 1867).
44. 210. 1962.

Harrow.[45] *Plus ça change!*

The *Poor Man's Guardian* had concluded on 25 October 1832 that, "The promoters of the Reform Bill projected it, not with a view to subvert, or even remodel our aristocratic institutions, but to consolidate them by a reinforcement of sub-aristocracy from the middle-classes." It then continued, "the only difference between the Whigs and the Tories is this - the Whigs would give the shadow to preserve the substance; the Tories would not give the shadow because stupid as the millions are they will not stop at shadows but proceed onwards to realities."[46] Nevertheless, the short-term reality was that the Whig government quickly broke up and Peel became prime minister for a few months after producing his Tamworth Manifesto in 1834 which helped swamp the die-hard Tories in the party with an accession of supporters from the new middle class voters. Then, after the Whigs had returned to government under Viscount Melbourne for six-and-a-half years, Peel and the Tories won a majority of about 80 in the general election of 1841.

But even under subsequent Whig governments there was to be a long gap before the advent of further reform. In the meantime it was Lord John Russell who led the opposition to the "realities" of increasing the size of the electorate or introducing the ballot by saying that such questions had been settled by the 1832 Act which was final. As a result the architect of the Reform Act became

45. Butler. *Op. cit.* 232.
46. Page 578 (27 October 1832).

known derisively as "Finality Jack" although it has been suggested that as his position was tactical rather than principled the sobriquet was undeserved. Furthermore, he actively promoted reform again in the 1860s. Nevertheless, that the Act should be final was a position he and Lord Grey had always maintained before, and often after, 1832. For his part, Peel always insisted that the ballot would make the Commons more democratic when it was too democratic already.

But, after all, as Grey and Russell, as well as the opponents of the Act, had always feared, the manner of its enactment as a result of public pressure made it crystal clear that change sparked by popular impulse was possible. Parliament had at last begun to represent opinion in the country and the seeds of future reforms were sown. Such success also led to a fever for reform of the antiquated and cruel criminal law, the poor law and local government. In fact, the Municipal Corporations Act of 1835 was to be more democratic than the Reform Act in that it gave all male ratepayers the right to vote in local government elections and this was extended to women in 1869.

CHAPTER 11

The Chartists

In the summer of 1834 an ageing Lord Grey resigned as prime minister following a dispute with Althorp, the Whig leader in the Commons, over an Irish Coercion Bill and Viscount Melbourne took his place.

Election

However, for the time being Melbourne was a reluctant leader of an unruly party in the Commons. Within a few months the king, who by this time had come to dislike the Whigs and was afraid that Russell, whom he distrusted, would be promoted, took the occasion to dismiss his ministers - although as a matter of form Melbourne resigned. Sir Robert Peel then took office without waiting for a general election. This was significant. It was to demonstrate that, unlike in 1783-4, when the king turned out the Fox-North coalition government and replaced it with one led by William Pitt which did not have a majority in the House until it secured one at the 1784 election, an imposed government could no longer since 1832 be assured of winning an election.

However an election could not long be delayed and meetings took place in many parts of the country although without raising much enthusiasm. Nonetheless, in Kidderminster a gathering of 10,000 people was addressed by their candidate, Mr Godston. Speaking in Northumberland, another candidate, a Mr Beaumont, revealed his dislike of Conservative principles. He said that despite his aversion to innovation causing him to be suspected of Conservatism he believed that in the Tories' hands the Reform Act would soon become little more than a dead letter and the rights of the people would be treated with contempt and scorn. At another meeting Lord Howick stated that he was not prepared to support any further changes; the Reform Act was as good as could be expected.[1]

The most important contribution in the campaign, however, was Peel's famous Tamworth Manifesto which, addressed through his constituents at Tamworth to the whole country, made clear that the Conservatives accepted the Reform Act as a "final and irrevocable settlement of a great constitutional question." This attempt to re-model the Tory Party was successful in that, despite its bitter opposition to the Bill and because of the increase in the middle class electorate, the party won about a hundred seats in the December 1834 election. Nevertheless, although the Tories remained without a majority Peel continued in office until he had been outvoted in the Commons six times in as many weeks. He finally resigned in April 1835 and was followed by the return of Melbourne.

---

1. *The Times*, 1 December 1834, p. 3.

Wakley's Effrontery

One consequence of the Reform Act was that some two years later, in the general election of July 1837, which by law had to be held following the death of William IV, Dr Thomas Wakley was returned as one of the two members of the House of Commons for the extensive constituency of Finsbury in London. The other seat was won by the sitting member Thomas Duncombe. Wakley's majority was the largest obtained by any candidate at this general election. On the Address in answer to the first speech to Parliament from the throne by the 18-year-old Queen Victoria, Wakley gave a spirited display of oratory and presented three amendments (in order that each could be voted upon separately). These called for an extension of the franchise, vote by secret ballot and the repeal of the Septennial Act.[2] He also contrasted the deep poverty, dirt and disease in which working people had to live with the expenditure on royalty and its palaces. To do so in reply to the Address to the young new queen was considered by many to be ungentlemanly and caused a great deal of consternation among members.

However, in the ensuing debate his speech secured from Lord John Russell an admission that corruption and intimidation had prevailed in the recent election to a "very lamentable extent". Votes, he said, were purchased widely and landlords continued to evict tenants who voted the "wrong way". Indeed, after a contest at Hertford

2. *Hansard.* [39] 37.

Duncombe is reputed to have spent £40,000 on finding homes for tenants ejected by Lord Salisbury.[3] Nevertheless, Russell declared that he could not countenance any attempts to reopen questions such as universal suffrage and the ballot that had been settled by the Reform Act. If they were brought in, he said, they would repeal that Act.[4] This was a rather surprising remark when what was being proposed was an extension of the Act. At the end of the debate Wakley's amendments attracted only 20 votes against 509 but he expected that and had made his point and drawn out Russell.

The result of the voting, and Russell's response to the amendments, caused bewilderment and anger in the manufacturing districts where it was widely, if erroneously, believed that the Reform Bill had been enacted simply as a first step to wider changes in the franchise and where there was deep resentment over the new poor law. Before 1834 the poor law was based on the important Act of Elizabeth I in 1601 which made every one of the 15,000 parishes in the land responsible for supporting its poor. This became open to abuse in the nineteenth century when the new manufacturers in the towns could take men from the villages when work was plentiful and return them there for outdoor relief when it was scarce.

Under the Speenhamland system, introduced on 6 May 1797 by Berkshire magistrates and adopted almost

---

3.   E.L. Woodward. *Op. cit.* 85.
4.   *Hansard. Op. cit.* 65.

universally in the Midlands and southern England, for 40 years the poor were kept at subsistence level but not starving. Unfortunately, corruption and abuse of the system became rife as relief became a subsidy for wages that were kept down and the cost of administering the poor law rose from £619,000 in 1750 to £8,000,000 in 1818. As a consequence, a select committee was appointed in 1817 to consider the question of poor-law reform but it made no positive recommendations and no action was taken. In 1824 another select committee reported in favour of abolishing the poor law altogether but it too was not acted upon.

The Reform Parliament's Poor Law Amendment Act of 1834 had three main objectives. The first was that parishes were to cease giving relief to the able-bodied except within a prison-like workhouse - the hated "Bastilles" as they were soon to be called. Secondly, such relief was to be "less eligible" than the most unpleasant means of earning a living outside and included low diet, severe discipline, a rule of silence and hard labour at stone-breaking, bone-grinding and oakum picking, much the same as in prisons. And thirdly, it was to enforce the separation of man and wife in order to prevent child-bearing. Fergus O'Connor, who was to become a famous Chartist orator, would delight his audiences at the time with his description of how he would treat Lord Chancellor Brougham and his wife on their arrival at the workhouse door: "I shall be sorry for Lady Brougham. I know no harm of her. But I would have no pity for him: 'No, no, Harry'," I will say to him, "You may not go with my lady; this is the way for you; otherwise you might breed."[5] It is difficult to believe that the pre-Reform Act Parliament would have passed such a measure.

Birth of the Charter

Following the euphoria brought about by the Reform Act these poor law provisions provoked widespread loathing and were seen as an attack on the poorer classes and family life.[6] As a consequence, once their effects were being felt they ignited an explosion of demands among the working classes for their own political representation and two conferences to discuss this were called in May and June 1837 by a number of Liberal and Radical MPs and trade union leaders. Five demands were formulated: (1) universal manhood suffrage, (2) annual Parliaments, (3) payment of MPs, (4) abolition of the property qualification for parliamentary candidates and (5) vote by ballot.

In themselves, it seems unlikely that these franchise demands, even if enacted, could have alleviated the misery to which the state of the economy and new poor law were giving rise and, despite the prominence given to

---

5.   G.D.H. Cole and Raymond Postgate. *The Common People 1746-1938*. 272. 1938.
6.   Revulsion at the new poor law was fully justified but a useful corrective to many newspaper exaggerations of its horrors is to be found in David Roberts' "How cruel was the Victorian Poor Law?" *Historical Journal* 6 97-107 (1963).

such demands, the Chartist movement was always activated by poverty and economic conditions. Nevertheless, the connection was perceived at the time and from these beginnings, and from an earlier meeting of the London Working Men's Association in February of that year, arose both the "People's Charter", in the form of a parliamentary Bill, and the working class Chartist movement that was to dominate domestic politics for a decade. The Charter was published on 8 May 1838.

The famous "six points" of the Charter included the above five and a further demand for 300 equal electoral districts to remedy the anomaly that some constituencies had populations of several hundred thousand whereas others had a mere 3-400 inhabitants. One of the early Chartist leaders, William Lovett who drafted the Charter, wanted to include women in the franchise but the others[7] thought such a demand would not be taken seriously and would be used to laugh the Charter out of court and damage their campaign. Accordingly, the proposal was abandoned. Nevertheless, a public meeting of women in Birmingham was held at the town hall on 2 April 1838 which pledged its support for the already known demands of the Charter.[8] And a leaflet issued in Birmingham on 16 August 1838 over the name of T. Clutton Salt claimed that "within a fortnight 50,000 women shall have signed

---

7. These included Henry Vincent, Daniel O'Connell, Henry Hetherington and J.A. Roebuck who could not overcome their prejudice on this issue despite their general forward-looking stand.
8. *Birmingham Journal*, 7 April 1838.

that National Petition."[9]

In reality the principal aim of the Chartists was nothing less than to change the system of government in an attempt to remedy economic and social grievances and regenerate society. Thomas Carlyle summed it up as "the cry of pent-up millions suffering under a diseased condition of society."[10]

Starvation, poverty and distress were indeed rife and the Charter was quickly endorsed at gigantic meetings held by torchlight all over the country; 300,000 people at Manchester, 250,000 at Leeds, 200,000 at Glasgow and 80,000 in Newcastle. It soon had 150 supporting societies and it was agreed that to secure acceptance of the six points by Parliament there would have to be set in train a mass petition, the calling of a Convention and, if the petition were rejected, a month's general strike, to be called a "Sacred Month". In the meantime, rumours of arms, riots and conspiracies began to circulate and crowded meetings applauded violent speeches by such tireless agitators as Joseph Rayner Stephens.

"Moral Force" v. "Physical Force"

As home secretary, Russell refused to panic however, and on 3 October 1838 at a dinner in Liverpool attended by

---

9. The leaflet is reproduced in Constance Rover's *Women's Suffrage and Party Politics in Britain, 1866-1914*. 9. 1967.
10. *Chartism*. 1839.

merchants and mill-owners, he declared his unwillingness to close down Chartist meetings and reluctance to sanction secret service expenditure for the purpose of infiltrating the movement.[11] He said he thought the people had a right to free discussion and a right to meet to declare their grievances. Nonetheless, in February 1839 he ordered that the correspondence of four Chartist leaders be henceforth intercepted by the Post Office.[12]

A tremendous problem for the movement arose when, facing obstruction by the entrenched authorities, it soon split into a "moral force" group relying upon the persuasive power of meetings and petitions and a "physical force" group talking of insurrection. It was a breach that seriously weakened both the movement's unity of purpose and its impact. The first group, comprised in the main of better-paid artisans, was led by the long-popular William Lovett and Thomas Attwood. The second was headed by James Bronterre O'Brien and the fiery giant of a man, Fergus O'Connor, who had entered Parliament in 1832 as member for Cork and whose strength derived from the support of many poorer workers, including miners and weavers, from the industries of the north of England and Wales where hatred between the workmen and their often cruel employers was intense.

The intellectual O'Brien was a lawyer turned Radical.

---

11. *The Times,* 9 October.
12. PRO. HO. 41/13.

In his own words in 1837: "About eight years ago I came to London to study law and radical reform. My friends sent me to study law; I took to radical reform on my own account. I was a very short time engaged in both studies, when I found the law was all fiction and rascality, and that radical reform was all truth and matter of dire necessity. Having a natural love of truth, and as natural a hatred of falsehood, I soon got sick of the law, and gave all my soul to radical reform."[13]

The schism reinforced Russell's view that there was no real danger of insurrection. When reports reached him that in some parts of the country workers were arming following violent and revolutionary speeches from some Chartists, he told the House of Commons that "their language was not exceeded in violence or atrocity during the worst times of the French Revolution but we owe it to the good sense of the people in general, that they have not listened to such exhortations."[14] This did not free him from complaints of excessive indulgence of what was occurring.

On the other hand Benjamin Disraeli, sitting in his first Parliament, took this opportunity to declare that "however much I disapprove of the Charter, I sympathise with the Chartists. They form a great body of my countrymen; nobody can doubt they labour under great grievances and it would indeed be a matter of surprise and little credit to the House if Parliament had been

---

13. *National Reformer.* (7 January 1837).
14. *Hansard*, third series. [49] 236.

prorogued without any notice being taken of what must always be considered a very remarkable social movement."[15]

Pressure for Reform

Following the Queen's Speech on 5 February 1839 the Radical MP Thomas Duncombe rose in the House of Commons to propose an addition which read: "That the amendment of the representative system enacted in 1832 has disappointed the people; that it is not, and cannot be, a final measure, and that it is the duty of this House to take immediate steps towards its further improvement." He did not look, he said, for any support from the gentlemen opposite - the Tories. They were not responsible for the Reform Bill. They were only responsible for having failed in their endeavours to strangle it in its birth. But he did look with confidence to his side of the House.

Duncombe claimed that nomination, intimidation and corruption were as rife as ever and the House still did not represent the democracy of the nation but represented the exclusive feelings of the aristocracy. What was needed was an extension of the suffrage and equal representation of constituencies.[16] Few members took up the challenge although Lord John Russell, who had earlier admitted

---

15. *Ibid.* [49] 250/1.
16. *Ibid.* [45] 64.

that corruption remained a serious problem, again opposed any suggestion that the Reform Act was not final. Not surprisingly, when the vote was taken Duncombe's amendment was defeated by 426 to 86. It took another three decades for his message to be taken up - ironically by his hated Tories in the unlikely figure of Disraeli.

A few weeks after Duncombe's move, on 21 March, another radical MP, Joseph Hume, presented a motion to extend the suffrage to all householders and all persons occupying parts of houses who were ratepayers. Like Duncombe, he asserted that the odious system of nomination was almost as bad as at any time before 1832. What he was proposing instead, he argued, was what Lord Grey had once said was the ancient right of voting under the Constitution. He was referring to a position which had been upheld by a committee of the House of Commons upon the Cirencester Election Petition in 1792[17] when it said, "every male person of full age, and not subject to any legal incapacity, who shall occupy any house or dwelling, the same being *bona fide* fitted for and applied to purposes of residence, shall, if duly registered, be entitled to vote in the election of Members to serve in Parliament."

Denial of reform, said Hume, had led to millions of working people becoming Chartists and their demands could be put an end to only by the grant of household suffrage on an extensive scale. Hume had done his homework and he submitted 13 detailed tables revealing

---

17. Quoted in 2 Fraser's *Election Cases*, pp. 449-51.

gross inequalities in the numbers of the population and their representatives similar to those that existed before 1832. His remedy, and a further set of tables set out his proposals constituency by constituency, would have given an additional 1,250,000 or more persons the right to vote.[18]

Once again, that erstwhile champion of reform, Lord John Russell, opposed the motion. He conceded that under the existing system four out of every five adults were excluded from voting and accepted that under Hume's proposal the number would be reduced to two out of every three. But failing to address the real issue he exclaimed, "Why, if his proposition were carried, we should have fresh applications the next day to change a constituency so narrowed, and we should have as many applications then from the two that were excluded as we have now from four."[19] His view prevailed and in a sparsely attended House the motion was rejected by 85 votes to 50.

Convention of the Industrious Classes

The first Chartist Convention, with 53 delegates, held its initial meeting at the *British Coffee House* in Cockspur Street, London on 4 February 1839 amidst great excitement. It was seen by many, including the

---

18. *Hansard.* [46] 1048.
19. *Ibid.* 1078.

ever-optimistic Duncombe, as potentially the new government. Indeed, many delegates vaingloriously described themselves as MC in place of MP. However, the mood quickly changed and the Convention dragged on for some months in a fog of acrimonious debate between its two wings.

But many people, contrary to what Russell said he believed, were listening to exhortations of violence. Early in 1839 there were reports that the Chartists of Norwich were arming; that some 300 men were already armed, mostly with halbards but some with pistols.[20] By April some supporters were drilling illegally and the hitherto moderate Whig government began to contemplate counter-measures including bringing over troops from Ireland and arming special constables.

John Frost, a JP at Newport in South Wales, held a Chartist meeting in Cirencester where the magistrates asked the home secretary to do something about him. Russell said he needed more information but *The Times* commented that no further information was needed about people who were despatched into the country to preach sedition and treason; it was one of a number of illegal assemblies and the government should put them down.[21]

In fact, Russell had already written to Frost on 16 January asking whether there was any truth in reports that he was a delegate to the National Convention and had attended meetings at Pontypool and elsewhere at

---

20. *The Times*, 8 March 1839, p. 7.
21. *Ibid.*, 26 March, p. 6.

which violent and inflammatory language had been used. If true, he said, Frost's name would be erased from the commission of the peace. In a lengthy and spirited reply on 19 January, Frost denied the allegations and took the opportunity to deplore Russell's interference with his right to express private views. In any event, he reminded the home secretary, there was a time when the Whig ministry were not so fastidious about violent language at public meetings - as in 1831-32.[22] It was to no avail. The lord chancellor was in no doubt about what to do and instructed the mayor of Newport to remove Frost's name from the list of magistrates.

A meeting of Chartists in Rochdale determined to arm themselves with pikes and guns, pistols, powder and ball in order to resist the putting into force of the new rural police and poor law. They also resolved that at any election they would support either a Radical or a Tory candidate for the Commons rather than a Whig. They claimed to have in their possession more than four thousand instruments of warfare.[23] It was reported that pikes were being manufactured cheaply in Lancashire and Yorkshire and were openly being sold in the marketplace from six pence to one shilling and six pence each. A "pike meeting" was held in Manchester for the purpose of advocating the People's Charter and opposing the introduction of the Rural Police Bill which, given the

---

22. BL. *Add. MSS. General Convention of the Industrial Classes. 1839.* Papers 34245A.
23. *The Times.* 29 March, p. 3.

Chartists' concern about police powers in France, led it to claim that the Bill was intended to "take away the last vestiges of our liberties."[24] During the preceding year a series of Police Acts had been enacted and the forces in Birmingham and Manchester reorganised.

Significantly, as it would turn out, arms were being sold in Monmouth and a letter from the home secretary to the lord lieutenant of Monmouthshire pointed out that any person attending a meeting for drilling, training or selling of arms was liable to transportation or imprisonment.[25] Pikes were being sold by Chartists in and around Wigan and a society in Trowbridge resolved to levy a sovereign from each member with which to procure firearms for Chartist purposes. They would then be taught how to use the weapons.[26]

The lord mayor of London issued an edict against the Chartists meeting in Smithfield as they had planned and as they had done twice before to what he described as "the alarm of the neighbourhood."[27] Large numbers of people in Preston were withdrawing their money from savings in order to buy pikes and firearms, and there was a similar report from Truro.[28] By this time Chartists were being arrested in many parts of the country. In Rochdale, for example, a Chartist was found to be in possession of a pistol and was committed to hard labour for three

---

24. *Ibid.* 2 April, p. 7.
25. *Ibid.* 10 April, p. 4.
26. *Ibid.* 18 April, p. 7.
27. *Ibid.* 6 May, p. 4.
28. *Ibid.* 8 May, p. 6.

months.[29]

Bull Ring Violence

On 13 May the Convention moved from London to
Birmingham and twelve days later a massive meeting of
some 300,000 people that was to become part of Chartist
folklore was held at Kersal Moor under the slogans:
"Slavery versus Liberty" and "Peace, Law and Order".
Twenty bands and 200 banners were present with one
banner displaying a picture of the Peterloo Massacre with
the words, "Murder demands Justice".

Along with O'Connor, Stephens spoke saying, "I ask
today, with such a sight before me as the world never
before beheld - I ask what is it that makes this mighty
movement of the masses of the people of England? What
is it that has shaken England herself to her very centre,
and brought her laborious, industrious, peaceable, loyal,
united, determined sons to this great, this glorious
gathering? I ask what means this mighty movement?
There must be something greatly wrong which these
hundreds of thousands have come here to right, or to have
righted for them."[30]

The government became alarmed but Russell was no
Sidmouth and there was no repeat of Peterloo. Instead, he
told the House of Commons that recent proclamations

---

29. *Ibid.* 14 May, p. 6.
30. Henry Jephson. *The Platform. Its Rise and Progress.* ii. 238. 1892.

against illegal torchlight meetings had produced salutary effects and he was now contemplating legislation regarding the possession of arms.[31] However, he may have been too late to prevent their production; a dagger and pike manufacturer at Heady-Hill had already abandoned his manufacture due to an entire cessation of demand.[32] The market was presumably saturated.

On 4 July a special body of London police was sent to Birmingham where it brutally attacked a demonstration in the city's famous Bull Ring. Bloody clashes resulted which led to rioting and the burning of houses. The Duke of Wellington told the House of Lords that he had never known a town taken by military storm to be worse treated by troops than Birmingham had been by the mob[33] but he was accused of exaggerating. The Convention, on the other hand, complained that "a wanton, flagrant and unjust outrage has been made upon the people of Birmingham by a blood-thirsty and unconstitutional force from London, acting under the authority of men" (ie, the Whigs) "who, when out of office, sanctioned and took part in the meetings of the people."[34] Dozens of people were arrested although most were subsequently discharged or acquitted by the courts. However, three men, one with a wooden leg, and a boy were tried on charges of arson and sentenced to death. This was later commuted to transportation on the grounds of possible mistaken

31. *Hansard. Op. cit.* [47] 1026.
32. *The Times,* 12 June, p. 3.
33. *Hansard.* [49] 588.
34. *Ibid.* 375.

identity[35] - which surely should have secured their pardon and release.

The disturbances spread to Glasgow, Newcastle and a number of other northern towns. The secretary of a Chartist association at Ashton-under-Lyne, near Manchester, was arrested by police for being in possession of a large quantity of muskets, bayonets, fowling pieces, rifles, single-barrelled guns and pistols. The Chartists in Cheshire were reported to be keeping up intimidatory agitation and a number were arrested and committed for trial.[36]

The prime minister, Lord Melbourne, warned the queen that troubled times were approaching and that there were fears of a revolutionary outbreak.

---

35. *Northern Star.* (10 and 31 August 1839).
36. *The Times,* 9 July, p. 6.

CHAPTER 12

Abortive Efforts

The First Petition

On 12 July 1839, the "National Petition", with 1,280,000 signatures at a time when the electorate numbered some 931,735, was presented to the House of Commons by Thomas Attwood. It was a large cylinder of parchment about four feet in diameter and had to be carried by 12 men. It reflected, said Attwood, the misery and distress of the people and their desire for relief by the restoration of their rights. Although the House was composed of men of the highest honour and virtue, he added, they legislated in the dark because they were not aware of the state of the country or of the misery and suffering they were inflicting on the nation and the working class in particular. Failure to redress genuine grievances would produce consequences that would "shake the stoutest nerves".[1]

Lord John Russell replied that he accepted that the sentiments of Attwood and those who had signed the petition were genuine in their belief that universal male suffrage would produce national prosperity. But it was not so. In a country depending on commerce and

---

1.   *Hansard.* [49] 220.

manufactures you could not prevent "low wages and consequent distress which at all times affect those who are at the bottom of the scale". Even in the United States, which he said had universal suffrage, the situation was similar. (He omitted to say that the US suffrage had existed only since 1837 - two years earlier - and, indeed, was hardly universal since it extended only to white males - except for a short period after the Civil War.) Those who had signed the petition, he said, had been deluded but, more importantly, the majority of the people rejected the demands it made.[2] In his general approach, on this occasion Russell was to some extent right in that the suffrage would not of itself have removed the poverty which was the result of economic processes. But the extent to which the economy was influenced by government policy was a factor on which an extension of the franchise might well have had an effect.

Disraeli, fully alive to the "two nations", again applauded the aspirations of the Chartists. He agreed with Russell that political rights did not necessarily bring social happiness; but it did not follow that they should not attempt to cure the disease. He maintained that the middle class had found political success without "simultaneous advances of the great social duties". Hence it was detested by the working classes. At this time he was sympathetic to universal male suffrage and gave his support to Attwood's motion to have the House go into

2.   *Ibid.* 237.

committee on the petition.[3] Daniel O'Connell pointed out
that the demands of the Chartists fell short of giving
women the vote and said he favoured the principle of the
petition but not its details. He would, however, support
the motion.[4]

Thomas Wakley thought it was preposterous for
Russell to suggest, as he had, that wages were high
enough for working men to deposit money in savings
banks. Agricultural wages were as low as six to seven
shillings a week. Furthermore, many harvest men were,
"sweating and toiling day by day under a burning sun
and resting at night under a barn, a shed, an outhouse,
covered with rags and suffering under a degree of poverty
which it was not in the power of language to describe.
Was that the condition in which the House wished the
industrious classes to be placed?"[5]

At the end of the debate the motion was defeated by
an overwhelming majority of 235 votes to 46. As a
consequence riots broke out in various parts of the
country and the government promptly banned meetings
and arrested a number of prominent Chartists. By late
July, although Birmingham was reported to be quiet,
rioting broke out in Newcastle. In Wellington a Chartist
billsticker was charged with having two loaded pistols in
his possession.[6] A letter from Lord John Russell to
magistrates advised that they should convict the large

---

3. *Ibid.* 246.
4. *Ibid.* 259.
5. *Ibid.* 268.
6. *The Times,* 25 July 1839, p. 5.

number of people who were going around to shopkeepers and householders and intimidating them into giving money for the Chartist cause. Meanwhile, meetings attended by huge crowds were being held virtually daily in Warrington, Blackburn, Lancaster and Wigan.[7] However, although a general strike was called for 12 August it did not materialise but turmoil continued until the Convention was dissolved on 14 September. The "moral force" Chartists had been defeated and the "physical force" men believed their opportunity had arrived.

In Hulme, Manchester, a disturbance occurred after the arrest of a Chartist who was a munitions manufacturer. The man, Scott, had strongly resisted but was finally taken by the police. Five others were apprehended and taken to Liverpool to await trial without bail at the assizes.[8] Shortly afterwards three Chartists, Francis Roberts, Joseph Howell and John Jones were sentenced to death at Warwick Assizes. The council of the General Convention called upon the queen to exercise her royal prerogative and extend a pardon to them.[9] Two days later 5,000 arms were seized in Chester. It was said they were for a Chartist attack upon the city and the liberation of prisoners committed for trial. The same night, a riot took place in Bolton and an attempt was made to fire the town. Two men were killed, a

---

7.   *Ibid.* 5 August, p. 3.
8.   *Ibid.* 6 August, p. 6.
9.   *Ibid.* 13 August, p. 5.

number wounded, some shops were gutted and the hall of the council chamber almost destroyed by fire.[10]

The Newport Rising

In November 1839 the highly respected John Frost, the former magistrate and mayor of Newport, reluctantly led a rising of miners in South Wales, ostensibly to free the charismatic Chartist leader Henry Vincent from Newport gaol where it was alleged he was being treated with great cruelty. The Chartist leader and historian R.G. Gammage wrote that Vincent was regarded as "the young Demosthenes of English democracy."[11] His appeal to miners in particular was remarkable. At the time he was known to be imprisoned in Monmouth which is some 20 miles from Newport and from which one contingent of miners was moving away during the march to Newport. The whole incident is shrouded in mystery. Frost really favoured a mass demonstration and not force but when he was urged not to take action by O'Connor (who, despite his fiery words, was careful never to become involved in violence and always walked away from it) he is said to have been afraid of being seen as a traitor to the miners and responded: "I might as well blow my brains out as try to hold back the Monmouth lodges now."[12]

---

10. *Ibid.* 15 August, p. 5.
11. *History of the Chartist Movement 1837-1854.* 11. 1894.
12. Cole and Postgate. *Op. cit.* 280.

The militancy of the miners is undoubted and was understandable when their lives, as well as their livelihoods, were so little valued and, indeed, were often at risk. Even in October 1913, when serious breaches of the Coal Mines Act by colliery owners and managers were proved to have caused the Senghenydd pit disaster in South Wales which led to the death of 439 men, the owners were merely punished by fines amounting in total to £24, or just over a shilling per head.[13]

In the dead of the night of 3-4 November 1839 many thousands of miners marched down their valleys in the unusually heavy blustering rain and storms of the moonless sky. Frost's detachment had assembled at Blackwood. Others, under the leadership of Zephaniah Williams, met at Nantyglo and yet more, led by the erratic and militant William Jones, at Pontypool. Whilst some were armed with muskets, pikes and pitchforks, many had no weapons of any kind. All were marching to meet at Risca, above Newport. However, the unprecedented weather not only drenched them to the skin but delayed their progress and prevented them meeting at the rendezvous on time.

Eventually, with dawn breaking, Frost, who had been the first to reach Risca, decided to proceed to Newport at the head of some 5,000 men without waiting any longer for the other two groups. Unknown to him in that fateful night Williams was only a short distance away. Unfortunately for the miners, as a consequence of the

---

13. *Mines and Quarries.* S. Wales Division Reports. Cmd. 8023-iv. 58/9.

delay, the authorities were fully warned and the dishevelled contingent walked into an ambush in the square outside the Westgate Hotel in Newport. Unaware that troops had been stationed in the hotel by the mayor only a few minutes earlier, the men approached the building (some gaining access) and stood exposed to bullets from soldiers of the 45th regiment and police who were sheltered behind the hotel shutters. Estimates of the number of miners killed vary between 11 and 33 and many more were injured.

Although the miners were dispersed the government immediately flooded South Wales with troops and in December Frost and 13 others were brought before a hastily appointed special commission at Pontypool and charged with treason in waging war against the queen.

Efforts were made to prejudice the public against Frost to which effect his 14-year-old son, Henry, was arrested and it was put about by the press that Frost's wife and daughters had joined the insurgents at Blackwood disguised as peasants. *The Times* in particular lost no opportunity to blacken Frost's name in a number of special reports and leaders. They found him guilty long before his case had even commenced. Yet public support for him was widespread throughout the country.

Although Frost's trial took place first and lasted eight days the prosecution could find no evidence to sustain their theory that the rising was a green light for a general insurrection throughout the country. The attorney-general, Sir John Campbell who was later lord chancellor, alleged that the revolt was to begin in Wales and the signal for its extension was to be the non-arrival in Birmingham of the coach carrying the Welsh mails.[14] However, this allegation was discredited by the fact that no coach at that time ran from Newport to Birmingham as was pointed out by defence counsel, Sir Frederick Pollock. Moreover, not even the slightest disturbance occurred in Birmingham or elsewhere, despite talk of such actions in a few places. Nevertheless, Frost, and the others, were found guilty of treason with three of them, including Frost, being sentenced to death.

The queen and Lord Melbourne believed execution was the right method of dealing with them but popular campaigning for a reprieve soon reached great intensity with mass meetings throughout the country. Indeed, the campaigning threatened to lead to such an upsurge as to mar the forthcoming celebrations to honour the queen's marriage, and possibly even to bring down the government. (In fact, in January 1840 the government survived a vote of no-confidence by only 21 votes.) Defence counsel and the lord chief justice appealed to the home secretary, now the bureaucratic Lord Normanby who, under tremendous pressure and concerned about the queen's marriage and the fate of the government, granted a reprieve. *The Times*, no longer the "thunderer" of the Reform Bill, misreported the rising and called for the resignation of Lord Normanby for being too sanguine about it. Although there were individual cases of

---

14. David J.V. Jones. *The Last Rising. The Newport Insurrection of 1839.* 190. 1985. By far the best account of the Rising.

intimidation the newspaper, with little understanding of the miners or their grievances which alone could account for the intensity of the rising, overstated the claim that marchers sacked villages in the valleys and threatened to kill instantly other miners who did not join them on the march. It also said that the mayor was shot whilst reading the Riot Act when in fact it never left his pocket.[15] The mayor, Thomas Phillips, was, however, given a knighthood for having called in the military.

Further appeals for pardons failed and Frost, Zephaniah Williams and William Jones were transported for 14 years to Van Diemen's Land, now Tasmania. At a Chartist meeting in Bristol in early 1841 it was announced that the three of them had been appointed to official situations at Port Arthur in Van Dieman's Land. In a letter to his wife Frost recorded that he was working as a clerk in the office of the commandant, Williams was superintendent of a coal mine and Jones was working in a juvenile establishment. Although there was much privation and suffering in Port Arthur their situation was one of comparative comfort and he said he was in excellent health and good spirits. After nationwide campaigning and an impassioned speech by Wakely in the Commons Frost was finally pardoned in 1854. He died in England 23 years later.

If the rising had been intended as a signal for insurrection elsewhere it failed to raise a spark. Significantly, there were no other risings by Chartists at

---

15. *The Times,* 6 September 1839, p. 5.

any time despite the widespread possession of arms and some fire-raising activities. Following Newport the "physical force" threat rapidly diminished.

Second Petition

After the rising the government arrested some 500 more Chartist leaders who were gaoled, this time including O'Brien and O'Connor. Reports of cruelty on the prisoners began to circulate. O'Connor was said to be suffering from the treatment at York castle and Henry Vincent in Millbank. But the treatment of Joseph Crabtree appeared to be even worse and a form of torture. He was held in Wakefield's House of Correction, said to be the most severe prison in the kingdom. The punishment inflicted was indeed dreadful. He was locked in a 6ft by 8ft cell from 6 pm until 6 am when he was taken to the day room where he had to sit on a form all day and face one direction. At 6 pm he was returned to his cell. He was not allowed in the yard unless sick. If he hung down his head or looked at another prisoner in the face he was placed in a dark cell in solitary confinement for three days with only half a pound of bread and some water a day.[16]

When Duncombe moved for a full inquiry into the harsh conditions of imprisonment Wakley seconded the motion and Disraeli supported it, although they could muster only 27 other votes. Wakley always opposed the

---

16. *Ibid.* 6 July 1840, p. 10.

"physical force" side of Chartism in the belief that its actions were counter-productive. For him all action had to be undertaken constitutionally and the place for achieving reform was Parliament. Clearly, without distancing himself from the mainstream of the movement, he had independently drawn important lessons from the failure of the Rotundists. This led to a meeting in St Pancras, London, calling on all true Chartists no longer to have any faith in him[17] but many Chartist leaders themselves abjured violence, and the movement's posters and literature constantly proclaimed the motto of "Peace, Law and Order".

Revival

On the subsequent release of many of its prisoners held in English gaols the Chartist movement revived and O'Connor's newspaper *The Northern Star* achieved a circulation of 50,000. A new convention was called with the aim of securing the release of all the remaining Chartist prisoners and making the Chartist programme the law of the land.

However, the general election of July 1841 brought about an acrimonious dispute on election policy between O'Brien and O'Connor who were still confined in prison. The issue was whether Chartists should support the Whigs or the Tories. The Whigs had imprisoned Chartists

---

17. *Ibid.* 6 October 1840.

but the Tories were more resolute as opponents of reform. O'Connor urged support of the Tories, a stand that O'Brien vehemently attacked. To do so, he said, would mean that the Chartists would, "annihilate themselves *morally* and prepare the way for their physical extinction as a political party by the very villains they would league with, covertly supported by the other villains they leagued against."[18] On his release from prison O'Brien addressed a Chartist meeting in Kendal but his talk met, according to *The Times*, with derisive laughter and when he spoke at a large gathering in Glasgow he spoke "lamely and unenergetically and only a small part of the 10,000 present seemed to take part in the proceedings."[19] Earlier, Henry Vincent, also recently released from prison and speaking at a meeting in Gloucester, had anticipated O'Connor in saying that the Chartists should throw all their influence and votes on the side of the Tories for, bad as they were, they were infinitely better than the Whigs.[20]

In the event the Tories won the election. In 1842, following a winter of industrial and trade recession, Chartist activity was renewed on a considerable scale and a new petition was taken to the House of Commons by a "vast multitude in procession". The petition was over six miles long having been signed by 3,317,702 people, more than half the adult male population. Its bulk was so great that the doors of the House were not wide enough for it to

18. Letter to *The Northern Star*. (19 June 1841).
19. *The Times,* 28 September, p. 8; 14 October, p. 5.
20. *Ibid.* 14 May 1841, p. 8.

be carried through and it had to be unrolled. When it was divided up on the floor of the Commons it rose above the level of the table and the chamber looked "as if it had been snowing paper".

At this time there was a Conservative government with Sir Robert Peel as prime minister and Sir James Graham, home secretary. The petition was introduced by Thomas Duncombe on 2 May with a motion the following day that six petitioners "be heard by themselves or their counsel at the bar of the House".[21] Duncombe quoted precedents for such a procedure being adopted. Sir John Easthope said he believed that the aims of the Charter would not relieve the distress in the country but the distress was so profound that he considered it proper to hear the petitioners at the bar. Otherwise members were saying to over three million people, "we will not hear you because you do not correctly describe the causes of your misery nor limit your prayers to appropriate remedies."[22]

For the government Sir James Graham found it impossible to deny the extent of distress in the country but decided that because it was well known no investigation was necessary. Furthermore, it would be disastrous to excite hopes about a change in the franchise. The remedies which were proposed would be "more hurtful" than the evils complained of.[23] He did not say why or, in a very short speech, offer an alternative

---

21. *Hansard.* [63] 32.
22. *Ibid.* 40.
23. *Ibid.* 41/43.

policy. During the debate Macaulay said he agreed with much of the Charter but universal suffrage, which was its essence, would be "fatal to all purposes for which government exists, and for which aristocracies and all other things exist, and that it is utterly incompatible with the very existence of civilisation ... which rests upon the security of property."[24] Lord John Russell expressed both his respect for the petitioners and his abhorrence of the doctrines of the petition.[25] His respect did not extend to allowing the petitioners to speak to the House, however. And he denied that anybody had the "right" to vote. Disraeli was not present but Gladstone voted against the motion which was defeated.

The rejection of the petition on 4 May 1842 by 287 votes to 49 was followed by a great series of strikes against wage reductions across Scotland, Wales, the Midlands and the north of England. Although the Chartist leaders had not started the movement, meetings of strikers began to pass resolutions that "all labour should cease until the People's Charter becomes the law of the land." In Lancashire, in what was known as the "Plug Plot", the cotton spinners went from mill to mill first raking out the fires from beneath the boilers and then knocking the boiler plugs out to bring the steam-engines and the mills to a standstill. But as the strikes were spreading O'Connor denounced them in the *Northern Star* and when the paper reached the streets

24. *Ibid.* 46.
25. *Ibid.* 70.

the movement collapsed. The impact of the actions before his intervention may be gauged from the fact that 1,500 persons on strike were arrested and 79 transported to Australia.

Despite these setbacks women were continuing to show a growing interest in the movement. A meeting of female Chartists was held for the purpose of forming an association to co-operate with the all-male association. A Mr Cohen caused a "sensation among the ladies" when he asserted that women would be more in their proper character and station at home than in the political arena. He did not consider that nature intended women to partake of political rights. When Miss Susanna Inge, who became secretary to the association, asked Mr Cohen why he considered women unqualified to vote as this required little physical force, he replied that if she were in the House of Commons a man could sway her vote by playing on her affections. Mary Ann Walker responded that she would treat such a man with womanly scorn and then to loud cheers gave a spirited speech and appealed to her countrywomen to come out and enrol their names in favour of the Charter.[26]

Kennington Common

Five years later O'Connor was elected to the Commons as member for Nottingham although by this time his

---

26. *The Times*, 20 October 1842, p. 3.

energies were largely directed to endeavouring to found a series of land colonies. However, he remained the most influential Chartist leader and another petition was put in hand in 1848 against a background of revolutions across Europe which overthrew Louis Philippe in France and Metternich in Austria.

When the petition was ready O'Connor was delirious with excitement at the millions of signatures he claimed were appended to it. With the Whigs back in office (after the election of July 1846) and Lord John Russell as prime minister, a monster meeting on Kennington common, London was called for 10 April 1848. But times had changed and an era of relative prosperity was opening. Nevertheless, the government was unnecessarily fearful and declared the meeting to be illegal.

The Duke of Wellington, now 78 years of age and commander-in-chief of the army, brought 9,000 troops from outlying barracks and enrolled 70,000 men as special constables. Over four days, some 4,000 policemen guarded the bridges, Palace Yard and Trafalgar Square. Mounted police were supplied with arms. Even 1,500 hundred Chelsea pensioners were taken out of retirement to defend Battersea and Vauxhall. Heavy gun-batteries were ferried over the Thames from Woolwich Arsenal and placed at various strategic points.

Notwithstanding these, and numerous other intimidatory measures, some hundred thousand or more people gathered on the common ready to march to Westminster with the petition. O'Connor then met with metropolitan police commissioner, Richard Mayne, at the nearby *Horns Tavern* where he agreed to abandon the procession to Westminster if the meeting were allowed to continue peacefully. The anger of the crowds at this "surrender" was manifest and it needed all O'Connor's powers of persuasion and demagogy to placate them. However, he managed to do so and the day did indeed pass off without serious incident as the last flare up of Chartism. A happy Russell reported to the queen that the meeting had proved "a complete failure". *The Times* agreed. A leading article claimed that whether considered as a display of physical or moral force the meeting was a "decided and conspicuous failure". No more than 7,000 people, it said, were in the centre of the common to hear the speakers and the orators were "second class". It claimed that the rain, which fell at the end, stopped any tendency to riotous or turbulent conduct although a pawnbroker's and a bakery were broken into and all contents removed.[27]

According to O'Connor the petition had 5,706,000 signatures, which an anonymous correspondent to *The Times* claimed was more than the entire adult male population of Great Britain. When it was presented to the House of Commons and examined by a staff of clerks, however, it was found to have only 1,975,496 names of which many were bogus, such as "Victoria Rex", the Duke, Sir Robert Peel, "Mr Punch" and "Pug Nose". Many others were written in the same handwriting. A heated exchange followed in the House of Commons with charges

---

27. *Ibid.* 14 April 1848, p. 8.

of insincerity against O'Connor who had probably fully believed in his wild claims.

Little Charter

Two months later, on 20 June 1848, Joseph Hume endeavoured to resurrect the issue of the franchise in the House of Commons with his "Little Charter". This provided for household (instead of manhood) suffrage, combined with the ballot, triennial Parliaments and the redistribution of seats to accord better with the population of various districts. In a lengthy speech, he moved that the Commons did not represent the population, the property or the industry of the country. He proposed that the franchise be extended to include all householders, that votes should be taken by secret ballot and that the duration of Parliament should not exceed three years. "Taxation and representation should go together," he said, "and those who did not assist in the election of members who were to sit in the House, and pass laws affecting their liberties and property, were, in fact, deprived of their rights. They were not in that condition which distinguished freemen from slaves." He complained that five out of every six male adults were without any voice in elections.[28]

In the debate on 28 June Disraeli accepted that as the country was governed by a woman, that peeresses were

---

28. *Hansard.* [99] 879.

part of an estate of the realm and that women could own land, if "right" came into the matter then they should have the right to vote. But the suffrage was not a right or a duty, it was a privilege and even to say that every man who lived in a house should have the vote was absurd.[29] Richard Cobden, with Hume, argued for household suffrage on the ground that the vote should be linked with taxation. "What danger," he asked, " can there be in giving the franchise to householders? They are the fathers of families, the persons who fill your Churches and your workshops, in fact the people of the country."[30] Lord John Russell opposed the motion saying that although it stopped short of the Charter it would ultimately lead to it. The motion was defeated by a majority of 267.

Although Chartism lingered on for a few years, with its surviving leaders, particularly Ernest Jones, loosely connected with Marx and Engels, it was no longer a human convulsion of despairing workmen but a spent force, succumbing to the advance of Victorian prosperity. The "Hungry Forties" were followed by the "Age of Equipoise" as the 1850s were labelled. However, its influence on the reviving trade union movement and the eventual birth of the Labour Party was considerable and five of the Charter's "six points" were eventually adopted (the exception was annual Parliaments). In the words of one writer, "It represented the first genuinely democratic movement for social reform in modern history and has a

---

29. *Ibid.* 950.
30. *Ibid.* [100] 185.

real place in the development of modern English politics and society."[31]

Further Efforts

After 1848 the issue of the franchise was to lay largely dormant for some 10 years. The storm had subsided and in the intervening period Parliament and the country were more concerned with the Great Exhibition at the new Crystal Palace in Hyde Park and with the Crimean, Chinese, Persian and Indian wars. The Exhibition was a celebration of internal harmony. Living standards were rising rapidly for the great majority of the population including the working classes. Demand for reform did not disappear altogether, however, and Lord John Russell introduced minor Bills in 1852 and 1854 although he subsequently withdrew both of them.

On 8 June 1858, H. Berkeley, the member for Bristol, moved to bring in a Bill to provide for voting by secret ballot. This was too much for Lord Palmerston who had told his constituents at Tiverton in 1852 that "to go sneaking to the ballot-box, poking in a piece of paper and looking round to see that no one could read it, is a course which is unconstitutional and unworthy of the character of straightforward and honest Englishmen."[32] Russell, who appealed to the tradition of open voting, also opposed

---

31. Mark Hovell. *The Chartist Movement*. 312. 1925.
32. Quoted in E.L. Woodward. *Op. cit.* 162.

it and after a short debate the motion was defeated by 294 votes to 97.[33]

But by now the question of franchise reform was again on the agenda and, also in 1858, John Bright, the famous Free Trade orator, at the urging of reformers in Birmingham, Manchester and Glasgow, introduced in the Commons a Bill to transfer the franchise from a number of boroughs to large towns and the counties, with universal vote by ballot. Sensing that a strong feeling for reform was beginning to emerge again in the country Lord Derby's government decided to introduce their own Bill which Disraeli, who was chancellor of the exchequer, presented to the House of Commons on 28 February 1859. This would have widened the electorate in the counties and redistributed 15 seats to large towns that still remained unrepresented and to certain populous county areas such as Middlesex. As usual, however, it was opposed by Russell and at the end of the second reading on 31 March was defeated by 330 votes to 291, after which Parliament was dissolved.[34]

A year later, with Lord Palmerston and the Whigs back in power, Russell himself, aware of the strength of feeling in the country for reform, introduced a Representation of the People Bill. The essential elements were to introduce a £10 occupation franchise for the counties and to reduce the borough franchise to £6. With partisan politics to the fore the Conservatives opposed the

---

33. *Hansard.* [150] 1793.
34. *Ibid.* [152] 966.

Bill with Disraeli saying it was, "a measure of a medieval character, without the inspiration of the feudal system or the genius of the middle ages." He did not elaborate on what the inspiration and genius were, but after the Bill received a mauling in debate Russell withdrew it on 11 June 1860.[35]

Further efforts to introduce a Reform Bill were made in 1864 but the Commons remained unreceptive although this was the occasion on which Gladstone clashed with his prime minister, Lord Palmerston, on the question. Henceforward, after the changes in the franchise wrought in the USA by the civil war had made an impact in Britain, Gladstone was to become the champion of Liberal reform and how he fared at the hands of Disraeli will be considered next.

---

35. *Ibid.* [156].

CHAPTER 13

Gladstone and Disraeli

By 1865 the adult male population of England and Wales numbered over five million but the sum total of voters was still only around one million. Five out of six adult males, including the greater part of the working class, were outside the franchise. Furthermore, although the distribution of the population had changed since 1832 the apportionment of seats had not. One half of the borough population of England had 300 seats and the other half a mere 34.[1]

Gladstone's Reform Bill of 1866

While on the other side of the Atlantic the American civil war to preserve the Union was drawing to a bitter close, the summer of 1865 saw an uneventful general election in the United Kingdom resulting in a substantial victory for the Liberals, as the Whigs were now known. But within three months prime minister Palmerston, who had consistently opposed franchise reform, was dead and Lord John Russell (now Earl Russell and in the House of Lords) succeeded him. The rising William Ewart

---

1.   E.L. Woodward. *The Age of Reform 1815-1870.* 175/6. 1954.

Gladstone was appointed leader of the House of Commons. Electoral reform was again in the air, with numerous meetings being held across the country to discuss how reform could be brought about. An analysis of the rents being paid in the borough of Leeds, for example, showed that a reduced franchise of £6 would double the number of voters in the constituency from 7,000 to 14,000.[2] Resolutions adopted at a meeting in Ayr were presented to the prime minister in favour of reform to include the extension of the franchise, redistribution of seats and increased representation for Scotland.[3]

An ageing Russell now decided he wanted to give his name to a second Reform Bill - provided it was moderate and did not open the door to democracy or involve manhood suffrage. The franchise had still to be tied to property.[4] Accordingly, on 12 March 1866 Gladstone, after having said that "the limbo of abortive creations is peopled with the skeletons of reform Bills" but anxious to increase the Liberal vote, introduced in the Commons a measure to extend the borough franchise to householders paying a minimum annual rental of £7 in place of the existing £10 threshold. This, he said, would add about 144,000 working class men to the electorate. In

---

2. *The Times*, 19 December 1865, p. 10.
3. *Ibid.* 6 March 1866, p. 9.
4. In 1866 Russell had written that the Reform Bill of that year went against "natural order" in "seeking to make the Governed Governors" and not "independent, thoughtful voters" who could combat "cholera, cattle pest, the Nigger Pest - white murder by blacks - and Fenians". Earl Russell. *The Final Reform Bill*. 7/8.

justification, if any were needed, Gladstone declared that the working class had advanced in education, in social conduct, in self-command and avidity for knowledge, but had not been sufficiently admitted to the franchise.[5] Despite such fine words, however, he was not prepared to reduce the annual rental to £6 that would have given another 242,000 working men the vote. Nevertheless, in linking the franchise with education Gladstone was breaking from the long-standing tradition that only ownership of property entitled a man to the privilege of voting. Gladstone seems to have been genuinely impressed with the moderation of many skilled workers and their trade unions but some members of his party welcomed the move declaring quite openly that they believed workers who were educated would vote Liberal.

In a further measure the county occupation franchise was to be reduced from a rent of £50 to £14 and would apply to those occupying not only land but a house or a house with land. Tenants of separate parts of a house and lodgers paying £10 a year for their lodgings were also to be enfranchised. Altogether this would bring within the fold another 172,000 voters, mainly middle class. In addition, adult males who had held £50 or more in a savings bank for two years were to be given the vote if they did not already qualify. On 7 May a Redistribution Bill was introduced to transfer some seats from small boroughs to large towns and Scotland.

The old disputes immediately re-surfaced with Sir

---

5. *Hansard*, third series. [182] 18 *et seq.*

Thomas Bateson declaring that the first Bill would lead to the "emasculation of the aristocracy" and the replacement of the hereditary monarchy by a president with a salary of £10,000 a year.[6] Some members of the Liberal Party also found this mild measure too strong. Two principal dissidents were E. Horsman, earlier chief secretary for Ireland, and Robert Lowe, *The Times* leader writer and, under a forgiving Gladstone, afterwards chancellor of the exchequer and home secretary.

John Bright, who was to be a member of Gladstone's 1868 Cabinet but at this time was seen to be too radical and a threat to Liberal cohesion, described their defection from the Liberal mainstream as a retirement into a political "cave of Adullam" - a reference to the distressed Biblical figures that David gathered around him in the cave of that name. "This party of two," Bright said, "reminds me of the Scotch terrier, which was so covered with hair that you could not tell which was the head and which was the tail of it."[7] But if Gladstone was not amused when a number of other Liberal MPs joined "the Cave", or "cave-men", as members of the group were henceforth known, he was stung to fury when Lowe, who feared democracy and even wanted to have freemen disenfranchised, described members of the working class as ignorant, drunken and violent. Gladstone retorted that they were "our fellow-subjects, our fellow-Christians, our own flesh and blood, who have been lauded to the skies

6.   *Ibid.* [183] 1856.
7.   *Ibid.* [182] 219/20.

for their good conduct."[8]

Lowe believed that, "The seven Houses of Commons that have sat since the Reform Bill have performed exploits unrivalled, not only during the six centuries during which Parliament has existed, but in the whole history of representative assemblies."[9] Proof that change was needed was required from the reformers. As an intellectual he opposed transferring power to those he dubbed "the ignorant", although this epithet did not prevent him from declaring incongruously that the working class were looking beyond political democracy to socialism. If reform gave them real power the economy and prosperity would be imperilled and the machinery of the state might be used to assist strikes. Lowe's passion in the Commons produced a great deal of outward support but members were also aware of the groundswell of public feeling against him on the issue.

Indeed, his remarks provoked a strong reaction in the country which Bright exploited in electrifying meetings throughout the land. And the bitter conflict continued in Parliament with Lord Cranborne, Conservative MP for Stamford and afterwards Lord Salisbury, describing Gladstone's speech claiming working men as fellow-Christians as "sentimental claptrap". Did the leader of the House, he asked, really see a moral principle in a £7 borough rental, and "were not tramps, paupers and lunatics also our own flesh and blood?" More to the point,

---

8. *Ibid.* [183] 1642.
9. R. Lowe. *Speeches and Letters on Reform*. 1867.

Mr Banks Stanhope asked, if this fellow-Christian theory were pushed to the utmost, why should not the five million adult women in the country be considered? Why not indeed?

There can be no doubt that the defection of the "cave-men", and their blistering speeches in the Commons, harmed their own party and encouraged the Conservatives to oppose the Bill. The Tories correctly believed that if enacted it would unduly favour the Liberals in elections but, despite the government's majority in the House, it could be defeated if they received support from a good many Liberal MPs. A determined Gladstone fought back and appealed to the House to admit nearly 400,000 more men to the franchise. In Birmingham, Bright told a large meeting that their representation in the Commons was a sham and a farce and that if they wanted an effective Reform Bill they would have to bring strong pressure to bear on Parliament. Meanwhile, Gladstone declared at meetings in Liverpool on 5 and 6 April 1866 that the Cabinet would stand or fall by the Bill. What would the defeat of the Bill procure, he asked? "An interval, but not an interval of repose; an interval of fever, an interval of expectation, an interval for the working of those influences which might possibly arise even to the formidable dimensions of political danger. Let the great English nation be wise, and be wise in time." To loud cheering he then declared, "We have passed the Rubicon; we have broken the bridge; and we have burnt the boats behind us. We have advisedly cut off from ourselves the means of retreat."[10]

Liberal Defections Defeat the Bill

On 12 April Gladstone moved the second reading of his Bill and Lord Grosvenor, normally a supporter of the government but now an Adullamite, moved an amendment to adjourn the debate which was intended to destroy the Bill.[11] To wild cheering by the Tories and Adullamites this was defeated by only a tiny majority of 318 votes to 313 in perhaps the highest attended division the House had ever seen. In the debate Horsman fatuously claimed that if the threshold of the franchise were indiscriminately lowered the privilege of voting would be extended to those of low character and those who had not been sufficiently provident as to lodge their families in comfortable houses. He went on to declare that "the whole Liberal Party, against its convictions, and still more against its interests, has been drifting to democracy."[12] T.B. Horsfall, the member for Liverpool, suggested that the Bill would create a problem of expense in holding elections in large constituencies such as his own.[13] Gathorne Hardy, a Conservative, argued against John Stuart Mill that reform was not needed because it was no more necessary for working men to be represented

---

10. 6 April 1866.
11. *Hansard.* [182] 1152.
12. *Ibid.* 1113.
13. *Ibid.* 1184.

by working men (as Mill had suggested) than it was necessary for clergymen to be represented by clergymen.[14]

Disraeli, not only opposed the Bill,[15] but seized the opportunity to attack Gladstone for a speech he had made at the Oxford Union as far back as 1831 against the Reform Bill of that year. Gladstone responded by telling the Tories:

"You cannot fight against the future. Time is on our side. The great social forces which move onward in their might and majesty and which the tumult of your debates does not for a moment impede or disturb ... are against you; they are marshalled on our side; and the banner which we now carry in this fight, though perhaps at some moment it may droop over our sinking heads, yet it soon again will float in the eye of heaven, and it will be borne by the firm hands of the united people of the three kingdoms, perhaps not to an easy, but to a certain and to a not distant victory."[16]

Then on 18 June in committee, Lord Dunkellin, Liberal MP for Galway and an Abdullamite, moved an amendment to the Bill to provide that in the boroughs a rateable value qualification should be substituted for rental. As rateable values were usually lower than rents

---

14. *Ibid.* 1741.
15. *Ibid.* [183] 94.
16. A. Tilney Bassett. *Gladstone's Speeches*. 359. 1916.

this would increase the number of voters. But Dunkellin argued that whilst his proposal would indeed admit the best qualified of the working class to the franchise it would also produce an insurmountable barrier to universal suffrage.[17] Not everyone could agree with such a drastic change, however. The eminent jurist, Walter Bagehot, had already complained that a rate-paying innovation would be favourable to "ignorance and poverty" and unfavourable to "cultivation and intelligence". To support his argument he wrote that in England and Wales:

The number of houses assessed at £10 and above is computed to be	990,000
The number of houses assessed at £6 and under £10	572,000
The number of houses assessed at under £6	1,713,000
Total:	3,275,000

Accordingly, he claimed, "More than half the persons who would be admitted by the rate-paying franchise are, therefore, of a very low order, living in houses under £6 rent and two-thirds are below £10, the lowest qualification admitted by the present law." Enfranchising them would stir "dangerous democratic passions".[18] But this took no account of Gladstone's intention to reduce the rental qualification. One member, R.B. Osborne, saw the other side of the coin. He found, he complained, that 217

---

17. *Hansard.* [184] 536.
18. *Essays on Parliamentary Reform.* 27. Published 1883 but written in 1859.

members of the Commons were either directly connected with or were actual members of the aristocracy. To all intents and purposes they were a trade union. And there were no less than 1,500 members of great families who constituted the whole of the Upper Chamber and one third of the Commons. Yet they heard talk of keeping out the artisan class.[19]

Nevertheless, Dunkellin's amendment secured a majority of 11 with 44 Liberals voting against their government. The House was in uproar and Gladstone recorded, "There was shouting, violent flourishing of hats, and other manifestations, which I think novel and inappropriate."[20] True to his promise the Cabinet resigned, but without seeking an election and possibly support similar to that achieved by the Whigs in the 1831 general election. In consequence, on 2 July, Lord Derby in the House of Lords became Conservative prime minister without a majority in the Commons where the Liberals had a nominal majority of over 70.[21] His spokesman there was Benjamin Disraeli whom he appointed chancellor of the exchequer. At this point Derby, who had been a member of the Cabinet which had carried the 1831 Reform Bill, was in favour of some further reform whilst Disraeli remained lukewarm, although not for long. In fact, what was involved behind all the rhetoric was, as

---

19. *Hansard*. [183] 1818/19.
20. Philip Magnus. *Gladstone*. 180. 1963.
21. Lord Derby once told Queen Victoria that an independent member of Parliament was a member who could not be depended upon.

Maurice Cowling has shown,[22] a battle for party advantage and not principle on electoral reform - as events were to prove.

Rioting in Hyde Park

On the defeat of the Bill, and in another period of economic distress, new reform associations sprang into being to affiliate to the National Reform League which was formed in London in 1865 and had many branches in the South and the Midlands. Although it was predominantly a working class organisation the president of the League was a respectable conveyancing barrister named Edmund Beales. Its objects were set out as to "procure the extension of the elective franchise to every resident and registered adult male person of sound mind and unconvicted of crime" and "to obtain for the voter the protection of the Ballot".

In an Address to trade unionists in June 1865 the League had declared that,

"During the last few weeks you have been called upon to witness a General Election. About 1,000,000 of our fellow countrymen have had the 'privilege' of recording their votes in the election of the 'Law Makers' of Great Britain.

Out of this number only about 100,000 or

---

22. Maurice Cowling. *1867 Disraeli, Gladstone and Revolution. The Passing of the second Reform Bill.* 1967.

one-tenth of the whole, belong to the *Working Class* of our population. Besides which there are about 6,000,000 of the adult males without *any vote* or direct voice in the great council of the nation.

Yet these 'Law Makers' enact laws binding upon us all; they impose taxes we all have to pay; aye, and spend these taxes most improvidently. Yet we have no voice to advise, no power to check any extravagance in the expenditure, or mismanagement in the government, or injustice in the laws."

A year later, on 24 July 1866, the League determined to hold a huge meeting for reform in Hyde Park. The law officers of the crown told the Cabinet that they could prevent the meeting taking place by closing the gates of the park. They could then deal with any who entered the park as trespassers. Sir Richard Mayne, chief metropolitan police commissioner, acted accordingly and the gates were closed at 5 pm. The League's procession, consisting of thousands of men and women, marched to the closed gates of the park at Marble Arch where they were confronted by more than 1,700 police. By this time the crowds were estimated at between 100,000 and 200,000 persons. Being repulsed by the police, most of them turned and walked along Oxford Street and thence to Trafalgar Square. However, some of the crowd remained at the park and pushed against the railings which were knocked down over a length of 1,400 yards. They then remained in possession of the park where they battled with the police until evening and some rioting continued for two more days. Considerable damage was caused to trees and railings and stones were thrown at the police, many of whom were injured. Some 40 to 50 people were arrested and next day sentenced to short terms of imprisonment or fines.[23] Heated exchanges over the meeting occurred in both Houses of Parliament.

Another result of the affair was that during the following months the trade unions entered into an alliance with the League and numerous joint meetings and huge protest marches were held. In London, in December, a demonstration included members of many unions and societies holding aloft banners bearing legends such as "Taxation without representation is tyranny". In recognition of the leadership of John Bright the slogan of the tallow chandlers was, "Bright and Light" and the cabinet makers' banners proclaimed, "No more oligarchical rule - the people are determined to be the cabinet makers" and "Bright Cabinet makers wanted - no Adullamites need apply". Consternation among Conservative leaders grew, particularly as they had no majority in the House of Commons.

Even the pro-Tory *Times* declared that the day's proceedings showed what the sturdiest Conservative would have to admit, namely that "the more intelligent mechanics were at least the equals, in all that constitutes good citizens, of the small shopkeepers who did possess the franchise."[24] Such public pressure played a part in

---

23. *The Times*, 24 July 1866, p. 9.
24. *Ibid.*, 4 December 1866.

convincing both the main political parties that reform had to come and cleared the way for the Act of 1867. In April of that year, as if to confirm that conviction, the government, after first banning another meeting of the Reform League to be held in Hyde Park, subsequently capitulated and allowed it to take place, which it did peacefully. Indeed, Lord Cranborne wrote in an article in the *Quarterly Review* in October, entitled "The Conservative Surrender", that many MPs had feared that "the pot should boil over ... The meetings in the manufacturing towns and the riots in Hyde Park had had their effect. The comfortable classes had no stomach for a real struggle." Nonetheless, undue importance should not be attached to the activities of the League. The point has been well made by Maurice Cowling in his *1867 Disraeli, Gladstone and Revolution. The Passing of the second Reform Bill:*

"The passage of the Reform Act of 1867 was effected in a context of public agitation: it cannot be explained as a simple consequence. Parliament in the sixties was not *afraid* of public agitation: nor was its action *determined* by it. Its members did not believe that public agitation necessarily represented public opinion. Public opinion included a variety of acquiescencies and protests, which interacted continuously with Parliament. The interaction took the form of dialogue: the dialogue was a real one. The interaction reached its most fruitful peak in Parliament. It is in Parliament, and in the light of

Parliament's view of public feeling, that the centre of explanation will be found."[25]

In any event, other circumstances also had an effect. For a time the Stock Exchange was in trouble, for three months the bank rate rose to 10% and unemployment became widespread. The 1866 harvest had been ruined and the repercussions were still being felt, cholera returned and Irish extremist action reached new heights on both sides of the Irish Sea.

Tory Response

Despite a minority government, and under pressure from Lord Derby, Disraeli determined to keep the parliamentary initiative. On 11 February 1867, as the leader of the Conservatives in the Commons, but with little prior discussion in a divided Cabinet, he tabled thirteen vague and general resolutions promising a reform of the franchise.[26] This was purely a tactic, however, and his true intention was to pave the way for an all-party commission of inquiry in order to delay the introduction of a Bill. Sensing this, some 20,000 trade unionists meeting in the Agricultural Hall, Islington immediately attacked the resolutions. And Disraeli was soon to be overtaken by events.

---

25. Page 3, 1967.
26. *Hansard.* [185] 214/243.

On 25 February,[27] with tongue in cheek, he told a crowded House of Commons that the resolutions aimed to increase the representation of the labouring class, which had been disregarded in 1832, but without giving them a majority as it would be against the Constitution to allow any class to predominate. To ensure that this would not happen he intended to neutralise the increased working class votes that the resolutions proposed with plural voting. This involved giving additional votes to all graduates of universities, to members of professions, to those with £30 or more in savings banks or £50 upwards in public funds, and everyone paying 20 shillings or more a year in direct taxation. Similar to some of the earlier proposals of the Liberals these were known as the "fancy franchises".

The Conservative Party had now accepted rateable value instead of rent as the basis for having the vote and the borough franchise was to cover householders paying rates of £6 or more annually in place of the £10 rental threshold. This was expected to enfranchise 130,000 new ordinary voters as against 212,000 new plural votes in the boroughs. In the counties the occupation franchise was to be a rating value of at least £20 instead of £50 rent. This, in turn, would add 82,500 new occupying voters against 105,000 new plural votes. As in 1832 the changes were intended to be permanent. For the opposition, Gladstone complained that the figures given for the number of new voters was grossly overstated.

---

27. *Ibid.* 937/52.

But Disraeli had other problems. Like his rival earlier, his supporters were divided. There was also a good deal of confusion, and in March General Peel and Lords Cranborne and Carnarvon resigned from the Cabinet on the ground that the household suffrage would survive but plural voting would not. Other Tories predicted a concession of Home Rule to Ireland following a large increase in voters in that part of the kingdom.[28] Such prophecies were to be fulfilled.

After the defections the new Cabinet translated Disraeli's resolutions into a Representation of the People Bill, which was introduced by him on 18 March 1867. He took the opportunity to say, "We do not live - and I trust it will never be the fate of this country to live - under a democracy. The propositions which I am going to make tonight certainly have no tendency in that direction."[29] The Bill revealed that the Cabinet had decided to extend the franchise in boroughs to the male heads of households with two years' residence who had paid their rates, however low the amount. In the counties householders who had resided for a year in property of £15 annual rateable value would qualify if the rates had actually been paid. To soften the impact of this increase in household suffrage (which continued to exclude women and others) the Bill also included a second vote for every borough voter who paid £1 a year in direct taxation, held £50 in government stock or held a professional

---

28. See speech of Brodrick. *Ibid.* [188] 578.
29. *Ibid.* [186] 6/25.

qualification. In the main, plural voting was to be replaced by dual votes. Further, planned redistribution would give fifteen extra seats to the counties, fourteen to the boroughs and one to the University of London. According to Disraeli the result of the plan would be that one quarter of the voting power would belong to the aristocracy, another quarter to the working class and the remaining half to the middle class.

Gladstone, on the other hand, said that the net effect would be to enfranchise not 240,000 people who paid rates as Disraeli claimed but fewer than 140,000 and he now suggested a rating of £5 in the boroughs.[30] He further urged that household suffrage was premature and not desired in the country. Nonetheless, he did not oppose the first reading of the Bill.

At a meeting in Trafalgar Square on 3 March a large crowd was told that the Tory government wished to make them believe that they were enfranchising the working classes by the addition of 100,000 votes, whereas the previous year's Liberal Bill would have given an increase of 200,000. George Potter, founder of the London Working Men's Association and its newspaper *The Beehive*, in addressing the meeting said that it was the working classes which in the main produced the wealth of the country and they asked to be permitted to have a voice in the management of its affairs. He wanted Disraeli to give them household suffrage and a lodger franchise. Despite the increase in the country of population, intelligence,

---

30. *Ibid.* 26/46.

power and wealth, he said, the great mass of the community were still deprived of the right of citizenship. A lodger who paid £20 for his apartment had no vote whilst the tenant who let the house out at a profit and lived in the kitchen had a vote.[31]

Second Reading

The second reading of the Bill, which lasted two nights, commenced on 25 March 1867. Gladstone, who could not contain his loathing for Disraeli, immediately entered the fray.[32] He denounced the Bill as a gigantic fraud and made five demands: (i) That there should be a lodger franchise. (ii) That the so-called 'compound householders' who paid rates via their landlords should have the vote. (iii) That the taxation franchise, plural voting and the dual vote be dropped. (iv) That the redistribution of seats be enlarged. (v) That the figure for the county franchise be reduced. Disraeli objected to Gladstone's air of the Inquisition in his speech, adding that "his manner is sometimes so very alarming that one might almost feel thankful that gentlemen in this House who sit on opposite sides of this table are divided by a tolerably broad piece of furniture."[33] Unsurprisingly, he was not prepared at this point to concede on any of his rival's

---

31. *The Times,* 4 March 1867, p.5.
32. *Hansard.* 472/504.
33. *Ibid.* 642/64.

demands although he did say that he was the father of the lodger franchise but had been unable to get the Cabinet to agree to it.

John Stuart Mill, MP for Westminster, said that it was the "very essence of constitutional liberty, that men come from their looms and their forges to decide, and decide well, whether they are properly governed, and whom they will be governed by." He then attempted to introduce some measure of female suffrage by replacing the word "man" in clause 4 of the Bill by "person".[34] Supported by a petition signed by 1,499 ladies in his constituency he declared, with a breathtaking disregard for reality, that women's suffrage was an uncontroversial issue. "More to the point," he added, "in our constitution there is no other exclusion which is so absolute." Despite arguing that taxation and representation should be linked, his amendment was defeated in the division by 196 to 73. Gladstone voted with the majority after a number of members had given what the *Annual Register* described as, "a jocular character to the discussion".[35] It never crossed the minds of the majority of members that women had the right to vote; as they saw it the franchise was a privilege to which they were not entitled - their husbands could vote on their behalf. Even Mill's proposal was far from democratic since married women would have been excluded because at the time the law was that on marriage women's property passed to their husbands and

---

34. *Ibid.*, third series. [187] 817.
35. *Annual Register*. 72. (1867).

therefore they could not be ratepayers. Only widows and spinsters would have qualified. Even after the Married Women's Property Act of 1870 women had control only of their property and earnings acquired after marriage and not other property, which, until 1882, remained with their husbands.

Mill was, however, deeply concerned about the franchise rights of minorities and also championed working men who had no vote. He told the Commons,

"While so many classes, comparatively insignificant in numbers, and not supposed to be freer from class partialities or interests than their neighbours, are represented, some of them, I venture to say, greatly over-represented in the House, there is a class, more numerous than all the others, and therefore, as a mere matter of human feeling, entitled to more consideration - weak as yet, and therefore needing representation the more, but daily becoming stronger, and more capable of making its claim good - and this class is not represented. We claim, then, a large and liberal representation of the working classes, on the conservative theory of the Constitution. We demand that they be represented as a class, if represented they cannot be as human beings."[36]

Mill also supported the more proportional system of voting first advocated by Thomas Hare in 1857. This

---

36. *Hansard.* [150] 1255/6.

involved the whole country forming one constituency which would return hundreds of members. A candidate would be elected by obtaining a quota of votes calculated by combining the number of votes cast with the number of seats to be filled. He believed this would protect the rights of minorities but it found no favour with either Gladstone or Disraeli. In any event, despite all Mill's efforts for women and the working classes, and his growing support for socialism, he really feared that democracy would destroy the higher cultivation because of its "collective mediocrity."[37]

---

37. On the last point see Maurice Cowling's *Mill and Liberalism*. 10. 1990.

CHAPTER 14

Disraeli "Dishes the Whigs"

After Disraeli's Bill was read a second time without a division (Gladstone was anxious to avoid a further schism in Liberal ranks) it was referred to committee on 8 April 1867.

Disraeli's Manoeuvres

In committee Disraeli, who was intent on defeating Gladstone and strengthening the Conservative Party even if it meant accepting amendments decidedly more radical than those of his rival, was now content to sit back whilst more extreme amendments were carried by majorities, and the dual vote was temporarily withdrawn after universal condemnation.

A significant amendment of Gladstone's was not carried. He proposed to bring within the franchise those whose rates were included in their rents to landlords believing this would mean the reinstatement of a £5 minimum. This was a move to win over the "cave-men"; that was dangerous to Disraeli who immediately announced that if it were accepted he would dissolve Parliament. At the same time he made a blistering attack on Gladstone whose amendment was, he said, a declaration of war made by "a candidate for power" who forgot that he "has had his innings". A glorious mixed metaphor!

There was still serious dissent in the Liberal Party and with Disraeli's connivance a group of some 63 Liberals opposed Gladstone's apparent acceptance of a rating qualification and because they met in the tea-room of the Commons their opposition to their leader became known as the "Tea-room Revolt". In the division on 12 April 1867 Gladstone's amendment was defeated by 21 votes[1] to thunderous applause. "A smash perhaps without example," said Gladstone who contemplated retiring to the back benches.[2]

The government then conceded a £10 lodger franchise in the boroughs, abandoned some plural voting, reduced the county qualification from the proposed £15 to £12 and improved the distribution of seats. It also reduced the qualifying residence in boroughs from two years to one.

Disraeli had made his mark on his party that hitherto had been distrustful of him. And he knew he had done so. Leaving the House at 2 am on 13 April he looked in at the Carlton Club an hour later to more applause and went on home to a bottle of champagne and a Fortnum and Mason's pie which his wife Mary Anne had waiting for him. He ate half the pie, drank all the champagne and turning to his wife made his famous remark: "Why, my

---

1. *Hansard.* [182] 1699.
2. Gladstone. *Diaries.* vi. 513.

dear, you are more like a mistress than a wife."[3]

After 13 weeks in committee the greatly amended Bill came before the House for the third reading and was quickly passed. Disraeli had manoeuvred to keep the Tory minority government in office and had gone so far as to accept radical amendments to a Bill he would not previously have dreamt of for that purpose and to thwart the more committed reformer, Gladstone, who otherwise would have received all the credit. For, of the 61 sections of the Act as passed only four came directly from the government. Amendments and clauses from Gladstone's 1866 Bill provided the remainder.[4] Disraeli largely gave up the dual vote and when an amendment was introduced to give the franchise in boroughs to occupiers regardless of whether they paid rates direct or through a landlord Disraeli, without consultation, caused a sensation by accepting the plan which he had previously rejected when it had been proposed by Gladstone. This added an additional 500,000 working class voters to the electorate. In this way the franchise was extended to nearly four times the extent that was originally contemplated by the government. The county franchise was lowered to a £12 rateable value, and by taking one member each from boroughs with a population of less than 10,000 Disraeli had 45 seats available for redistribution. Twenty-five of these were given to the counties, 15 to new boroughs, a

---

3.　T.E. Kebbel. *Lord Beaconsfield and Other Tory Memories.* 40. 1907.
4.　H. Cox. *Whig and Tory Administrations during the Last Thirteen Years.* 51/2. 1868.

third member each to Manchester, Liverpool, Leeds and Birmingham and a member to the University of London. As electors in three-member seats continued to have only two votes Disraeli left them alone calculating that this would increase Conservative votes as would restricting reform largely to the Liberal boroughs and lowering the franchise level for ratepayers in small boroughs. As Maurice Cowling has pointed out the Act was "an incident in the history of party".[5]

As now drawn, the Bill passed in the Lords and received the royal assent on 19 August 1867. In what has been described as a victory disguised as defeat Disraeli had "dished the Whigs", to use Lord Derby's memorable phrase. Yet for Disraeli was it not really a defeat disguised as victory since, by clever tactics in order to keep himself in office, someone who initially at least was not really interested in reforming the franchise had given the vote to far more people than the 1832 Act? The authoritarian, Thomas Carlyle, commented that, "Traitorous Politicians, grasping at votes, even votes from the rabble, have brought it on."[6] But the Reform League was still not satisfied. Its council announced that nothing short of universal manhood suffrage and vote by ballot would be satisfactory and these had not been achieved.[7] Lord Cranborne, on the other hand, complained of a political betrayal, saying that the principle of monarchy

---

5. *1867 Disraeli, Gladstone and Revolution. The Passing of the Second Reform Bill.* 2. 1967.
6. *Shooting Niagara: And After?* (1867).
7. *The Times,* 29 August 1867, p. 12.

was dead, that of the aristocracy doomed and the democratic principle triumphant: a prettily balanced sentence but untrue in all three respects.

A Leap in the Dark

Certainly Disraeli was determined to hold on to power, and commenting on the passing of the Bill the *Edinburgh Review* said that the Conservative Party, "sore at its long exclusion, and determined to clutch the prize it had obtained, was in a humour to bear much. Unlimited abandonment of principles and policy on Reform, deceit in any quantity, vacillation without end - for these it was well prepared."[8] That may have been the case but Disraeli had genuine compassion and feeling for the working class and also took the realistic view expressed by his character, Charles Egremont, in a speech in Parliament in the novel *Sybil* that "if you wished for a time to retain your political power, you could only effect your purpose by securing for the people greater social felicity."[9] In any event, whatever the motive, the statute was a milestone in the struggle for the franchise and democracy.

The Act, which Lord Derby described as "a great experiment and taking a leap in the dark"[10] abandoned the property qualification for the franchise and was far

---

8.   *Edinburgh Review.* 543. (October 1867).
9.   Benjamin Disraeli. *Sybil, or the Two Nations.* 82. 1845.
10. *Hansard.* [189] 951/2.

more sweeping than the one the Conservatives had wrecked a year before. It added 938,000 voters to an existing electorate of 1,056,000 in England and Wales. This gave working class voters in the towns a majority whilst most of the new country voters were members of the middle class. Not that the newly enfranchised would necessarily vote according to class and both Disraeli and Gladstone believed that the new working class voters would wish to be represented by their "betters" and not by working men. Significantly, the need to woo all the new voters greatly increased the importance of party organisation.

Both leaders claimed victory. Gladstone, in a moment of groundless elation, claimed the Act was "the highest triumph of a party ... to see our opponents themselves compelled to be the organs of giving effect to our principles and fulfilling our wishes."[11] Disraeli, on the other hand, asserted that the Tory Party was the national party of England and that "when change is carried out in deference to the manners, the customs, the laws and the traditions of the people ... then the Tory Party is triumphant."[12]

Some four months later, in a rare letter to *The Times*, Disraeli claimed that he had announced in relation to parliamentary reform five conclusions. (I) That the measure should be complete. (ii) That the representation of no place should be abrogated. (iii) That there must be

---

11. *The Times,* 20 December 1867.
12. *Ibid.* 30 October 1867.

a real boundary commission for redistribution. (iv) That the county representation should be increased. (v) That the borough franchise should be established on the principle of rating. He concluded by saying that all five points were accomplished in the 1867 Act.[13]

In 1868, supplementary Bills were introduced for Ireland and Scotland. Ireland had, of course, been in the background of events in England in 1867 when Fenian violence there reached a peak. The Irish Bill proposed to retain the occupation vote in the counties and reduce the borough franchise from £8 to £4 householders in towns and certain county boroughs, with votes for lodgers as in England. Some boroughs, were to be included in county constituencies and an extra seat was also provided for Dublin. The existing occupation franchise of £12 in the counties was retained. However, the House of Commons objected to redistribution but the Act as passed did include the enfranchisement clauses. In Scotland the county vote was extended to £5 owners and £14 occupiers. Seven new seats were also provided after the withdrawal of the vote from some small English boroughs with fewer than 5,000 inhabitants.

In July, the secretary of the London Working Men's Association wrote to the prime minister to point out that as polling took place from 8 am until 4 pm half of the working men on the electoral register in the metropolitan boroughs were deprived of their franchise since their working hours meant that many left home at 5, 6 or 7

---

13.   7 March 1868, p. 9.

o'clock in the morning and did not return home until 7 pm in the evening. He suggested that polling should be extended until 8 pm but a reply from Downing Street said that Disraeli was unable to hold out the hope that any change could be made before the general election.[14]

That the Act proved to be a "leap in the dark" was shown in the December 1868 general election which was based on the new franchise and in which the Conservatives were the losers, although they reaped the fruits in later years with a prolonged period of power. Before the election a *Times* leader had mistakenly indicated that the provisions of the 1867 Act would not come into operation until 1 January 1869. The reason, claimed the paper, was that the Act "was excessively ill-drawn and the original defects of expression had been exaggerated by a number of interpolations and alterations effected by various hands". It was "an inartistic patchwork".[15]

Suffrage for Women?

In 1870, with John Stuart Mill no longer in the Commons, Jacob Bright introduced a private member's Bill entitled the Women's Disabilities Bill. This required that in any Act dealing with parliamentary elections "wherever words occur which import the masculine gender, the same shall

---

14. *Ibid.*, 30 March 1868, p. 9.
15. 12 May 1868, p. 12.

be held to include females for all purposes connected with and having reference to the right to be registered as voters." This would give the vote in boroughs to women who were householders and paid rates and in the counties to those who were householders in houses rated at £12 or more. It meant that married women would still be excluded because their property belonged to their husbands. As the saying went, "The woman, the cat and the chimney should never leave the house."

Bright pointed out that "According to the common law of England a married woman in regard to the rights of property, is in the position of the Negro in the southern states of America before the American Revolution," by which he probably meant the civil war. "She cannot," he continued, "control her property and she has not the possession of one farthing of her earnings ... Be the woman ever so prudent, be the man ever so imprudent - be the woman ever so sagacious and be the husband ever so imbecile, still he has absolute control, not only of his own but of hers."[16] But while he considered the law unjust he saw no hope of changing it in regard to the franchise, and made no attempt to do so in his Bill.

Jacob Bright was the brother of the better known John Bright the Anti-Corn Law League orator and subsequently a member of Gladstone's Cabinet. But whereas John Bright was opposed to women's suffrage in the belief that women would vote Conservative, Jacob was a strong supporter alongside his wife and two

---

16. *Hansard, third series.* [201] 199.

daughters. The Bill passed its second reading on 4 May by 124 votes to 91 but as a result of Gladstone's manifest antagonism it was thrown out in committee.[17] Despite this defeat Jacob Bright continued his efforts with a similar Bill in the following year which received its second reading on 3 May 1871.[18]

In the debate he deplored the fact that on Mill's proposal in 1867 members had considered the question with feelings of curiosity and amusement. Now, he said, 170 members agreed with the principle of his Bill. It was claimed by others, he added, that the franchise would be a curse to women, but it might be assumed that women were the best judges of that. And there had recently been presented to the prime minister a memorial in support of his Bill signed by women and headed by the names of Florence Nightingale, Harriet Martineau, Miss Carpenter and several ladies of title. The principal argument of opposition, he concluded, was that women stood in too high a position to be subjected to the dirt and mire of politics, but "everything in this world has its baser side including religion, literature and art, and we do not attempt to exclude women from them on that account."

Mr E.P. Bouverie, a barrister and Liberal MP for Kilmarnock, opposed the Bill on the ground that the lives of women would be made a burden to them during a contested election as they would be assailed, bothered, annoyed and persecuted to give their votes and this

---

17. *Ibid.* 622.
18. *Ibid.* [206] 68.

should not be imposed upon them. Presumably men did not mind these excesses. However, he also believed the Bill would disturb the whole foundation of society and obliterate the distinction of sex, as well as the separate functions of the sexes in society which had always existed in every civilised community. The pride and glory of women were their modesty and their purity and they could not be brought into contact with the rough occupations of men without defiling that modesty and purity. In a tortuous speech aimed at avoiding giving offence to anyone, Gladstone nevertheless indicated that he would again vote against such a Bill. When a member suggested that the female mind could rarely follow a logical argument W. Hunt promptly retorted that if they were to go into the question of who was able to follow a logical argument they would have to bring in Bills of disenfranchisement. When the House divided the Bill was postponed for six months, and effectively killed, by 220 votes to 151.[19]

It is interesting that a few years later Arabella Shore was to tackle the question of how long women had been denied the vote, in a lecture at a meeting called by the London National Society for Women's Suffrage on 14 May 1877.[20] Women's suffrage, she said, meant household suffrage the same as with men. This was no constitutional innovation, it was against no custom from

---

19. *Ibid.* 121.
20. See *Before the vote was won: arguments for and against women's suffrage.* Ed. Jane Lewis. 282. 1987.

time immemorial and was contrary to no statute until 1832. Indeed, she declared, in Saxon times the Witan included women as did early local government and shire and borough courts. And when parliamentary representation was established there was no limit of sex; freeholders were entitled to the franchise and freeholds could be held by women. When in the reign of Henry VI the franchise was limited to 40 shillings freeholders the voters were described in the statute as "people", not "men".

In the reign of James I, she continued, on two occasions women's votes were recorded and when this was raised before the courts in Westminster Hall it was decided that "a *femme sole*, if a freeholder, might vote for a Parliament man". And in the Record Office were to be found the names of several women electors with some as returning officers. It was the Reform Bill of 1832 that first confined the suffrage to males. Then, in 1850, Lord Brougham's Interpretation Act (not Lord Romilly's as she said) declared that in all statutes the masculine gender should be taken to include women unless the contrary intention was expressly stated. When in the Reform Bill of 1867 the words "male person" were changed to "men" the question was taken to the court of common pleas in a test case[21] from Manchester where 5,750 women had placed their names on the register. Here John Coleridge QC, representing the appellants, argued that the "women's vote was an ancient constitutional right that

---

21. *Chorlton v. Lings. Law Reports.* CCP. iv. (7 November 1868).

had never been rescinded". Nevertheless, the resourceful male judges decided that the word "men" in the Act included women for the purposes of taxation but not for representation. Since then, Arabella said, the cause had had to be fought constitutionally and was quickly gaining ground.

The Secret Ballot

Seasons and leaders change. In February 1868 Disraeli became prime minister on the retirement of Lord Derby through ill health and Gladstone replaced Earl Russell as Liberal leader. Disraeli told a friend that he had at last, although perhaps too late, "climbed to the top of the greasy pole", and, as if to justify his pessimism, in December the Liberals regained power.

Four years later Gladstone, who was now prime minister, reluctantly submitted to the idea of the ballot and after 40 years of public debate the Parliament and Municipal Elections Bill of 1872 was introduced by his government to make voting for Parliament and local authorities secret for the first time in British history. It defined in great detail the procedure for elections and the functions of the returning officers (who were to have a vote only in the event of a tie). The ballot paper would have a list of candidates' names and outside each polling booth there would be a placard with all the directions for voters.[22] An amendment to the Bill to prevent anybody from displaying his ballot paper after he had marked his vote was defeated by 274 to 246.[23]

Members of both parties claimed the ballot would increase their side's representation although Disraeli said there was no demand for it in the country. After being passed by the Commons the Bill was thrown out by the Lords and Gladstone's anger was aroused. It was re-presented and, with the prime minister threatening a dissolution which Disraeli and the Conservatives did not want, it was accepted by the Lords by a majority of 30 although a number of peers, including Earl Russell and the archbishops of York and Canterbury, left the chamber before the division was called.[24] According to the *Annual Register* the Act passed, "in spite of the all but unanimous hostility of the House of Lords, the secret disapproval of the House of Commons, and the indifference of the general community."[25] As the Lords had no doubt foreseen when they rejected the Bill, the Ballot Act, as it became known, weakened the power of the landed interests, particularly in Ireland where it led to the rise of Charles Stewart Parnell. Despite the ballot, however, well into the twentieth century the fear of losing their tied cottages remained a serious matter for farmworkers at election times.

Immediately after the Bill was passed, a council

---

22. *The Times,* 15 February 1872, p. 4.
23. *Ibid.* 20 April 1872, p. 5.
24. *Ibid.* 11 June 1872, p. 10.
25. 1872. 72.

election in Gloucester on 20 July had to be abandoned at 2 pm when a telegram was received indicating that, since the Ballot Act had received the royal assent the day before, the election, which was being held under the earlier procedure, was null and void.[26] However, two days later an election for a vacancy on the council at Boston, Lincolnshire, in which the ballot was adopted, was conducted successfully.[27]

One of the first prosecutions under the new Act took place in Liverpool when three agents of the Conservative candidate were accused of copying the register-number of voters as they cast their votes and ascertaining for which candidate the voters had given their votes, with the intention of conveying the information to the Conservative committee room. For the defence it was argued that there was no communication between the agents and the committee, and that the Ballot Act was passed to prevent bribery and intimidation. Nothing the defendants communicated could harm the voters. The charges were dismissed by the stipendiary magistrate.[28]

When the Act was passed it was intended to be merely experimental and to require renewal, but it has of course survived. Not that it was always welcomed in its early days. On 6 April 1883 Sir W.B. Barttelot nostalgically recalled the time when an elector could speak freely in declaring his vote and not have to record a "sneaking"

---

26. *The Times*, 23 July 1872, p. 11.
27. *Ibid.* 25 July 1872, p. 6.
28. *Ibid.* 20 November 1872, p. 7.

vote. He complained about the "hole and corner" measure of 1872 which, he said, had widened the gulf between Parliament and the people and cut politicians off from access to "the current of public feeling" and prevented them seeing "in what way persons of different classes, different creeds, and, in a certain sense, persons of different nationalities exercised the franchise."[29]

Corrupt and Illegal Practices Act, 1883

By introducing secret voting the Ballot Act went some way towards restricting direct corruption but it was by no means enough. Indirect bribery with parties and entertainments continued as did the filing of incomplete and fictitious election accounts. As a consequence, in 1883 Sir Henry James, the attorney-general, carried the first reasonably effective Corrupt Practices Act to prevent abuses at elections. An earlier Act of 1854, which for the first time defined bribery and undue influence, was largely unsuccessful owing to its failure to ensure strict accountability.

Shocked by revelations of continued corruption and illegal practices the Commons approved, with the 1883 Act, a measure to strictly limit the amounts which might legally be spent by parliamentary candidates and their agents. The number of electors determined the amount that might be spent in a constituency. In a borough with

---

29. *Hansard.* [278]. 1724/5.

2,000 or less maximum expenditure was limited to £350. If there were more than 2,000 electors the limit was £380 plus £30 for each additional 1,000. In the counties the figure was £650 for 2,000 or fewer electors and if there were more than that number the amount was increased by £60 with another £60 for each additional 1,000. There could be only one committee room for every 500 electors. A candidate might incur personal expenses up to £100. Settlement of accounts had to be within one month of the election and before the elapse of 35 days the agent had to send to the returning officer a certified statement of all sums expended together with receipts for every payment exceeding £2.

The Act listed practices that were declared to be illegal. These included the payment of travelling expenses and the hiring of conveyances (which infuriated taxi drivers) banners, ribbons and bands. Overspending or paying money not directly authorised was also illegal. For such acts the first penalty was a fine of up to £100 and disqualification from voting. For a candidate responsible personally he was also disbarred from representing the constituency for seven years and an elector lost political rights for five years. Corrupt practices were: bribery, treating, undue influence and personation. For these, in addition to a fine of up to £100 there was a further penalty of up to one year's imprisonment with hard labour and loss of political rights.

There can be no doubt that the Act was a success. It reduced estimated election costs for candidates from

£1,737,000 in 1880 to £777,429 in 1900.[30] And cases of corruption fell dramatically although they still arise occasionally today as instanced by the Neill Committee and a few prosecutions. With the advent of modern means of communication new laws governing election expenses are now on the agenda. Another effect the Act produced was to shift to some extent election spending away from the localities to central party funds.

The Reform Act of 1884

After 1867 there were different electorates in the boroughs and the counties. In the boroughs, householders were entitled to vote as such but not in the counties. The towns, therefore, were more democratic with a higher proportion of men in the population being electors. As a result, agricultural labourers were disgruntled. In 1872 Sir George Trevelyan moved in the House of Commons, "That this House would be more likely to devote due and adequate attention to the wants and interests of our rural population if householders outside the boundaries of parliamentary boroughs were in possession of the franchise; and that it is expedient to extend to counties the occupation and lodging franchises now in force in boroughs." The motion was rejected as were similar attempts by the persistent Trevelyan in succeeding years.

Gladstone's arch enemy Disraeli died on 20 April

---

30. W.B. Gwyn. *Democracy and the Cost of Politics in Britain.* 55. 1962.

1881. In 1884 General Gordon was sent to the Sudan to evacuate Egyptian troops from Khartoum which was under threat from rebels led by the Muslim mystic, al-Mahdi. January of the following year saw the rebels break into Khartoum and kill Gordon. The British public acclaimed the immensely popular Gordon as a martyr and blamed the government for the delay in sending a relief force which resulted in his death. Earlier, on 28 February 1884, unflustered by the uproar already occasioned by the sending of Gordon to the Sudan, Gladstone moved for leave to introduce a new Representation of the People Amendment Bill. By this, he said, he intended to extend the household franchise to the counties and "increase the strength of the state ... which lies in the representative system."[31]

Perhaps unwittingly, or possibly deliberately, he also helped largely to diminish the influence of the landed interests in Parliament that Earl Grey and Lord John Russell had fought so hard to protect in 1832. The Bill proposed giving the counties the £10 occupation vote, and the household and £10 lodger franchise which had been given to the boroughs in 1867. This stung Lord Randolph Churchill to exclaim that he could say, "without fear of contradiction, that the agricultural labourer, as a general rule, was absolutely unfitted for the exercise of the franchise."[32] After some debate on an amendment to increase the representation from Scotland the Bill

---

31. *Hansard.* [285] 106/134.
32. *Ibid.* [285] 175.

received its first reading on 3 March.

Another Women's Suffrage Debate

Just prior to that, Millicent Garrett Fawcett had argued in the *Pall Mall Gazette*[33] that the majority of Liberals were now in favour of giving the parliamentary suffrage to women on the same terms as it was granted to men. Nearly a month later a conference of women held in the House of Commons resolved to procure an amendment to Gladstone's Bill with the object of securing for women the parliamentary franchise on the same terms as for men.[34] A few weeks later a crowded meeting in Scotland sent a resolution to Mr Gladstone requesting that the government should not offer any opposition to the claims of women householders and that no measure of reform would be satisfactory if it did not recognise their claim.[35]

The Times thought the idea silly. A leader on 27 May listed women's arguments before attempting to knock them down. Taxation and representation went together; women were taxed, therefore they should be represented. They did not fear comparison with the mass of agricultural and urban labourers who could barely write their names but who were admitted to the franchise whilst educated and cultivated women were excluded.

---

33. 14 January 1884.
34. *The Times,* 8 February 1884, p. 11.
35. *Ibid.* 24 March 1884, p. 6.

Yet if women were to have a vote for members of Parliament, *The Times* asked tongue in cheek, why should they not be allowed to sit there? Although the Bill as it stood would add some two million male voters to the register it was a step along the old lines, whilst to admit women would be a new thing unknown in any country in the world. Women did not really want the vote and the "small band of ladies" who sent a memorial to Mr Gladstone could hardly suppose themselves representative of their sex generally. They spoke only for themselves. Women, the paper concluded, had no case and were well satisfied to leave things as they were. However, a rebuttal came swiftly from no less a personage than Elizabeth Garrett Anderson, England's first woman doctor, who said that their opponents underestimated support for women's suffrage.[36]

On 11 June 1884, with the Commons in committee on Gladstone's Bill, William Woodall proposed an amendment to extend the suffrage to women on the same basis as men.[37] To widespread astonishment, the leader of the Tories, Lord Salisbury, said he would give the proposal his support in the House of Lords. But Gladstone had already made it clear in a fatuous statement that he believed the question of female enfranchisement should be discussed totally apart from all political and party considerations as he feared that it might jeopardise the Bill as a whole. Not surprisingly, however, he was

---

36. *Ibid.* 31 May 1884, p. 9.
37. *Hansard.* [289] 92.

ignored by back-benchers and a spirited discussion took place although the leader of neither Party took part.

In an openly sexist speech E.A. Leatham told members that "so far as the feminine element penetrates into your electorate, a feminine alloy will penetrate into your policy. You will have ... a feminine flutter in your courage at the moment when you require to be most manly and robust." He then put the true situation succinctly when he added, "It is not because men pay rates or taxes, or own or occupy property, that they have votes, but because they are men."[38] Sir Wilfred Lawson responded that "I wish there was a feminine alloy - an alloy of truth and humanity - in our policy. It will be a good day for England when that alloy does enter into our policy."[39] Lawson and other speakers who favoured the proposal nevertheless expressed the view that it could not succeed and indeed when the committee divided it was defeated by 271 votes to 135.

This was not an inconsiderable minority at that time, particularly as Gladstone was firmly opposed and had told his MPs that if a women's suffrage amendment were carried the Bill would be dropped and the government would resign. As a result the *Daily News* suggested that the Tories might with advantage take up the women's cause.[40] Some Conservatives did indeed take up the idea in the belief that many women were likely to vote for

---

38. *Ibid.* 103.
39. *Ibid.* 179.
40. 12 March 1884, p. 5.

their party and there was some support among Irish and Liberal MPs. However, nothing came of it against Gladstone's opposition to the issue being considered for inclusion in his Bill.

Reject the Bill

Five days after the women's suffrage amendment was moved, C.N. Warton from the Conservative benches raised the question of a redistribution of seats without which the Tories considered the Bill to be grossly unfair to their supporters in the country and likely to deprive them of 47 seats. "The Conservative side of the House," he said, "was quite able to see the position in which it was put; they quite understood the alternative offered to them, to have this Bill passed without redistribution, so that when redistribution was proposed it could be handed to them, as it were, with a pistol at their heads" ... But "they held one trump card; and with all respect to 'another place' he trusted that that card would be played. He hoped the House of Lords would reject the Bill."[41]

In the House of Lords itself the Conservatives demanded that a redistribution Bill be passed at the same time,[42] hoping that both Bills would founder, and called for Parliament to be dissolved. They were careful not to appear in public eyes as opposed to franchise reform as

---

41. *Hansard. Op. cit.* 655.
42. See Lord Cairns's motion. *Hansard.* [289] 1770.

such although the real concern of Lord Salisbury, the Tory leader in the Lords, was to preserve the influence of the landowners in the counties. Gladstone denied that the Lords were entitled to force a dissolution on the issue and called an autumn session to proceed with the original Bill which passed its second reading in the Commons on 7 November by 372 votes to 232. Lord Salisbury declared that the Conservatives would not be guided by the public opinion of the streets. In response, Gladstone attacked the Lords by threatening their existence and was rebuked by the queen who gratuitously added that the Lords reflected the true feeling of the country better than did the Commons. Gladstone told a friend that it was useless to quarrel with "Her Infallibility" but he also had to consider his radical supporters.

Once again the country was stirred into agitation with huge demonstrations taking place and slogans such as "Peers against the People" and "Mend them or end them" resounding throughout the land. Joseph Chamberlain threatened to lead 100,000 Midland men on London and break Lord Salisbury's head on the way. He was also involved in the Aston Park riots in Birmingham, in which Randolph Churchill and Sir Stafford Northcote narrowly escaped with their lives, and made fiery speeches around the country. So strong was the feeling for reform that it led to the queen sponsoring a compromise to avoid a crisis similar to that in 1832. This involved Gladstone as prime minister and Salisbury the leader of the Conservative peers agreeing privately to a proposed redistribution of seats, drawn largely by the Radical, Sir Charles Dilke, in the next session of Parliament. Boroughs with a population of fewer than 15,000 were to be merged into the counties and those with fewer than 50,000 were to return one member each instead of two.

The result was that the Franchise Act of 1884 was passed by the Lords,[43] after Gladstone had introduced the Redistribution Bill, and received the royal assent on December 6.[44] The latter Bill became law the following year. Following these two measures the United Kingdom electorate was raised from some three million to about five million - the largest increase in the numbers entitled to vote of the three nineteenth century Reform Acts. Seventy-nine towns with a population of fewer than 15,000 were disenfranchised and 36 with fewer than 50,000 inhabitants lost one of their two seats. Over 160 seats became available for redistribution. Boroughs with between 50,000 and 165,000 continued as two-member constituencies and that persisted until 1950. Otherwise two, three and four member constituencies disappeared when the remainder of the country, urban and rural, was divided into single-member divisions. Instead of the boroughs and counties retaining their historic role as the foundation of the House of Commons the individual had become the basis of the electoral system for Parliament, as it remains today. But the belief that single member constituencies would produce more proportionate results has proved unfounded as British politics has tended to

---

43. *Ibid.* 1455.
44. *Ibid.* [294] Index.

become polarised around a conflict of social classes. As Martin Pugh has said, "It is a paradox that Lord Salisbury played a key part in such a development."[45]

The English franchise was extended to Ireland whilst maintaining all the Irish seats. This led to an increase in the electorate there from 200,000 to 700,000 voters and a tremendous growth in the Nationalist Party of Parnell, with serious and largely unanticipated consequences in Parliament. But in England the increase in the franchise brought little comfort to the working class until the formation of the Labour Party in 1900, combined with a period of industrial confrontation in the years leading to the First World War, caused Asquith's Liberal government to introduce trade union and welfare legislation. By this time the 1867 and 1884 Acts were bearing fruit for men, with some 65 per cent of them entitled to vote, and this caused women who were still outside the pale to feel the injustice of their exclusion more deeply. The consequences of this will be considered in the next chapter.

---

45. *The Evolution of the British Electoral System 1832-1987.* 12. 1988.

CHAPTER 15

Votes for Women

In January 1892, Herbert Henry Asquith, himself a somewhat languid Liberal home secretary and future prime minister, in a comment to the House of Commons said that the great mass of women were watching the struggle for the emancipation of their sex "with languid and imperturbable indifference". If he was correct for the moment it would not be long before the climate changed, and it is not surprising that when it did he never really understood what the suffragette storm was all about.

The Agitation Commences

After more than 10 years of Tory government, January 1906 saw a dramatic general election with a Liberal landslide win[1] and the return of no fewer than 53 working class members of Parliament of whom 29 took the Labour whip, the rest sitting with the Liberals. Some three months earlier, on 13 October 1905 just before the election campaign, another event occurred, less

---

1. Conservative prime minister A.J. Balfour had resigned on 4 December 1905 and the following day the Liberal leader, Campbell-Bannerman, took office before the general election.

sensational but destined to lead to political turmoil. On that day two young girls, Christabel Pankhurst and Annie Kenney, a cotton mill operative, interrupted with demands for votes for women a Liberal Party meeting in Manchester addressed by Sir Edward Grey who, ironically, was a strong supporter of women's suffrage. The purpose of the meeting was to endorse the local candidate, Winston Churchill, a recent convert to the Liberal cause and also at the time a keen advocate of votes for women.

Both girls were charged, Christabel with a technical assault on the police officer who arrested them, Annie with creating a disturbance, and both were convicted and fined. However, they refused to pay the fines and were sent to Strangeways prison in default, Christabel for seven days and Annie for three. Their incarceration in such circumstances, even though for short periods, aroused immense sympathy and publicity throughout the country.

As we have seen, this was by no means the first time women had demanded the vote. In fact, in 1897 all the extant women's suffrage bodies had united to form the National Union of Women's Suffrage Societies (NUWSS) which attracted the affiliation of some 500 groups. Under its president and tireless advocate of votes for women, Mrs Millicent Garrett Fawcett, sister of Elizabeth Garrett Anderson the pioneer woman doctor, the Union was campaigning for democratic reform by lawful means and its members became known as the suffragists or constitutionalists. Public meetings and petitions were their weapons.

However, in October 1903, a more militant Women's Social and Political Union (WSPU) had been formed in Manchester by Emmeline Pankhurst, a member of the Independent Labour Party and the mother of Christabel and Sylvia. She was supported by James Keir Hardie, the first Labour Party MP, who became Sylvia's lover. But it was the publicity and support that Christabel Pankhurst and Annie Kenney received on their imprisonment that marked the real birth of the suffragette movement.[2] After their release from custody they resolved to interrupt many more Liberal meetings during the lengthy election campaign which lasted for some weeks and their efforts breathed fresh and defiant life into Mrs Pankhurst's Union. At first they looked to the recently-formed Labour Party for help but found most, although not all, of its leaders more concerned with gaining universal male suffrage than votes for women. Indeed, it was not only the leaders. Successive Labour Party conferences passed resolutions taking the same stand.

The Suffragettes

In the WSPU Emmeline Pankhurst found a keen associate in a wealthy socialist, Emmeline

---

2. The term "suffragette" was first used by Charles E. Hands, a *Daily Mail* journalist. The WSPU adopted it to distinguish themselves from the suffragists.

Pethick-Lawrence, who became treasurer of the Union and did a great deal to help the movement to expand. Mrs Pethick-Lawrence also chose what were to become the well-recognised colours of the WSPU, namely green (for hope), white (for purity) and purple (for dignity). Dresses were run up in these colours and were worn with matching sashes or ties. So extensive did the activities of the organisation become that no Liberal meeting or Cabinet minister could escape the attention of its members, usually unexpectedly in indoor meetings from underneath the platform or high up in the rafters. Liberals were chosen for their attentions, they said, as only the government could enact a suffrage Bill. Consequently even ministers favourable to their cause such as Grey, Churchill and Lloyd George were subjected to disruption.

In time the tactics of the suffragettes of the WSPU became more violent with the breaking of windows and the interruption of the proceedings of Parliament from the galleries of both Houses. In one sense the violence was out of keeping with the aim of securing the vote but the suffragettes were also seeking equality of the sexes and the opposition they received incited them further when frequently that opposition was itself violent and derogatory. Undoubtedly, their tactics produced a backlash but that only stimulated them the more. Eventually they would alienate Churchill and Lloyd George, both of whom were their partisans in Cabinet, as well as George Lansbury and even Keir Hardie. But that lay in the future and even then did not mean they changed their minds about the merits of the case.

The Mud March

In the meantime, on Saturday 9 February 1907, the constitutional societies held a march from Hyde Park to Exeter Hall in the Strand, two days before the state opening of Parliament. Despite heavy rain, between 3,000 and 4,000 women, dressed mostly in black, joined the procession which was a great success, although dubbed by the press "The Mud March".

The Times, no friend of women's suffrage, admitted that the demonstration was remarkable as much for its representative character as for its size. Ladies "of title and distinction" walked through muddy streets on a cold February afternoon and were undaunted by the rain or the jeers of amused spectators. In Exeter Hall, it said, after speeches by ladies representing various factions of the suffragette (*sic*) movement, the crowd was addressed by the distinguished novelist, Israel Zangwill, who declared that if ever there was a subject on which women had a right to a voice it was surely the recent Education Bill.[3] After that monumental example of male mismanagement, he said, who could wonder if women began to take the law into their own hands. The government that refused to grant female suffrage was the enemy and

---

3.   This introduced the principle of medical inspection of school children and was surrounded by controversy.

the secret was to damage the government. Keir Hardie also spoke, saying that he was still on the same side and would not turn his back on the women's cause.[4] But he and Mrs Fawcett caused some consternation among the non-militant audience when they praised the suffragettes.

The *Manchester Guardian* was also impressed with the meeting and procession. A leader said that it required some courage for women to step out of their drawing rooms into the street and walk through rain and tramp through mud in a mixed throng in a cause probably distasteful to many or most of their acquaintances, and to see themselves pilloried in the newspapers next morning. The crowd was well-mannered but neither enthusiastic nor sympathetic. The position taken by a small portion of the suffragists (ie, suffragettes), the leader continued, in insisting that the government should introduce a suffrage Bill and force it into law, was indefensible. If the WSPU continued to do such things they would defeat their own ends and if the suffragists as a whole were to be led by them they would invite disaster for their own movement.[5]

Then, as a counterblast to the march, a few days afterwards Mrs Pankhurst called "A Women's Parliament" in Caxton Hall. After a number of speeches, she and Mrs Charlotte Despard led the women present in a march to the precincts of Parliament where the police rode into them on horseback and scattered them. Some 54 women were arrested and, after refusing to pay fines,

4. *The Times*, 11 February 1907, p. 11.
5   *Manchester Guardian,* 11 February 1907, p. 6.

were sent to Holloway prison. The question of police violence was raised in the Commons but the Home Secretary, Herbert Gladstone, blatantly refused to acknowledge there had been any.[6] However, it was real enough and served further to inflame the suffragettes and their supporters.

A Private Member's Bill

Two days later Willoughby Dickinson, the Liberal MP for St Pancras North, introduced in the House of Commons a Women's Enfranchisement Bill. This came up for its second reading on 8 March when in anticipation of a demonstration the ladies' gallery was closed to visitors. The Bill provided that in all franchise statutes words of masculine gender should be deemed to include women and that women should not be disqualified by marriage from voting. The reason for the second point was that although the Municipal Corporations Act of 1869 gave the vote to women ratepayers in local elections the courts had ruled that married women could not vote even if they paid rates.[7] This was considered by the women's suffrage societies as untenable since women should have the right to vote on the same basis as men. Although they wanted all adult women to have the vote they saw the lesser demand involving a property qualification as the thin end

---

6.   *Hansard*, fourth series. [169] 272.
7.   *R. v. Harrald*. 7 QB. 361 (1872).

of the wedge to universal suffrage.

Although he was not proposing full adult suffrage, Dickinson said, he based the Bill on the concept of democracy and claimed that there were 400 members who agreed with women's suffrage in principle and, in order to avoid defections from that number, he declared that the cause was not helped by incidents taking place outside the House. He added that the example of Australia, where women had enjoyed the franchise since 1902, showed that they not only wanted the vote but exercised it responsibly.[8]

During the debate the Liberal prime minister, Sir Henry Campbell-Bannerman, a warm supporter of women's suffrage, said it was wrong that a woman who paid taxes had no direct representation and no power of influencing those who controlled the taxation. She had to obey the laws and act upon matters that affected her personal liberty in a thousand ways but had no share in shaping them. In line with these views he announced that there would be a free vote of the House and that he himself would vote for the Bill.[9] Nonetheless, the Bill retained the property qualification for voting which discriminated against working class women and, apart from the fact that it was therefore not democratic, many Liberal and Labour MPs who should have acted from principle were instead concerned that it would simply enfranchise a body of well-to-do women who would vote

---

8.   *Hansard. Op. cit.* 1102.
9   *Hansard.* 1109/1112.

Conservative. As is often the case, playing party politics came before principle and in consequence the Bill was talked out the same day with the Speaker refusing to call a division.

Women on Local Authorities

Nevertheless, by the Summer of that year a useful stepping stone towards women's enfranchisement was achieved with the enactment of the Qualification of Women Act, 1907. The genesis of the statute is to be found in 1890 when a court decided that three women who sat on the newly formed London County Council had no right to do so. As a result Lord Meath had introduced a Bill to remove the disability but the House of Lords threw this out by a majority of more than two to one. Subsequently, several Bills which provided for women to sit on borough councils were all rejected by Parliament. Then, in 1907, Lord Crewe, the influential parliamentary president of the council, moved for a similar Bill. This received its second reading in the Lords on 12 June.[10]

In the ensuing debate Lord Halsbury, a Tory former lord chancellor, decried the fact that if the Bill were passed there would be no reason why women should not have the parliamentary vote.[11] If they qualified they could already vote in municipal elections but he was not

10. *Ibid.* [175] 1343.
11. *Ibid.* 1351.

prepared to adopt the logical consequence and instead opposed the Bill. He was supported by the Marquess of Lansdowne who was worried that local councils might be flooded by women and particularly by women who enjoyed the hurly-burly of political life,[12] unlike men presumably. Like other Lords and MPs before him, he thought women should be quiet and unobtrusive. Indeed, it was often claimed by politicians at the time that it would be unbecoming for women to enter a polling booth alone to vote or, if a candidate, to canvass on the doorsteps of men's homes.[13]

Despite such shallow arguments the Bill was passed and enabled women, married or single, to sit as councillors, aldermen, mayors or chairmen (so called at that time) on borough and county councils. That, however, still fell far short of the principal aim of being able to vote for MPs and sit in the House of Commons. Nor did it prevent *The Times* in the following year making the extraordinary assertion in a leader that, "Again the underlying assumption in the national franchise is that the voter, who has to decide on the well-being and even the existence of his country, can argue out his views for his country's good on equal terms with his fellow, and in the last resort can knock him down if he chance to be the better man. No such assumption could be possible were women to have the vote."[14] If force

---

12. *Ibid.* 1355.
13. In spite of such views some women were already involved in canvassing.
14. 15 June 1908.

was so important perhaps voting was unnecessary.

Schism and Successes

By the summer of 1907 the militant suffragettes, whose WSPU now had 70 branches, conceived a policy of not only heckling but fully opposing Liberal candidates in by-elections. Such tactics swelled the growing criticism of the Pankhursts in their own Union. There were complaints that the executive never met and that the Pankhursts dominated the emergency committee that ran the Union as dictators. As if to prove the critics' point, at the next meeting Mrs Pankhurst simply abolished both the constitution and the annual conference of members of the Union and announced that in future she would not have anyone on the emergency committee who did not agree with her. This caused a split in the movement and a number of members, including the prominent and formidable Charlotte Despard, broke away in September 1907 to form the more democratic Women's Freedom League of which Mrs Despard became President. It was at this point that the WSPU launched its journal *Votes for Women*.

In the following year, Londoners saw two impressive demonstrations in favour of women's right to vote. On 13 June the constitutional suffragists (NUWSS) organised a march of 13,000 women from the Embankment to the Albert Hall. *The Times*, hostile as ever to the suffragettes, had allowed suffragist Mrs Fawcett to write about the demonstration on the day before it took place. She even produced a plan of the starting place so great were the numbers expected to march. This covered a square bounded by Whitehall and Parliament Street to the north, the Embankment to the south, and by Horse Guards Avenue and Bridge Street. In the event, eminent women graduates from Oxford, Cambridge and Dublin were in the procession that included women writers, doctors, artists and musicians as well as a large contingent of what the press called "working women". Special trains brought many of the participants from Liverpool, Manchester, Sheffield, Leeds, Leicester, Birmingham, Hull and Bristol. At the meeting Mrs Fawcett emphasised that there was no rivalry between the procession that day and the suffragettes' Votes for Women demonstration due in Hyde Park on 21 June. They were different societies but they had the same end in view.[15]

According to a leading article in *The Times* two days later the procession was "not only interesting but impressive". But more interesting, it believed, was the attitude of the spectators who lined the three-mile route. Their keen interest was purely "the detached interest of curiosity that never at any moment kindled into enthusiasm". The demonstrators could congratulate themselves on having attracted so much public attention and having been received with such extreme politeness, but they could not pretend they moved the public heart. If the objective of the demonstration was to prove to the

---

15. *Ibid.* 13 June 1908, p. 9.

general public that the great masses of the people were deeply moved on the suffrage question it could not be regarded as an unqualified success. But, the paper conceded, in every other respect its success was beyond challenge.[16] The *Manchester Guardian* was strangely silent: it carried no comment on the meeting but only a large photograph showing the huge crowd.[17]

Eight days later, on a Sunday, the suffragettes' rally in Hyde Park was attended by more than a quarter of a million people, including some prominent men such as Thomas Hardy, George Bernard Shaw and H.G. Wells. Mrs Flora Drummond, known as "The General", had advertised the meeting by mooring a motor boat opposite the terraces of the House of Commons and using a megaphone to invite members having tea to attend.

After the rally *The Times* was even more effusive and even more damning than before. "Last Saturday week," it began, "the National Union of Women's Suffrage Societies showed the capacity of women to organise a beautiful and impressive procession through the streets of London, and yesterday the more militant National Women's Social and Political Union made an even more imposing appeal to the attention of the public by their remarkable demonstration in Hyde Park." Some 30,000 women converged on the park where thousands of people were already present, the largest crowd seen there for 25 years. "A quarter of a million, indeed, seems hardly to be an

---

16. *Ibid.* 15 June, p. 9.
17. *Manchester Guardian.* 22 June 1908.

exaggerated figure at which to place this immense crowd gathered round the 20 platforms from which well-known advocates of the cause addressed those near enough to hear them. We can but offer a tribute of admiration to the wonderful organisation displayed by those responsible for this remarkable demonstration, especially to its chief, Mrs Drummond."

After the patronising velvet glove came the dismissive iron fist. The paper said it would be idle to deny that a great many women were for the time desirous of the franchise but of course 30,000 demonstrators and a crowd of a quarter of a million who watched them was no proof that an overwhelming majority of the women in the country demanded the vote. And it was certainly time that a corresponding demonstration of strength should be made by the women who disbelieved the suitability of their sex for the franchise, as well as by the men of the same opinion whose views also had to be considered. There was to be no receding from its opinion that women were less strong in persistence and physical power than men. It believed it would "weaken the moral fibre of the nation" if the supreme decisions of the state were determined partly by women who could not feel the same responsibility for seeing them carried through as men.[18]

---

18. *The Times*, 22 June 1908, p. 11.

In Court

On 12 February 1908 Campbell-Bannerman made what was to be his last speech in the House of Commons and the next day went down with a serious illness. He died on 22 April but had already resigned on 6 April when he was replaced as prime minister by Herbert Asquith, who was less than warm towards votes for women. Against a background of growing unemployment and hunger marches, the struggle now grew more intense. The suffragettes called a meeting for 13 October in order, as they put it, to "rush the House of Commons". Fearing that the unemployed who were holding a demonstration in Parliament Square earlier the same day might join the suffragettes, the government had all approaches to Parliament sealed off and obtained from the Bow Street magistrate, Mr Curtis Bennett, a warrant for the arrest of Emmeline and Christabel Pankhurst and Flora Drummond. They were charged with conduct likely to lead to a breach of the peace. In the meantime huge crowds gathered as near to Parliament as they could get and two suffragettes managed to break through the police cordon and "rush" into the House of Commons where Mrs Travers Symons shouted to the startled MPs, "Leave off discussing the Children's Bill and attend to women first".

The case against the arrested leaders opened on 21 October at Bow Street magistrates' court when Christabel, who had read law, subpoenaed the chancellor of the exchequer, Lloyd George, and the home secretary, Herbert Gladstone, to give evidence. As Lloyd George had taken his six-year-old daughter, Megan, to see the demonstration he was hardly in a position to say a breach of the peace was "likely" although the charge depended upon that word only, and not on whether a breach of the peace actually occurred.

In giving evidence Lloyd George said that he was present for about 10 minutes at the Trafalgar Square meeting and had received a handbill inviting him to "rush the House of Commons". He understood this to mean to force an entry to the Commons. Christabel, who was examining him, disputed his interpretation of "rush" and offered "eager demand", "urgent pressure" and "in a hurry" as alternative readings. However, although Lloyd George would not accept them he agreed that he did not hear any speaker threaten violence or urge people to go armed or suggest that property be damaged. The home secretary said in answer to a question from Christabel that it was impossible to rush without violence but he confirmed that he did not see the crowd attack either property or persons.

During the case Christabel revealed that another magistrate had admitted that in sentencing a suffragette to six weeks' imprisonment he had "done as I was told" by the government. Furthermore, she claimed that the crowd at the "rush" on the Commons had not been as violent as that which watched the wedding of Winston Churchill in the previous month. She also complained that the government had ensured the defendants would be tried by a "star chamber of the twentieth century" and denied them trial by a jury who would acquit them. For her part,

Emmeline Pankhurst told the court, "I come here not as an ordinary law-breaker. We are here not because we are law-breakers; we are here in our effort to become law-makers".

At the resumed hearing a few days later the magistrate, in making his decision, pointed out that in consequence of the publication of the handbill between 5,000 and 6,000 policemen had had to be placed on special duty. In the ensuing fracas 10 people were taken to hospital, seven policemen were on the sick list, 37 people were arrested and 40 had property stolen. A serious breach of the peace had occurred and he ordered Mrs Drummond and Mrs Pankhurst to be bound over in their own recognisance of £100 each and to find two sureties of £50 each to keep the peace for 12 months with the alternative of three months' imprisonment. Christabel was asked to find sureties in half these sums with the alternative of ten weeks' prison. As they all refused to accept the binding over they were sent to prison for the terms stated. A week later, in a gesture of solidarity with their former colleagues, three members of the Women's Freedom League, chained themselves to the grille of the ladies' gallery in the House of Commons and commenced shouting "Votes for Women". This continued until officials found they were unable to break the chains and release the women and removed the entire grille with the women attached to it.

Forced Feeding of Hunger Strikers

Despite the huge success of the suffragettes' Hyde Park rally in June 1908 the Women's Freedom League and the constitutional societies outnumbered the WSPU both in numbers of branches and members. However, a turning point in militancy occurred in June 1909 when Miss Marion Wallace-Dunlop, a suffragette in prison, on her own initiative went on hunger strike against the harsh second-division treatment reserved for serious criminals in contrast to the more lenient first-division treatment. Among other things this involved wearing the prison dress with its broad arrows and being forbidden to receive visitors. After she had fasted for 91 hours, ministers, fearing that she would die whilst in their charge, released her. Following this retreat it should have come as no surprise when other suffragette prisoners soon followed Miss Wallace-Dunlop's example.

Now faced with a new dilemma, the government determined that hunger strikes should not result in freedom. Instead they introduced forcible feeding in prisons with meat extract and lime cordial passed through tubes; a treatment that could prove dangerous. As a response the WSPU decided to attract greater publicity by destroying property. Initially this was confined to breaking plate glass windows of shops, which caused at least one MP, with Asquith's support, to suggest that the funds of the WSPU be made available for compensation orders. But according to Mrs Pankhurst, "The argument of the broken pane is the most valuable argument in modern politics".

The policy of opposing Liberal candidates in by-elections was also gaining momentum. At a huge meeting in the Albert Hall, Mrs Pethick-Lawrence summed up the suffragettes' position as "so far as the power lies in us we do not intend to allow a single Cabinet minister to speak in public. We have to make these absurd little tin potentates who call themselves the Liberal party the laughing stock of the civilised world. We have to make it impossible ever again for a Liberal candidate to be returned at a by-election. (Loud cheers)."[19] No exceptions were to be made and in consequence, incredible as it must have seemed, when Bertrand Russell, encouraged by the constitutionalist women, stood for election at Wimbledon in the summer of 1909 on a platform which included women's suffrage, he was opposed by the suffragettes. Even so, he polled nearly 4,000 votes. Since during the campaign he had also advocated Liberal Party policies Sylvia Pankhurst argued that he had grievously misled women.[20]

Conciliation Bills

In February 1910, eight months after the first hunger strike, 54 MPs under the guidance of Lord Lytton, the brother of suffragette Lady Constance Lytton, had formed

---

19. *Votes for Women*, p. 97. (5 November 1908).
20 *Ibid.*, p. 1106. (27 August 1909).

a parliamentary committee to advance women's suffrage. They speedily produced a "Conciliation Bill" (officially, the Women's Enfranchisement Bill) which was acceptable to suffragists of all colours, and which provided, on the same terms as men, that every single woman with either a household or a £10 occupation qualification would be entitled to vote. This received a second reading in the House of Commons in July when Lloyd George and Winston Churchill, after reiterating their support for women's suffrage, spoke against the Bill as being undemocratic because it excluded the majority of married women since they were not occupiers in their own right.[21] Nevertheless, it passed by 299 votes to 189 but was then referred to a committee of the whole House where it expired when the government, fearful that women would not vote Liberal, refused to find time for it.

In any event it would have given the vote to just one woman in 10 and many Liberal and Labour members remained opposed to enfranchising what they thought would be only women of property, who were likely to vote Conservative. Deeply anti-Tory, Lloyd George, for example, claimed that the Bill would "on balance add hundreds of thousands of votes throughout the country to the strength of the Tory Party".[22] As a supporter of women's suffrage, however, he might have been expected to back the Bill which embraced the principle instead of

21. *Hansard.* [19] 224-7.
22. Quoted by Martin Pugh in *Women's Suffrage in Britain 1867-1928.* 15. 1980.

helping to destroy it. Perhaps he was more concerned about his position in the Cabinet.

This same year also saw the replacement of Herbert Gladstone as home secretary by Winston Churchill. One of Churchill's first actions was to introduce improved prison conditions including a change whereby non-serious offenders were no longer required to wear prison clothing, would not be searched, would be allowed to receive food from outside and be permitted to take regular exercise during which they could talk. Women suffragists, he explained, were included among those who would benefit, provided they abided by the ordinary prison rules.

On 5 May 1911 Sir George Kemp introduced in the Commons a new Conciliation (Women's Enfranchisement) Bill which included the word "conciliation" in its title in order to admit free amendment and which omitted the £10 occupation qualification.[23] It received a second reading by a majority of 167. However, Asquith's government refused further time for it although the prime minister, who had vehemently opposed women's suffrage from 1892, did, under pressure from the Cabinet and particularly Lord Grey, David Lloyd George and Winston Churchill, promise it "a week or more" the following year. A month later, Arnold Ward MP drew the attention of the home secretary to a speech made by a Cecil Chapman, a magistrate in London, in support of women's suffrage in which he attacked the law as unjust and unequal and accused the government of cruelly sweating the women in

---

23. *Hansard,* fifth series. [25] 738.

their employment. The secretary of state for the home department, Wedgwood Benn, replied that he was communicating with the magistrate.[24]

In February 1912 a protest meeting *against* women's suffrage was held at the Albert Hall presided over by Lord Cromer. Speakers included Lord Curzon, F.E. Smith and Violet Markham, the well-known anti-suffragist who had once said she regarded women as superior to men and did not like to see them trying to become men's equals.[25] As reported by *The Times*, Lord Cromer said that the British Empire was built up by men and should be governed by men as they alone were physically capable of defending it. He said there was no unanimity among women in wishing for enfranchisement. He warned that what had happened in Norway (where women obtained the vote in 1909) could happen in this country. Every office there was open to women with the exception of the Cabinet, the diplomatic service, the ministry, the bar and the army - rather a long catalogue of exclusions. He thought that to accede to the present request would be "a constitutional outrage" and a fraud upon the electorate.

In a leader in the same edition *The Times* contrasted two meetings held in the Albert Hall a week apart. In the anti-suffrage meeting, it wrote, the speakers set forth with gravity and responsibility reasons powerfully appealing to common sense and political sagacity. But a week earlier, it continued, Lloyd George had exhorted his

24. *Ibid.* [26] 1210.
25. *Anti-Suffrage Review*. 9. (November 1910).

audience to take advantage of a unique opportunity (after the passing of the Parliament Act of 1911 which reduced the power of the House of Lords to veto legislation) to carry a suffrage measure over the head of the Lords without allowing the opinion or wishes of the nation to be heard. The leader concluded that it was nothing short of cynical political immorality to attempt a gigantic leap in the dark of this kind while elaborately denying to the country every opportunity to express its considered opinion.

Reaction to Militancy

A month later, in March 1912, the suffragettes revoked the truce they had declared during the passage of the 1910 and 1911 Conciliation Bills and renewed militant activity, including arson and hunger strikes. This produced a backlash and resulted in a new Conciliation Bill (identical with that of 1911) being defeated by 14 votes in the Commons in contrast to the majorities for the earlier Bills. At the same time the Pankhursts forced out of the WSPU Mr and Mrs Pethick-Lawrence, their hitherto valued comrades, who then formed the Votes for Women Fellowship. The glass-breaking of "Mrs Pankhurst and her maenads", wrote *The Times*, resulted in thousands of pounds worth of damage. The paper could understand similar news coming from China or even from South Wales, but not from London where the destruction was the work of a "few unbalanced women" whose "only grievance lies in an insignificant point of parliamentary procedure". The movement of public opinion from indifference to hostility to their cause had reduced them to despair.[26]

It is hardly surprising that the paper welcomed the ensuing arrest of Mr and Mrs Pethick-Lawrence and a warrant issued against Christabel Pankhurst. Such government action, it said, might help to bring the less infatuated of the extreme suffragists to a wholesome sense of their position. Several women "who had been breaking shop windows in order to prove their fitness for the franchise" were sentenced to hard labour, a punishment that "was not too severe for the offence which these people committed" . Men and women of all classes had realised that the movement had grown from a nuisance to a danger. *The Times* did not agree with Christabel that the government would not dare send her and her associates to penal servitude but, on the contrary, thought that such a sentence would commend itself to a public sense of justice. "We are glad to believe that after what has happened no measure to extend the suffrage to women in any degree is likely to pass the House of Commons in the present session."[27]

On 16 March the paper believed it had identified, probably for the first time, what has since come to be known as crowd psychology and which it called "Insurgent Hysteria", the title given to a leading article.

---

26. 2 March 1912, p. 9.
27. 6 March, p. 9.

The writer could "scarcely doubt" that in a large number of cases even though insanity was not present among militant suffragists there was a tendency to some forms of hysteria or morbid moods. This had culminated in senseless outrages against property and other acts of hooliganism. Physicians, the writer claimed, came across many cases in which there was so much mental instability that any public excitement disturbed the balance and produced fits of hysteria that showed itself in violent conduct or loquacity. The editorial ended by suggesting that militancy could be used to further various aims such as enforcing vegetarianism or releasing interesting criminals and concluded that the militant movement was only partly understood if it were not seen that it attracted many "aspiring incapables and a mass of persons who prefer notoriety to obscurity".

As if to demonstrate that clever people can say stupid things another example occurred in the form of a letter to *The Times* 12 days later from Sir Almroth Wright.[28] Wright came from an outstandingly brilliant Irish family. His father Charles was a noted theologian, Hebraist and Arabist. His uncle Edward was a professor of botany and founder of the *Natural History Review* and his brother Sir C.T. Hagburg Wright was secretary and librarian to the London Library for 47 years. Almroth Wright himself shone even in such a family. He graduated in modern literature before qualifying in medicine. He was a professor of pathology continuously from 1892 until just

---

28.   28 March, p. 7.

before his death in 1947, first at the Army Medical School and then for 44 years at St Mary's Hospital, London, where he was responsible for the introduction of anti-typhoid inoculation and other vaccines, latterly with his younger assistant Alexander Fleming. He was made a Fellow of the Royal Society and knighted in 1906.

His three-column-long letter to *The Times* must have attracted every misogynist reader like moths to a lamp. He began by relating what he called women's peculiar behaviour to their physiology, referring to "serious and long-continued mental disorders developing in connection with the approaching extinction of a woman's reproductive faculty. The upsettings of her mental equilibrium were the things that a woman had most cause to fear. The doctor cannot shut his eyes to the fact that there is linked up with this women's movement much mental disorder." He continued that "the recruiting field for the militant suffragist is the half million excess of our female population - that half million that had better long ago gone out to mate with its complement of men beyond the seas."

He then discussed different kinds of women including those who believed they might, whenever it was to their advantage, lawfully resort to physical violence; "sexually embittered" women who hated men, and those who wished to convert the whole world into an epicene institution where men and women everywhere worked side by side. He considered it fatuous that a woman should receive the same wages as a man for the same work because the man was physically stronger. He believed that the institution of matrimony could possibly not endure without some willing subordination on the part of the wife. Wright ended his letter by saying that peace would come again when woman ceased to resent the fact that men could not and did not wish to work side by side with her and that she could without sacrifice of dignity give a willing subordination to her husband or father who, "when all is said and done, earns and lays up money for her".

As if that were not enough Wright also published his *Unexpurgated Case against Woman Suffrage,*[29] another, and longer, puerile attempt to show that all women were mentally inferior to men. At least he had the effect of bringing the various women's suffrage organisations together for a time in opposition to his madcap ideas.

A Male Suffrage Bill

On 13 March 1912 Reginald McKenna, who had replaced Churchill as home secretary in the previous October, stated in reply to a question by George Lansbury that 76 suffragettes were undergoing hard labour in prison and 42 others were also in prison of whom nine were in hospital.[30] A month later he agreed that they could have a weekly food parcel sent in to them. In the following year as many as 240 suffragettes were imprisoned of whom 57

---

29. 1913.
30. *Hansard.* [35] 1098.

were being forcibly fed.[31]

On 17 June 1912, the president of the board of education, J.A. Pease, introduced a government reform measure entitled the Franchise and Registration Bill.[32] It proposed that no person should vote in more than one constituency; that electors should be qualified by residence or occupation of property of whatever value and in no other way; and that the qualifying period be reduced from one year to six months. Despite Asquith's earlier promise of a "week or more" for a women's suffrage measure the Bill applied only to men although Asquith had told a deputation of suffragettes in the previous November that it could be amended to include women. Pease, however, said that if women were included on the same terms as men ten-and-a-half million women would be added to the register and that was more than the number of men.[33] Despite violent opposition from the fiery F.E. Smith, a later lord chancellor, the Bill received its first reading by 274 votes to 50. Its second reading was passed by 290 votes to 218 on 12 July and the committee stage (which will be considered later) was then postponed to 24 January 1913.

---

31. *Ibid.* [50] 1663.
32. *Ibid.* [39] 1326.
33. *Ibid.* 1342.

CHAPTER 16

The Women's Struggle Continues

Whilst questions were being raised in the House of Commons on 25 June 1912 about the forcible feeding of suffragette prisoners, the Labour MP George Lansbury left his seat below the gangway and walked to the ministerial bench above the gangway. Face to face with Asquith he cried, "You call yourselves gentlemen, and you forcibly feed and murder women in this fashion! You ought to be driven out of office ... It is the most disgraceful thing that ever happened in the history of England! You will go down in history as the man who tortured innocent women." The Speaker asked Lansbury to leave the House for engaging in grossly disorderly conduct. "I am not going out," Lansbury replied, "while this contemptible thing is being done" (Shouts of "Withdraw" and "Order, order") - "murdering, torturing, and driving women mad."[1] After this blast he was finally persuaded to withdraw but only for the remainder of the day.

Torture of Innocent Women

How dangerous forcible feeding might be was revealed by

---

1. *Hansard.* [40] 217/19.

Keir Hardie on 27 June 1912 when he questioned Ellis Griffiths QC, the secretary of state for the home department, about the case of Mrs Myra Sadd Brown. Was the secretary aware, asked Hardie, that "when forcible feeding was about to be resorted to, the prisoner informed the medical officer that owing to a fracture of the nose forcible feeding by the tube through the nose would not be possible; that the doctor refused to pay any attention but ordered three wardresses to hold her in a chair; that the feeding tube was forced three times up the nostril but returned by way of the mouth?" What action, he persisted, would be taken to prevent a recurrence?

A complacent Ellis Griffiths replied that "The difficulty in feeding her arose entirely from the unusual power which she possessed of contracting the throat muscles and bringing the tube out through the mouth ... If she suffered any pain it was due entirely to the violent resistance she offered to what was necessary medical treatment."[2]

The following day Labour MPs secured a further debate on the imprisoned suffragettes by means of a motion of no confidence in Reginald McKenna, the home secretary. The Conservative MP, Lord Robert Cecil, said he deplored militant methods but he produced evidence to show the serious ill-effects of forcible feeding even, in one case, leading to madness in a victim who had not struggled against the indignity. He also revealed an example of unequal treatment in the case of Lady

---

2. *Hansard*, fifth series. [40] 500.

Constance Lytton, daughter of a former Viceroy of India, who was sent to prison for throwing a stone at the bonnet of a motor car. Examined by a doctor she was found to have a chronically weak heart and was immediately released. Subsequently, dressed as a working woman, she made sure she was arrested for another suffrage offence in a different part of the country and gave the false name of Jane Walker. This time, being apparently of lower rank, she was not medically examined. As a consequence she was subjected to forcible feeding which seriously injured her health.[3]

In the same debate Keir Hardie produced a copy of a document sent to the home secretary by 117 medical practitioners. It read:

"We, as members of the medical profession, strongly protest against the forcible feeding to which certain prisoners are at present being subjected. We consider that tube feeding in cases where the operation is resisted by the patient, is accompanied by immediate risk to life, in addition to the danger of permanent damage to the health, both of body and of mind. We urge that this practice be discontinued."[4]

J.S. Fletcher quoted the case of Miss Emily Davison who attempted suicide in prison for the cause and that of Mrs Sadd Brown raised earlier by Keir Hardie. In support of

---

3. *Ibid.* 650/51.
4. *Ibid.* 659.

the home secretary, Cathcart Wason accused Lord Robert Cecil of trying to "harrow our feelings by going into nauseous details as to forcible feeding". "Will he say," he asked, "what he is going to substitute for it?" Cecil pointed out that Wason was a Scotsman and reminded him that forcible feeding was never resorted to in Scotland. Wason admitted he had not known that and added feebly, "We are not here to tackle the pure technicalities of the law."[5]

George Lansbury then indicated that there were one hundred suffragettes languishing in prisons. Ninety-seven of them were convicted of damaging property against common law and three for conspiracy to incite others to commit such damage. Yet the three leaders, Mrs Pankhurst and Mr and Mrs Pethick-Lawrence, were in the privileged first division in prison where they did not have to wear prison dress with its broad arrows, could receive visitors and would not be subjected to forced feeding whilst the others, whose offences were less serious, were in the harsher second division.[6] Members had sneered, he declared, that these women wanted cheap martyrdom. "I suppose," he continued, "every tyrant has said the same thing in the history of the world ... These women are fighting for a real and definite principle, for something which to them is dearer than life." Furthermore, he added, William Ball,

---

5. *Ibid.* 664.
6. The Prisons Act 1865 had actually introduced the divisions to enable less serious offenders and "political" prisoners to receive more favourable treatment.

a transport worker, had gone into prison sane and had come out insane after forcible feeding. Ball's case was also taken up by Hugh Franklin, a nephew of a Liberal Cabinet minister and a member of the Men's Political Union, who himself had experienced being forcibly fed. It was argued by the government that Ball's insanity was not caused by his treatment in prison.

After saying that he denied the right of society in the name of punishment physically to injure any human being in this kind of way, Lansbury produced a statement of Mr Forbes Ross which read:

> "As a medical man without any particular feeling for the cause of the suffragettes, I consider that forcible feeding by the methods employed is an act of brutality beyond common endurance, and I am astounded that it is possible for Members of Parliament, with mothers and wives and sisters of their own, to allow it, however wrong the methods of the women may be ... Even in asylums people who have to be fed in this way die as a rule. I have seen men dying after being fed artificially for one or two weeks."

"That is pretty strong evidence," added Lansbury, "and some of these women have been fed for weeks and weeks."[7]

---

7. *Hansard.* 666/673.

Pedantry

In his reply to the debate, the "sensitive" home secretary said that the questions raised by Lord Robert Cecil concerning Lady Constance Lytton, William Ball and others, "although important in themselves, are but of secondary importance compared with this charge he has made against me ... of discrimination in the exercise of my duty of treating all prisoners on the same footing." He then indicated that the three leaders, whose jury had recommended leniency but who had been given longer sentences than their followers, had been placed in the first division after giving an undertaking that they would not use the more lenient facilities there to incite persons to commit illegal acts.

After denying that he had the power to transfer a class of prisoners from one division to another (An Hon. Member: "You did it") McKenna, tortuously argued that he was really only giving effect to the discretion of the judge who had wanted to put them in the first division but felt that he could not. "What pedantry!" exclaimed Lord Robert Cecil in despair. John Ward, a Lib-Lab member, regretted that so much time had been spent on the rights and wrongs of "wealthy and influential people well able to look after themselves". McKenna was constantly and acrimoniously interrupted but in the division he was sustained by 213 votes to 69.[8] So much for the compassion of members of the Commons and the

---

8.   *Ibid.* 718.

Liberal government which remained unsympathetic to the arguments and was unwilling to retreat under the onslaught.

To the dismay of the Labour Party leadership, in November 1912 George Lansbury resigned his seat at Bow and Bromley in London's East End and stood for re-election in order to test opinion on his platform of women's suffrage. One of his aims was to strengthen the hand of the growing number of supporters of votes for women in the Labour Party. Unfortunately for his plan the Pankhursts descended on the constituency and, according to Martin Pugh, Lansbury's working class men were "so unappreciative of shrill harangues from middle class ladies that Lansbury's comfortable majority was easily overturned in a straight fight with a Conservative anti-suffragist"[9]

Debate on the Government Bill

On 23 January 1913 the Conservative leader, Andrew Bonar Law, asked the Speaker whether amendments to the government's June 1912 Reform Bill relating to the franchise for men were so materially different from the essential nature of the Bill that it should be withdrawn and a new measure introduced. The Speaker replied that the request was premature as they should see how the Bill emerged from committee but he went a stage further

---

9. *Women's Suffrage in Britain 1867-1928.* 24. 1980.

and also indicated that "other amendments relating to female suffrage would make a huge difference if they were inserted."[10] When on the same day the Commons discussed the allocation of time for the various stages of the Bill, Bonar Law, with special pleading, argued that if women's suffrage were added then the electors who already had the vote would be swamped and disenfranchised.[11] How they would actually lose the vote he did not say.

The following day it was revealed in committee that three amendments relating to votes for women had been put forward and it was widely believed that one of them would be accepted. In the light of disagreements in the Cabinet it was decided that ministers should be allowed to speak on different sides. The secretary of state for the colonies, Lewis Harcourt, admitted he was opposed to any form of female suffrage for parliamentary elections and said he would vote against the Bill. He also complained strongly that Sir Edward Grey could see no deficiency in the female mind which he (Harcourt) firmly believed existed.[12] He accused members of wanting to make "woman man's master".

Lord Hugh Cecil said the colonial secretary's bitter speech had filled him with amusement. Harcourt was an apostle gone wrong who if he had turned his warmth of feeling into happier channels might have been a Peter the

---

10. *Hansard.* [47] 643/4.
11. *Ibid.* 666.
12. *Ibid.* 893/4.

Hermit. As for "deficiency of mind" did he really believe that of Queen Elizabeth or women who served on municipal bodies with credit? The function of voting, he said, was a simple one. Active politicians of the parties in a district chose their candidates and the voter had to choose between two or three of them. Surely women were as capable as men in exercising that political function? Nonetheless, he would not have them as members of the Commons because "as a Conservative I like the House of Commons as it is"[13] - that is as a "gentleman's club".

In the event the Speaker ruled that the character of the Bill was being altered and that it should be withdrawn and a fresh one prepared. This destroyed not only the amendments but the entire Bill which Asquith immediately withdrew despite his earlier pledge that he would accept any amendment in favour of women's suffrage that the Commons might approve. In fact, the Speaker's ruling had been postponed for four days and it is difficult to believe that the prime minister was taken by surprise. Instead, he now said the government would give facilities for a private member's Bill on the issue but that, of course, was not the same as a government-backed Bill.

Not surprisingly the suffragettes were furious. A deputation led by Mrs Drummond went to see Lloyd George. Lloyd George told them he would meet them at 11 am the next morning but Mrs Drummond and Sylvia Pankhurst refused to leave and were arrested. At this,

---

13. *Ibid.* 909/17.

windows were broken at government offices in Whitehall and there were a further 30 arrests.[14] Mrs Drummond was fined forty shillings with the alternative of 14 days in prison. In a foretaste of what was to come, on the same day Grace Edith Burbidge was charged with damaging letters by putting "liquid phosphorus" into a letter box in Camden Road, severely burning her arm in the process.[15]

A More Violent Policy

Certainly Christabel Pankhurst believed that such a Bill as Asquith was suggesting had no prospect of success and decided upon a more violent policy. As has been seen, Mrs Pethick-Lawrence and some other members of the WSPU who were not in agreement with extended violence had been driven from the Union. Mr Pethick-Lawrence had continued to edit *Votes for Women* and the WSPU had started an alternative paper *The Suffragette*. Now the violence was to increase.

The new policy involved more extensive and secret arson with paraffin-soaked rags being placed in pillar boxes, houses, pavilions, a grandstand, a railway station, boat-houses and schools. It was secret because the suffragettes were no longer actively seeking arrest although they were prepared for it if caught. Before long bombs were being used, pictures in public galleries,

14. *The Times,* 29 January 1913, p. 7.
15. *Ibid.* 30 January, p. 12.

including the "Rokesby Venus" by Velasquez, were slashed, the Tower of London and the British Museum were attacked, golf greens were damaged in the Birmingham area and letters destroyed in post-boxes in various parts of London. Four postmen were badly injured in Dundee when the letters they were sorting burst into flame. According to *The Times* tubes containing phosphorus contained in envelopes addressed to Asquith were found among the letters.[16]

The refreshment rooms at Regent's Park were burned down with damage estimated at £6-700. The Orchid House at Kew was destroyed. Telephone wires were cut in Dumbarton, Birmingham and other areas with notices fixed to their poles bearing the words "votes for women".[17] Hundreds of windows of government buildings and of shops in London's West End were smashed. Less serious, but disturbing to the government, on the golf course at Lossiemouth militants tried to tear the clothes from Asquith who was saved only by the intervention of his daughter Violet and the police who grabbed the women and took them to Elgin police station.

The secrecy was not to the liking of Mrs Pankhurst, however. After Lloyd George's new house at Walton Heath was bombed causing extensive damage, and a second bomb failed to explode, she publicly declared, "We have tried blowing him up to wake his conscience. I have advised, I have incited, I have conspired. The authorities

---

16. *Ibid.* 6 February, p. 6.
17. *Ibid.* 8 February, p. 10.

need not look for the women who have done what they did last night. I accept the responsibility for it." Arrested for incitement, she was tried at the Old Bailey and on 3 April 1913 sentenced to three years penal servitude whilst her supporters in court defiantly sang the *Marseillaise*. She was taken to Holloway prison where she immediately went on hunger strike.[18]

Meanwhile, the tea pavilion at Kew Gardens was burned to the ground and a card with the words "votes for women" was found in the vicinity. Two women were arrested and charged and one of them threw a book at the chairman of the bench. Unsurprisingly, they were refused bail. Mrs Drummond said, "We are proud of such women. We stand by them."[19] Two weeks later five women were arrested in The Mall whilst trying to break through police lines in order to present a petition on women's suffrage to the king.[20]

To remain at liberty to organise the campaign Christabel, under the pseudonym Amy Richards, opened an office in Paris, outside the jurisdiction of the English courts. Some people, however, both inside and outside suffragette circles, believed she was seeking a safe haven away from imprisonment and forced feeding, although she continued to direct WSPU policy and write the editorials of *The Suffragette* from her self-imposed exile.

---

18. Antonia Raeburn. *The Militant Suffragettes*. 190/91. 1973.
19. *The Times*. 21 February 1913, p. 6.
20. *Ibid.*, 11 March, p. 8.

"Cat and Mouse"

Shortly afterwards the home secretary hurriedly secured the ingenious "Cat and Mouse" Act which was presented on 25 March 1913 and received the royal assent on 26 April as the Prisoners (Temporary Discharge for Ill-health) Act.[21] With this he was able to abandon forced feeding in order to avoid hunger-strikers (whose plight was securing them great public sympathy) dying whilst in government care and instead to keep them in jail until they appeared to be weakening from starvation. They were then released on licence but could be rearrested and again submitted to forcible feeding if they made speeches in public. Sidney and Beatrice Webb who were unsympathetic to the suffragette cause, nonetheless argued in the *New Statesman* that putting women who were on licence back in prison was illegal and asked what law there was for returning them without another trial.[22] McKenna responded that during the period of the licence the prison term was not running. The Webbs knew that only if a person committed an offence whilst on licence could he or she be returned to prison and that speaking in public was not an offence. McKenna simply chose to ignore this.

Sylvia Pankhurst now formed a "People's Army" to protect women from such rearrest. "Athletic Amazons

---

21. *Hansard.* [52] 763.
22. *New Statesman.* (26 April 1913).

with broomsticks" ridiculed the *Daily Citizen*[23] but they registered some successes in protecting the women. Nevertheless, Sylvia Pankhurst herself was repeatedly rearrested and imprisoned for breaking her licence, going to Holloway nine times in one year alone and suffering cruelly from her self-starvation whilst there. In June 1913 she commenced a vigil by lying on the steps of the House of Commons to secure some attention from Asquith. The prime minister had always doggedly refused to meet her but this time he was influenced by the fact that very recently Emily Davison had died after throwing herself under the flying hooves of the king's horse at Tattenham Corner on Derby Day and he relented and agreed to see her deputation. Nothing came of the meeting, however, and suffragettes continued to be released from prison so emaciated as to be scarcely able to speak or stand.

Unsuitable Men

On Asquith's promise that the government would not obstruct it, W.H. Dickinson moved the second reading of a new Representation of the People (Women) Bill on 5 May 1913. Women's suffrage, he said, was of supreme importance both to the country and all civilisation. He deplored that earlier efforts in Parliament had been impeded by militancy and said that his Bill included married women and would enfranchise some four or five

---

23. 24 November 1913.

million women over and above those who were already able to exercise the municipal vote. "It brings on to the register", he said, "a stable and reliable class of women representing all grades of rich and poor."[24] As if to emphasise the need for women in Parliament two speakers in the debate then unwittingly revealed how unsuited some men were to run the country. J.M. Henderson claimed he had been in favour of a limited franchise for women but he could not accept a Bill that would double the existing number of seven million voters. "You may call it prejudice if you like," he said, but "If you give women the vote to such an extent as this you must be prepared to see them in this House on the Front Bench governing the country, and on the Opposition Bench opposing the government." Women might be qualified for that, he grudgingly conceded, after three or four generations.[25] It was, of course, his "optimism" that was wrong by three or four generations.

A Liberal knight, Sir John Rees, relied for his opposition to women's suffrage upon a doctor and the Bible. The doctor was Otto Weininger who, in what Rees claimed was "the greatest work that has yet been written upon this subject," had said, "The emancipated woman is not a normal but an abnormal woman. It (*sic*) is not a natural but a perverted type..." Unfortunately for the gallant knight another member pointed out that the doctor had committed suicide through madness at the age

24. *Hansard.* [52] 1704.
25. *Ibid.* 1749/50.

of 24. Rees grotesquely replied that this put him on a par with Socrates. In fact Socrates was 70 when he died, was not mad and was executed (although he administered the hemlock himself). So far as the Bible is concerned, Rees was content to quote St Paul as saying "Neither was the man created for the woman, but the woman for the man" and "He suffered not a woman to teach, nor for the married woman to have authority over her husband."[26]

For the Labour Party Philip Snowden and Ramsay MacDonald supported the Bill in well-reasoned speeches and Sir Alfred Mond, the Liberal industrialist, pointed out that during the year 1911, among other bodies such as the Women's Liberal Federation, no less than five county councils and 108 city and town councils, including Birkenhead, Birmingham, Cardiff, Dublin, Edinburgh, Glasgow, Manchester, Leeds, Sheffield and Nottingham, had petitioned Parliament for women's suffrage.[27] Asquith, on the other hand, asked the House, "Would our political fabric be strengthened, would our legislation be more respected, would our social and domestic life be enriched, would our standard of manners - including the old-fashioned virtues of chivalry and courtesy - be raised and refined if women were politically enfranchised?" He thought not and said he would vote against the Bill.[28] In the event, it was defeated by 266 votes to 219 in the last important parliamentary vote on the issue before the

---

26. *Ibid.* 1758/67.
27. *Ibid.* 1791.
28. *Ibid.* 1915.

outbreak of the First World War more than a year later in August 1914.

Commenting on the defeat of the Bill by 47 votes *The Times* stated that there were two good reasons for expecting a decisive rejection. The first was the large number of women, about six million, who would get the vote at a single stroke, an increase of the electorate by 75%, hardly a gradual extension of the franchise to women. The paper believed that Asquith was about right when he said that they had no mandate for such an increase. The second reason was that the militant suffragettes had done their own cause a great deal of harm. It was what happened "when persons of weak minds and excitable dispositions take up a cause."[29]

A Derby of Two Incidents

The Derby in 1913, which was attended by the king and queen, was run on 4 June and the race was noteworthy for two unusual incidents, both reported in *The Times* the next day.[30] The favourite, Craganour, pulled away from the horse lying second, a 100 to one outsider called Aboyeur, in the home straight and won by a neck. However, the stewards disqualified the winning jockey for jostling and the race was awarded to Aboyeur.

The other incident, just prior to the end of the race, and to which *The Times* gave far less space, occurred as

---

29. *The Times,* 7 May 1913, p. 9.
30. *Ibid.*, p. 8.

the horses rounded Tattenham Corner when a woman rushed towards the king's horse, Anmer, with the apparent objective of seizing the reins. The horse fell and rolled on to its jockey who was lightly concussed when it sprang up again and dragged him by a foot caught in a stirrup. The woman, who had also fallen under the horse, was taken unconscious to Epsom Cottage hospital. She remained unconscious all night and was identified as Miss Emily Davison, known as a prominent suffragette who had been in prison a number of times for suffragette activity, the last time in November 1912 for 10 days for assaulting a Baptist minister whom she mistook for Lloyd George. And before that, in December 1911, she was given six months for setting fire to pillar boxes in Westminster. She was also the suffragette who was earlier injured by a fall in prison that appeared to be an attempt at suicide. Notwithstanding her record, the queen sent a messenger that evening to inquire after her.

Miss Davison continued to deteriorate and underwent surgery next day[31] but she died the day after. A number of her friends visited her before she died and draped her screen with the colours of the WSPU which she had joined in 1906. A graduate of London University with a first class degree from Oxford, she was well known for her militancy.[32]

The funeral took place at Morpeth, Northumberland on 15 June. The body was brought from Epsom by train

---

31. *The Times,* 7 June, p. 8.
32. *Ibid.* 9 June, p. 8.

and escorted across London from Victoria to King's Cross by thousands of sympathisers. Mrs Pankhurst had expressed her intention to attend the ceremony and a carriage had been reserved for her, but when she left her Westminster flat dressed in deep mourning she was immediately arrested and removed to Holloway prison by taxi. The interment at Morpeth was private but after the ceremony the suffragettes walked in single file to the graveside each bearing a floral tribute.[33]

Never a week went by now without the suffragettes causing disturbances and damage to property. At the end of the year suffragettes at St Ethelreda's Church in Fulham sang "God Save Mrs Pankhurst" and shouted "Votes for Women!" before being ejected, and two suffragettes were charged with setting fire to an unoccupied mansion and remanded in custody for a week before being released on account of their hunger strike.[34] And to ring in the New Year of 1914 *The Suffragette* carried a huge headline: "One Year's Militancy Ends" and continued, "Enormous Damage during 1913; Mansion Gutted at Bath; Serious Fire at Cheltenham; Valuable Yacht Destroyed, £40,000 damage; Many Haystacks in Flames."[35] When Emmeline Pankhurst was freed from prison for the third time on licence *The Suffragette* headline was "Mrs Pankhurst again triumphs" and triumph she had. She was out of prison again after five

---

33. *Ibid.* 16 June, p. 5.
34. *Ibid.* 29 December, p. 9.
35. 2 January 1914, p. 270.

days of hunger strike, although released in a state of utter exhaustion.[36]

Appraisal

A great deal has been written here about the suffragettes because their battle was waged at enormous cost in suffering on behalf of votes for women. They have an honoured place towards the end of the drawn-out and bitter struggle for the franchise. However, an important assessment of their full impact has been made by Martin Pugh in his *Women's Suffrage in Britain 1867-1928* (written in 1980) to which we are indebted for some of what follows.[37]

Apart from Sylvia Pankhurst the leading suffragettes fought, with a great deal of fanaticism, a single-issue campaign. But there were other issues such as married women's property rights, education for girls and lack of employment opportunities that exercised the minds of many women who did not think the vote was a panacea. Of the Pankhursts only Sylvia linked the vote with wider social issues and female equality which were left to be tackled later by the feminists of the 1960s and after. And, when she proclaimed that, "Every day the industrial and suffrage rebels march closer together," Christabel responded with, "Independence of all men's parties is the

---

36. 20 March, p. 511.
37. Much of Pugh's assessment is borne out by other writers, including women.

basis of the WSPU"[38] which, unlike the NUWSS, confined its membership to women. There were no allies within her vision. Also in contrast to the suffragettes, in 1912 Mrs Fawcett's NUWSS sought a working alliance with the Labour Party in by-elections by providing it with finance and experienced working class helpers as well as new candidates in elections for seats held by anti-suffrage MPs. By 1914 it had 480 branches and 53,000 members.

Emmeline and Christabel Pankhurst have widely been seen as personifying the women's campaign. However, according to Pugh "what we now know of the rest of the women's movement suggests that the Women's Social and Political Union played a far less significant part than the Pankhursts admitted. Moreover, investigation of the WSPU itself destroys their exaggerated claims."[39] He adds, "Their switch to attacks on property was the Pankhursts' way of obscuring the fact that they had failed to convert and had abandoned further attempts to persuade the country."[40] Nevertheless, it will also be acknowledged that they were dedicated to the women's cause. And although their violent methods alienated many of the public they stirred the suffragists into greater activity; and they did put the question of women's suffrage at the top of the political agenda, although not always with the effect they desired.

At the peak of their militancy, many politicians, the

---

38. Antonia Raeburn. *Op. cit.* 221.
39. Martin Pugh. *Op. cit.* 22.
40. *Ibid.* 24.

suffragists, voters and other members of the public turned against the Union. It was not only the violence, however, but their intervention in by-elections in support of Tory candidates who opposed women's suffrage that was politically damaging for them. At the same time their strident support for their parliamentary champion George Lansbury in Bow and Bromley helped bring about his crushing defeat. Whilst Sylvia worked among the poor women of London's East End and shared their problems her mother and sister obsessively saw them only as political fodder.

Public reaction to the suffragettes became so hostile that they ceased to hold meetings. And considerable antagonism arose from women when Christabel launched her "Chastity Campaign" in 1913 urging women to avoid marriage on the ground that three-quarters of men were infected with venereal disease. In doing so she reduced "to absurdity what was in fact a serious issue".[41]

Christabel and Emmeline were divisive and caused damaging splits in the WSPU as we have seen. In 1914 even Sylvia was forced out of the Union and a number of former militant members left and founded the United Suffragists. Furthermore, the Pankhursts' writings are largely self-serving. Christabel's *Unshackled,* which was published in 1959, is unashamedly hostile to the suffragists, and Emmeline's "autobiography", called *My Own Story* (1914) is a sham which was written by an American journalist. The best of them is Sylvia's *The*

---

41. *Ibid.*

Suffragette Movement (1931) which, although not always accurate, contains some useful material.

The First World War

With the outbreak of war in August 1914 the home secretary released all suffragette prisoners and the Pankhursts threw themselves into the cause of recruiting men and women into the armed forces. In July 1915 Christabel Pankhurst staged her last demonstration with 30,000 women marching down Whitehall under the slogan, "We demand the right to serve". In fact, 1,600,000 women joined the armed forces and nearly 100,000 the auxiliary services.[42]

In 1916, shortly before Lloyd George replaced him as prime minister, and with so many voters serving abroad and a general election possible, Asquith invited the Speaker of the House of Commons (J.W. Lowther) to convene an all-party conference to consider the franchise. The 32 MPs and peers chosen reported shortly after Lloyd George became prime minister and unanimously recommended manhood suffrage with a six months residence qualification, instead of the payment of rates. The plural vote, except for business and university representation, was to be abolished and the single transferable vote system was to be introduced in cities and large towns entitled to return three or more members

---

42. A.J.P. Taylor. *English History 1914-1945*. 38. 1965.

each. This was to be accompanied by the alternative vote for elections in single-member constituencies contested by more than two candidates.[43] A majority also proposed votes for women, not based on residence as with men but on the old householder qualification, and not at 21 years of age. They were to have the vote if they were either local government electors or the wives of local government electors and only at the higher age of 30 or 35.[44]

Franchise and Electoral Changes

Against some Conservative and Unionist protests the War Cabinet accepted the report, confirming that women's suffrage could commence at the age of 30, it being feared that if they could vote at 21 they would outnumber the men. This issue and that of proportional representation were left to a free vote in the Commons which passed the Bill on 7 December 1917 [45] after women's suffrage had been accepted in committee by 385 to 55. However, the Bill was delayed in the Lords over the rival merits of proportional representation and the alternative vote[46] and did not finally become law as the Representation of the People Act, 1918 until the following June. The alternative

---

43. For the meaning of different voting systems see chapter 17, *post*.
44. Cmd. 8463. (1917).
45. *Hansard*, fifth series. [100] 827.
46. *Ibid*. Lords. [30] 88. It was decided that there would be an experiment with proportional representation in 100 constituencies which returned three or more members but it was never put into effect.

vote had been proposed in committee in the Commons by Herbert Samuel. Following a fairly acrimonious debate[47] it was approved by a majority of one but it was opposed by the House of Lords and dropped before the Bill was enacted.

The Act meant that compared with 13 million men, 8.4 million women won the parliamentary vote; 10 years later they were to be the majority of the electorate. The Act meant for many Liberals that they had largely achieved their pre-war aim of votes for married as well as for single women, universal male suffrage and reduced plural voting. The electorate was no longer confined to a small propertied group and four voters out of 10 were now women. However, as with the suffrage for men, the enfranchisement of women would not quickly change the economic or political structure of society.

The Act also allowed for a second vote to be cast either in a University constituency or for occupancy of business premises worth £10 a year. An innovation was that those absent in the armed forces could appoint a proxy to vote on their behalf unless they were in France or Belgium when they could vote by post. All voting at a general election was to take place on the same day instead of being spread over several weeks, the £150 deposit was introduced and the Act included a redistribution of seats aimed at creating constituencies with about 70,000 voters each returning one member. Ten two-member boroughs remained as curiosities but otherwise the age-old

47. *Hansard*, fourth series. [100] 309.

distinction between boroughs and counties vanished. Women could stand for Parliament after the passing of the Parliamentary Qualification of Women Act, 1918, and at the Lloyd George-Bonar Law coalition "coupon election" in December 1918, 17 of them did so, including Christabel Pankhurst who was a coalition candidate. None were returned except the Irish-born Countess Markievicz who was elected for the St Patrick's division in Dublin with a 4,000 majority. But as a member of Sinn Fein she refused to take the oath of allegiance and never set foot in the House of Commons. The first woman to sit at Westminster was Nancy, Lady Astor who won Plymouth in 1919, succeeding her husband who had gone to the House of Lords.

In writing about the achievement of the large measure of women's suffrage in his *Memories and Reflections* in 1928 Asquith claimed that "the changed conditions brought about by the war" were responsible.[48] In a sense they were but other pressures for democracy were also at work and, indeed, seven countries gave women the vote before Britain, including Australia in 1902. Even Asquith himself had told a deputation of the East London Federation of Suffragettes in 1914 that women's suffrage must come and would be part of a thorough and democratic overhaul of the British electoral system.

Social reforms for women followed in quick succession. In 1919 the Sex Disqualification (Removal) Act abolished all existing restrictions upon the admission of women into

---

48. 1928. 140.

professions, occupations and civic positions including appointment as magistrates and selection as jurors. Three years later the Infanticide Act abolished the charge of murder for infanticide and the Law of Property Act enabled husbands and wives to inherit each other's property. And in 1925 the Widows Pension Act gave widows a pension of 10 shillings a week with children's allowances of five shillings for the first child and three shillings each for subsequent children.

Post War Attempts to Secure Political Equality

On 8 March 1922 Lord Robert Cecil introduced a Bill to extend women's suffrage[49] and Isaac Foot did so a little over a year later.[50] Both were defeated. Then, in January 1924, the first (minority) Labour government was formed. Almost immediately William Murdoch Adamson, MP for Cannock, introduced a Bill to provide, among other things, for the equalisation of the franchise for men and women.[51] The government claimed to be sympathetic but avoided promising any facilities for its passage. The Duchess of Atholl, an improbable representative of millions of women or soldiers who believed they were fighting for freedom, opposed the Bill on the ground that women did not want an extension of the franchise and

---

49. *Hansard*. [151] 1286.
50. *Ibid.* [163] 469.
51. *Ibid.* [170] 859.

that to allow more women than men on to the electoral register would be an insult to the 740,000 men killed in the war. Other speakers suggested that the qualifying age for women should be reduced from 30 to 25, Lord Eustace Percy claiming that the electorate was becoming too large and that 21 was too young for a person to make a balanced judgment.

Events overtook the Bill, however, when the government was defeated in the November 1924 general election which followed the *Campbell* case. In this J.R. Campbell, a leading Communist, was charged under the Incitement to Mutiny Act of 1797 with publishing in the *Workers' Weekly* an appeal to soldiers not to turn their guns on fellow workers in either a class war or a military war. Campbell was an ex-serviceman who was crippled by war wounds and the Labour attorney-general, Sir Patrick Hastings, caused the prosecution to be dropped. Hastings was attacked for interfering with the course of justice and on a vote of censure the government was defeated by 364 votes to 191 and the general election followed.

During the election campaign, Stanley Baldwin who was to become Conservative prime minister, said that his party was in favour of equal political rights for men and women. This was followed after the election by a statement in the House of Commons by Sir William Joynson-Hicks, the new home secretary, that the government would carry out the pledge made by the prime minister and would do so within the lifetime of that

Parliament.[52] This it did in 1928, the year in which Emmeline Pankhurst died, when a measure was introduced to give the parliamentary franchise to men and women on equal terms.

The easy-going Baldwin promoted the Bill which Joynson-Hicks described as the culmination of the process begun in 1832 with the number of electors increasing from 9%[53] of the population in 1832 to 48% prior to the Bill.[54] The onetime supporter of women's suffrage Winston Churchill joined the always virulent antagonist F.E. Smith, by then Lord Birkenhead, in opposing the Bill on the ground that the 1918 reform was sufficient. Some MPs again attempted to establish the minimum voting age at 25 but they were laughed out of court when the home secretary pointed out that this would dis-enfranchise two and a half million men. Despite all the efforts of opponents of the Bill it was passed by a resounding 387 votes to 10 and added another five-and-a-quarter million women to the electoral roll; they now formed 52.7% of all those eligible to vote. When enacted as the Equal Franchise Act, 1928 it finally swept away the gender distinction by lowering the voting age for women from 30 to 21 and giving them the same residence qualification as men.

The old Radical slogan "One man one vote" had finally come to fruition as "One adult one vote", except for

---

52. *Ibid.* [180] 1496.
53. In fact it was 4.7%.
54. *Hansard.* [215] 1361.

business and University franchises which gave some half a million people (mainly men) a second vote. These were finally abolished by the post-war Attlee-led Labour government with the passage of the Representation of the People Bill which received the royal assent on 30 July 1948.[55] This Act also removed the qualifying period of six months residence. The postal vote introduced for servicemen in 1918 was extended to civilian occupations and in the 1951 election three-quarters of a million such votes were cast. This was considered to have brought Conservative victories in at least 10 vital seats.[56]

A Minimum Age

At that time reducing the voting age to 18 was not a matter most people thought about. However, it was to be canvassed in the late 1950s and once a Labour government was re-elected in October 1964 the issue was bound to resurface particularly when a new Speaker's Conference on Electoral Reform was appointed. The following year the national executive committee of the Labour Party declared unanimously for votes at 18 - and submitted evidence in support to the Conference. It took three more years before the report of the Conference was published on 27 February 1968. It recommended by 24

---

55. 11 & 12 Geo. 6. c. 65.
56. Martin Pugh. *The Evolution of the British Electoral System 1832-1987.* 9. 1988.

votes to one that the voting age be lowered to 20 years. A minimum age of 18 was rejected by 22 votes to three. Both the government and the Tories gave the recommendation their support.[57]

Then came a twist in the story. On 10 April 1968 the attorney-general, Sir Elwyn Jones, announced in the House of Commons that the government hoped to introduce legislation to implement most of the recommendations on the age of majority made by the Latey Committee whose report[58] had been presented to Parliament in July 1967. "The government," he said, "think it would be right to reduce the age of majority to 18 and propose to follow the recommendation of the majority of the committee. Legislation to be introduced will reduce from 21 to 18 the age at which a person has full powers to enter into a binding contract, to give a valid receipt and to hold and dispose of property. This intended legislation will not affect the age of voting" (cries of "Why not?") "which was outside the committee's terms of reference and concerned the Speaker's Conference on electoral reform which has recently reported." He also explained that the need for parental or court approval for the marriage of a person between 18 and 21 would be removed.[59]

On 16 May the Labour Cabinet considered the question of votes at 18 but was unable to reach

---

57. *The Times*, 28 February 1968, p. 4.
58. Cmnd. 3342.
59. *Hansard*, fifth series. [762] 1401/8.

agreement. Richard Marsh and Barbara Castle were among those who doubted the wisdom of giving the vote to young people whilst those in favour included Richard Crossman and Peter Shore, as well as Tony Benn who threatened to resign from the Cabinet unless 18-year-olds got justice.[60] Two weeks later the Cabinet had more or less decided to reduce the age-limit not to 18 but to 20 for fear that young people in Scotland and Wales would vote for Nationalist candidates. As ever, party advantage was to the fore in the minds of the politicians. When, however, Lord Chancellor Gardiner pointed out the anomaly in that they had endorsed the recommendation of the Latey Commission that the age of majority be reduced to 18 it was accepted that to suggest the age of 20 for voting would provoke ridicule. Accordingly, on 24 July, a White Paper[61] was published in which Harold Wilson's government proposed that the voting age be reduced to 18 and not 20 as suggested by the Speaker's Conference and so recently desired by a majority of its own ministers.

Subsequently, on 14 October, James Callaghan, the home secretary, told the House of Commons that it was illogical not to give votes at 18 in view of the provision of the Family Law Reform Bill then before Parliament that the age of majority should be 18. He said if the Speaker's Conference recommendation of the age of 20 were adopted it would mean 1,500,000 new voters whereas votes at 18 would mean 3,000,000 new voters. "It is my conviction,"

---

60. *The Crossman Diaries*. 493/4. 1979 edn.
61. Cmnd. 3717.

he said, "that these young people have new vigour, and perhaps a new idealism, certainly less prejudice than those of us who are older, and open-mindedness to the problems we have to consider." For people to vote at the age of 18, he continued, would create a greater sense of participation.[62] No doubt he also thought it would secure more Labour votes in the country generally.

On the same day as Callaghan's speech *The Times* leader said,

"The votes-at-18 question was not to be settled by contradictory generalisations about the maturity and political responsibility of people at that age. Our system of universal adult franchise does not concern itself with people's fitness to exercise the franchise, provided they are in possession of their wits and their liberty. It assumes everyone of age ought to have the vote, whether wise or foolish, and whatever his knowledge or ignorance of public affairs. There has to be a threshold of age since in the extreme case infants in their prams must be considered ineligible but the place at which the line is drawn is bound to be arbitrary. It has coincided hitherto with the legal age of majority which makes good sense. If Parliament intends to follow the inconclusive reasoning of the Latey committee and reduce the legal age of majority to 18, as the government does, it would have to find very strong reasons for not following suit with the

---

62. *The Times*, 15 October, p. 8.

minimum voting age. No such reasons have been advanced so far."[63]

On 18 November Callaghan moved the second reading of the Representation of the People Bill which included the proposal. In the debate Labour MP George Strauss thought that giving the vote at 18 would inject a measure of idealism into political affairs. But idealism, he added, untempered by experience and knowledge, in short by maturity, could be dangerous. It could easily be inflamed by demagogy and lead to activities which mature people deplored. It had happened in other countries in a vicious way. Mr Boyd-Carpenter (Conservative) said that if young men and women could be conscripted at 18 for war service they should certainly be treated as of age to vote. Quintin Hogg, also a Conservative, praised votes at 18 but said it was very strange that the grammar school boy should be given the vote at a local election at 18 when the person who paid business rates had his right to vote taken away. That, of course, was not true. What the businessman had taken away was the "right" to vote twice or more. The argument for the business vote was a specious variant on "no taxation without representation" - that businessmen paid rates both as individuals and as businesses, and possibly to different authorities. Plural voting in this way had been restricted by the Parliament Act of 1911 to one extra vote, for either property or degree holders. It was abolished by the 1948 Act, though of

---

63. *Ibid.*, p. 9.

course the business vote survives in the City of London. When the House went into committee an amendment to have the voting age reduced only to 20 was defeated on 26 November, with the help of a government two-line whip and a free vote for the Tories, by 275 votes to 121.[64] Royal assent to the Representation of the People Act 1969 was given on 17 April and 18-year-olds became eligible to vote at the next general election.

Twenty years later the Thatcher government followed the example of Gladstone, Disraeli, Wilson and others in providing votes for people who did not have them and who were likely to support their Parties. This time it was United Kingdom citizens living overseas. Before 1989 such people, widely known as "ex-pats", had a postal vote in UK general elections if they had lived abroad for no more than five years. This was now increased to a maximum of 20 years. According to the *Sunday Times* of 30 July 1989[65] Conservative Party officials planned to register 250,000 "ex pats" to vote Tory at the next general election. Voting would be for the constituencies in which they last voted before leaving the UK. The newspaper also disclosed that 10 branches of an organisation called "Conservatives Abroad" had already been set up in Spain where there were 300,000 Britons, and others were to be formed in the USA and the Far East.

But was this to be the end of electoral change in the United Kingdom?

---

64. *Hansard*. [774] 309/436.
65. *Sunday Times*, p. A2.

CHAPTER 17

The Jenkins Report

In December 1997, Tony Blair, the prime minister of the Labour government elected the previous May, set up an "Independent Commission on the Voting System" presided over by Lord Jenkins of Hillhead OM. If its recommendations were to be accepted in a promised referendum then, along with other electoral measures that the Labour government has fashioned, the United Kingdom will experience the greatest shake-up of its voting system since the 1832 Reform Act. It is worthwhile therefore to consider briefly electoral systems by which the franchise can be exercised.

Context

In the 1850s and 1860s some people were already pointing to what they saw as shortcomings of the electoral system. Thomas Hare was a political reformer who early on raised the question of proportional representation for all classes including minorities. His views were first set forth in 1857 in a pamphlet entitled, *The Machinery of Representation* and subsequently enlarged upon in his *Treatise on the Election of Representatives, Parliamentary and Municipal*, published in 1859. Eight years later John

Stuart Mill presented Hare's plan to the House of Commons, in the debate on Disraeli's Reform Bill, as an amendment to secure representation for minorities. According to Mill's explanation in the House votes should be received in every locality for others than the local candidate, and if there were found in the whole kingdom other electors in the proper number who fixed their choice on the same person that person should be declared duly elected. Mill believed such a system would secure representation in proportion to numbers and no elector would be represented by someone he had not chosen.[1]

Although his amendment was defeated, in 1861 Mill raised the matter again, this time in his *Considerations on Representative Government.* In the same year Catherine Spence in Australia laid the foundations for the Single Transferable Vote in *A Plea for Pure Democracy.* Walter Bagehot responded to Mill in a debate between them that the purpose of elections was to elect governments not just representatives, so that representation in proportion to numbers did not matter.[2] Such opinions are often repeated today.

In committee on the early stages of the Reform Bill of 1884 some 31 MPs supported proportional representation but were told by ministers that this was a matter best dealt with on redistribution on which at the time the government was stalling. At this Leonard Courtney,

1. *Hansard.* [187] 1347.
2. *Cf.* Martin Lonton and Mary Southcott. *Making Votes Count.* 79 *et. seq.* 1998.

financial secretary to the treasury and a strong supporter of PR, resigned. Nevertheless, once the Tory Lords had pushed Gladstone into accepting redistribution he promised that PR would be considered fully "in connection with the redistribution of seats"[3] - a promise on which he later reneged when he realised that there was little public support for the system and believed that it might well reduce the number of Liberal MPs. Probably for similar reasons the Tories refrained from attacking the government on the issue which sank without trace.

In 1909 a royal commission on electoral systems was appointed and it reported on 9 May 1910.[4] It defined an electoral system as involving: (i) the method of recording a vote; (ii) the method of determining successful candidates; (iii) the number of members returned by each constituency. It rejected proportional representation and unanimously advocated the Alternative Vote which its members believed was the best method of removing the most serious defect of the single member system, namely the failure to return minority candidates. However, there was no debate on the report in a Parliament that was too involved in the acrimonious conflicts over the Liberals' Parliament Bill, which set out to destroy the House of Lords veto on legislation, to take any notice. *The Times* considered the report was "cautious to the point of timidity" and claimed that most people wanted a strong government which an accurate reproduction of the state

---

3.   BL. *Add. MSS.* Gladstone Papers. 44768. f. 2.
4.   Cd. 5163/1910.

of the parties would not necessarily yield.[5]

In the debates on the Representation of the People Bill in 1917 the House of Lords wanted a form of proportional representation which involved the grouping of constituencies, as proposed in the report of the all-party Speaker's Conference of that year. However, this was not in the Bill as enacted and a proposal to carry out an experiment in PR in 100 constituencies was never implemented. A second all-party Speaker's Conference on electoral reform was held in 1930 during the minority Labour government of Ramsay MacDonald but it proved abortive. A third was held in 1944 at the invitation of Winston Churchill in the wartime coalition government. This made a number of recommendations but apart from one or two minor ones the government failed to implement them and it was left to the post-war Labour government to introduce more of them in the Representation of the People Act of 1948. Others were abandoned and the Act abolished University seats and plural voting against the recommendations of the conference. Nothing was done about proportional representation which the conference had rejected.[6]

Background to the Jenkins Report

Early in 1997 Labour and the Liberal Democrats held

---

5. 16 May 1910, p. 9.
6. For full details of these conferences see J.F.S. Ross. *Elections and Electors. Studies in democratic representation.* 1955.

talks to try to find an agreed programme of constitutional reform. Their Joint Consultative Committee on the Constitution, as it was called, presented its report on 5 March of that year and its recommendations were incorporated into Labour's election manifesto. They were:

1. Support for a proportional representation system for elections to the European Parliament.
2. The setting up of an independent commission on voting systems to recommend a proportional alternative to the first-past-the-post system.
3. A referendum on the voting system for the House of Commons. There were also proposals regarding a Scottish Parliament, a Welsh Assembly and for a mayor of London.

When, on 2 May 1997, a Labour government was returned with 418 MPs out of 659, it was widely believed that it would be reluctant to change a system that had delivered them a landslide in seats. However, even this landslide was achieved by winning less than half the vote and with fewer total votes than Labour had gained when they lost the 1992 election. In the event, most of the above manifesto pledges were carried out although the prime minister was known to be lukewarm about the likely findings of the proposed commission on voting systems. The effects in Northern Ireland, Scotland and Wales have been described in the Preface to this book.

The Independent Commission on the Voting System for the House of Commons was duly appointed and in addition to Lord Jenkins its members were Lord Alexander of Weedon QC, Baroness Gould of Potternewton, Sir John Chilcot GCB and David Lipsey. Their 30,000-word, 90-page report was published on 29 October 1998.[7] In spite of the word "Independent" in its title and the high standing of its members, the terms of reference of the commission asked it to *recommend an alternative* (our italics) to the present system for parliamentary elections. It was to take into account what the commission calls "four not entirely compatible requirements" . These were broad proportionality, the need for stable government, an extension of voter choice and the maintenance of the link between MPs and their constituencies. Yet as the report itself admits there had been "no surging popular agitation for change" and nine public meetings addressed by members of the commission on an issue that might possibly result in an erosion of representative democracy attracted fewer than 1,000 people in total.

The Commission Examines

An acknowledged assumption lying behind the work of the commission is its conception of "fairness" in electoral outcomes. It sees fairness to voters as being primary, with voters getting the representatives they want as more important than parties getting the seats to which they

---

7.   Cm. 4090-1.

think they are entitled. This is, however, a curious way to describe its own recommended system which includes a number of top-up members. The gross and persistent under-representation of a substantial minority, the commission says, cannot be justified. But equally it would be undesirable to correct that by giving to the minority such a permanent hold upon power that neither of the larger groupings could ever exercise independent authority without the permission of the minority. Yet this is precisely what some believe the report's recommendations would bring about.

The commission regards MPs as having four functions: to represent their constituencies; to provide a pool from which holders of ministerial office can be chosen; to shape and enact legislation; and to enable the party in power to sustain its legislative programme whilst also being held to account for its executive actions. The House of Commons, it says, is effective in regard to the first two. As to the third, it considers that in the past there has been a great deal of legislation that was hastily conceived because it was not very effectively scrutinised. On holding the executive fully accountable for its actions the task is difficult when governments elected by, albeit large, minority votes can command huge majorities in the House. However, it lamely concludes that if a reformed electoral system could bring about some improvement in these matters that would be a mark in its favour.

The report then considers various different electoral systems.

The Current System

First, the report considers the advantages of the present First-Past-the-Post system (FPTP). It is, it says, familiar to the public, votes are simple to cast and count and there is no surging popular agitation for change. By usually (although not invariably) leading to a one-party majority government it enables electors to vote not only for a local representative but also to choose the party they wish to form a government. It also provides each MP with a direct link with a constituency and enables the electorate sharply and cleanly to rid itself of an unwanted government.

Although the report does not mention it, this last point is of considerable importance when comparing Britain with nations that use varying forms of proportional representation. Since the Second World War voters in four countries using FPTP (Britain, Canada, India and New Zealand) have turned out governments in 25 out of 58 elections. In four countries with PR (Germany, Italy, Japan and Switzerland) the main governing party has not been ousted by the electors in the course of 54 elections - until 1998 in Germany. In three other PR countries (Belgium, Netherlands and Sweden) in only six out of 103 elections was a government ousted. On average, in these seven PR countries it took 58 years for the electors to defeat the ruling party whereas in

FPTP nations it took on average every eight years.[8]

However, the Jenkins Report also sees demerits in the system. It considers that FPTP has a natural tendency to disunite the country. It exaggerates movements of opinion and can produce mammoth majorities in the House of Commons. Moreover, the large majorities in 1987 and 1997 were secured with total votes of only 42.3% and 43.2% respectively. FPTP also creates a geographical divide between the two leading parties. Thus the 1997 election drove the Conservatives out of Scotland, Wales and the big provincial cities of England. Equally, the Labour party was virtually excluded from the southern half of the country in the 1980s. What Jenkins fails to mention, however, is that even during the Thatcher years (1979-1990) Scotland, Wales and northern England were already Labour strongholds and that Labour's disadvantage in the 1980s did not prevent it from regaining power in 1997.

Another criticism the report makes of the present system is that it narrows the terrain over which the political battle is fought so that the two main parties fight over about 100 to 150 marginal seats out of a total of 659. Thus in safe seats many voters can never vote for a winning candidate or have any realistic hope of influencing a result. Perverse results are also possible: for instance a party can lose a general election despite obtaining more votes than in elections it had previously

8.   See Michael Pinto-Duschinsky. "Send the Rascals Packing". *Times Literary Supplement.* (25 September 1998).

won. But this has occurred in only two out of 15 elections since the war, namely in 1951 and 1974. There is also, it says, a built-in bias as when the total number of votes won by Labour in 1997, which produced an overall majority in the Commons of 179, was similar to that won by the Conservatives in 1992 which yielded a shaky majority of only 21.

The report also suggests that single-party government is not quite the time-hallowed British tradition its supporters claim. During the past 150 years Britain has been governed for 43 of them by overt coalitions and for 34 years the government of the day was dependent on the votes of other parties. Thus for only 73 of those years has the country been governed by a single party. Moreover, although FPTP can produce effective, stable and democratically elected single-party governments, during those coalitions or minority governments formative changes were made, including the beginning of the welfare state with the National Insurance Act of 1912 (says Jenkins!). Nevertheless, although Jenkins does not mention it, many of the coalitions were deeply unpopular in the country. And for most of the period of the Liberals' welfare reforms early last century they had a huge majority, whereas once they lost their working majority in 1910 and were dependent on the Irish Nationalist members, the spate of legislation began to dry up.

Alternatives

After considering the working of systems of proportional representation in various other countries the Jenkins Report turns to possible solutions for Britain without involving constituency changes. It argues that the simplest change would be from the present system to the Alternative Vote (AV). Instead of the customary cross on the ballot paper voters would rank their preferences for candidates in order ie, 1, 2, 3, 4 and so on. A candidate getting 50% of the vote would automatically win. But if no one did the bottom contender would drop out and his or her second preference votes would be redistributed among the survivors until someone achieved an overall majority.

This, says the report, would maintain the link between an MP and his or her constituency, would increase voter choice, would be unlikely to reduce the stability of government and might, in fact, lead to larger parliamentary majorities. It is acknowledged, however, that the second or subsequent preferences of a losing candidate, if decisive, would be seen by some as having less value and so contributing less to the legitimacy of the result than first preference votes or the second preferences of the most powerful candidates which would not count. In other words, why should the second preferences of weak candidates have the same value as the first preferences of the strongest candidates?

And, there is a "stark objection" to AV. It offers little prospect of greater proportionality and in some circumstances it is even less proportional than FPTP. In the 1997 election AV might well have given Labour 452 seats instead of 419, the Conservatives 96 instead of 165 and the Liberal Democrats 82 instead of 46. Some partisans might applaud such a change but it could hardly be proportional when the Conservatives obtained 30.7% of the vote that should have given them 202 seats on a proportional basis. The commission concludes that AV is capable of adding to disproportionality; that its effects are "disturbingly unpredictable"; and that it can be unacceptably unfair to the Conservatives. Accordingly it rejects AV *on its own* as a solution. In its eyes the Supplementary Vote (SV), where the voter can exercise only a second choice, must also be discarded for having the same defects.

The commissioners believe that the Second Ballot system as used in France could not be easily dismissed by Labour and Conservatives opposed to change since it is similar to the method both parties have recently used for selecting their party leader and therefore, in many cases, of an actual or future prime minister. In the voting in France unless one candidate secures an outright majority, a second round is held a week later with only the two most successful candidates from the first ballot left standing. However, the report promptly dismisses the system as suffering from most of the deficiencies of AV and involving the electorate going twice to the polls which it says many of them are reluctant to do even once.

The "Weighted" Vote is also considered. Under this system MPs would be elected as at present but where their party was under-represented nationally this would be corrected by giving them an additional voting strength in the division lobbies of the House of Commons. Thus, in the present Parliament each Conservative member would be entitled to one and a quarter votes. "Whether," says Jenkins, "they would carry these numbers round their necks or on their backs, rather like prize bulls at an agricultural show, is not clear, but what is clear is that there would be great problems if one of these vote-heavy beasts were to find himself in a lobby different from his party leader and whips, or worse still, if he were permanently to lumber off across the floor. There would inevitably be the most excited attempts to re-corral him." The system is therefore rejected in the report as likely to arouse more mockery than enthusiasm and to be incompatible with the practical working of a Parliament.

The Single Transferable Vote (STV)

This would be a more proportional system, undertaken in multi-member constituencies. Voters could rank as many candidates, both within parties and across different parties, as they wished in order of preference. Any candidates who reached a certain quota would be deemed to have been elected. The surplus votes of candidates elected on the first count and the votes of those with fewest votes after subsequent counts would be distributed on the basis of preferences to the remaining candidates until sufficient candidates reached the quota and were elected.

This system, the report claims, has several substantial advantages. It maximises voter choice; achieves a great degree of proportionality; avoids having two classes of member (as with the Additional Member system in which voters cast two votes - one for an MP and the other for a party); and also avoids the proliferation of small splinter parties. There are, however, serious disadvantages. Constituencies and the number of electors would have to be very large which would entail a very long ballot paper and a degree of choice that might be "oppressive rather than liberating". In a choice example of Jenkins' idiom the report says that, "Where the choice offered resembles a caricature of an over-zealous American breakfast waiter going on posing an indefinite number of unwanted options, it becomes both an exasperation and an incitement to the giving of random answers". Exasperation might discourage voters going to the polls at all and whilst some people want to be able to choose between candidates of the same party, many are interested only in voting for parties and would not appreciate being forced into choosing between candidates of the same party about each of whom they know little. Accordingly the report does not recommend STV, although the Republic of Ireland manages to cope with it. And if the commission had really wanted to maximise voter choice it would have gone for this system.

A Mixed System

In the event, the commission decided to recommend a

mixed system, similar to the method used in Germany, with what it calls a principal advantage of flexibility. This it calls "AV with Top-up", with which, it claims, degrees of priority can be given to both proportionality and the constituency link for MPs. It does not, however, amount to proportional representation. The essence of the system is that the elector would have the opportunity to cast two votes, the first for his choice of constituency MP and the second for an additional or Top-up member who would be elected for the primary purpose of correcting the disproportionality left by the constituency outcomes. Thus, it could be crucial in determining the political colour of the government. It would be possible to cast the second vote either for individuals or (as in Germany) for a party list without regard to the individuals on it. The report opts for such a list being open and not a closed party list in order to give voters the opportunity to discriminate between individuals. It declares that it would count against the new system if any candidate, by gaining party machine endorsement for being at the head of a list, were to achieve a position of effective immunity from the preference of the electorate as has now occurred in elections to the Scottish Parliament and the Welsh Assembly.

The report recommends between 15-20% Top-up members of the Commons (between 98 and 132 members out of 659) and sets out how the Top-up seats would be allocated:

(i)   After the total number of second votes cast for

each party have been counted, these numbers are then divided for each party by the number of constituencies gained in the Top-up area by that party, plus one (adding one avoids the impossibility of dividing by zero and ensures that the party with the highest ratio of votes to seats receives the Top-up seat).

(ii)   A Top-up member is then allocated to the party with the highest adjusted number of votes.

(iii)   Where there remains a further Top-up member to be allocated this process is repeated but taking into account any Top-up members already gained by each party.

Additionally, parties should not be eligible for Top-up seats unless they had contested at least 50% of the constituencies in the Top-up area.

Under this system, the report says, voter choice is manifestly enhanced by the ability of electors to cast their two votes in different political directions. To complaints that electing members by two different methods involves having two classes of MPs, the report replies that this is unavoidable unless the search for greater fairness is abandoned or a solution sought through universal STV or having all members elected on a list system, all of which would be less acceptable. In any event, the report continues, having two classes of MPs is not really a break with British tradition. Throughout the nineteenth century there was a considerable difference of category between county and borough members. And some constituencies were regarded as having a greater prestige than others. Further, university seats which were elected by STV persisted until 1950. These appear to be weak arguments in favour of different classes of MPs, however, and in fact such differences were abolished precisely because they were unfair.

The report proposes that for the whole of the United Kingdom there should be 80 Top-up areas with two of them in Northern Ireland, eight in Scotland and five in Wales. They would be divided between counties and metropolitan areas and would comprise an average of eight current constituencies. All 80 would have at least one Top-up member with the more populous areas and those in Northern Ireland having two. Top-up members would serve a new role by representing in the House of Commons the broader interests of the counties and cities and they should have fully equal status with MPs elected in constituencies. It is noteworthy, however, that if a party does very well in direct constituency elections, as Labour did in 1997, there would be little scope for them to receive Top-up members in addition.

According to the report the new mixed scheme would enable an elector to vote for a candidate of one party for the constituency and then cast his or her second vote in a different direction for the Top-up representative. At the same time if electors do not wish to discriminate between candidates of the same party as they know nothing about them they will be able to tick a party box. "The desirability of freedom of choice is not invalidated by the fact that not everybody wishes to exercise it."

Nevertheless, this means appointment of Top-up members from above.

The report sets out what it considers would have been the likely results of the 1992 and 1997 general elections (with 17.5% Top-up members) in the following tables:

	CON	LAB	LIB DEM	SNP/ PC	Various NI parties	Other
1992						
FPTP	336	271	20	7	17	-
AV Top-up	316	240	74	11	18	-
1997						
FPTP	165	419	46	10	18	1
AV Top-up	168	368	89	15	18	1

Thus, under the proposed new system in both elections the Liberal Democrats would have received a considerable increase in seats, with a hung Parliament in 1992. In 1997 Tony Blair would still have received a substantial overall majority (although with 64% of seats reduced to 56%) but with just 44% of the vote, which says something, but not a great deal, about proportionality. However, looking further back to 1983 and 1987, when the Conservative share of the votes was similar to that of Labour in 1997, the overall Conservative majorities would have been 30 and 20 respectively instead of 144 and 102 as they actually were.

Problems

Some proportional representation enthusiasts say that

FPTP is now exceptional in the world. This is hardly true, however, since it is used in 62 countries involving 49% of the electors in the world. In contrast, AV is used by only 0.5 of the world's electors and AV Top-up is non-existent. Furthermore, a number of countries, including Japan, Israel, France and Italy, are dissatisfied with their PR systems and may change or even abandon them.

In Britain FPTP in elections has in the main led to stable government. On the other hand, proportional representation in various forms, as in France, Italy, Israel and New Zealand frequently produced coalition governments which, despite what Jenkins says, are still not popular in Britain. Where major parties receive a similar number of seats PR often allows very small minority parties a role in a nation's affairs as coalition partners well beyond what their support entitles them to or what the electorate had in mind and voted for.

The report describes the German system of AMS and AV Top-up as being, although different, recognisably of the same broad family. And it believes AMS has worked very well in Germany for half a century. Nevertheless, it acknowledges that it had made coalition the norm and has led to the "permanent hinge position of the very small Free Democratic Party ... which was continuously in office from 1969 to 1998, with a perpetual grip on the foreign ministry and of two or three other Cabinet seats as well." This period of 29 years of almost guaranteed continuous if subsidiary power, for 13 years with one ally and 16 with another, was obtained for the Free Democratic Party with an average of 8.7% of the vote. Whether that can be described as having "worked very well" is open to question.

Would a similar position arise in Britain? It has been argued in *The Times* by Michael Pinto-Duschinsky that the Jenkins plan would mean that nine of the 14 post-war elections would have led to coalitions, with the Liberals or Liberal Democrats in a position to decide who should form a government.[9] Furthermore, such coalitions arising from forthcoming elections could deny the largest party in an election the opportunity to enact its programme.

Related Issues

The commission also considered some issues which, although outside its terms of reference, it believes will affect the conduct of the referendum to be held on its recommendations and the implementation of the new system if it is approved by the public. The first of these is the role of the boundary commission. It is suggested that the commission should work to the present fixed number of MPs, namely 659, and that the over-representation of Scotland and Wales and the inequality of constituency size should be remedied.

The second is the need for a publicly-funded and impartial civic education programme to prepare the public for the referendum on the voting system. The report recommends that the overview of elections and

---

9. *The Times,* 30 October 1998.

electoral administration should be undertaken independently of government by an electoral commission. Such a commission should also oversee the conduct of elections and the planning of the civic education programme but if it is not in place in time an independent referendum commission should be established. Since the report was published the home secretary, Jack Straw, has indicated that the proposed election commission, recommended by the Neill Committee in October 1998 to produce a new scheme for the funding of election campaigns, should also be the body to consider measures to increase electoral turnout and clarify the rules applying to future referendums. This, he said, was likely to reduce government control of both the proposed civic education and the referendums themselves.[10] In particular, the Committee declared that "in any referendum campaign there must be a fair opportunity for each side of the argument to be properly put to the voters."[11]

However, the government's draft Bill on the future conduct of referendums published in the White Paper *The Funding of Political Parties in the United Kingdom*[12] does not appear to meet the safeguards recommended by Lord Neill of Bladen. For example, the period during which the government would be forbidden to attempt to influence the voters is only 28 days before polling day. Further,

---

10. Jack Straw. Interview with *The Times*, 29 December 1998.
11. CM. 4057, October 1998.
12. CM. 4413, July 1999.

there is no reference to the wording of the referendum question. And all parties that have more than two MPs will be allowed to spend up to £5 million each which the Neill Committee has suggested could favour one campaign.

Thirdly, says the Jenkins Report, the new electoral system, if approved, should be reviewed after two general elections have taken place under it, possibly by the electoral commission. And, in any event, fundamental change such as a return to FPTP or substantially increasing or decreasing the ratio of Top-up members should not be introduced without a further referendum.

Note of Reservation

One member of the Independent Commission on the Voting System, Lord Alexander of Weedon, submitted a note of reservation to the report. He agrees with the Top-up proposals but does not share the view of his colleagues that AV, rather than FPTP, is an appropriate way of electing constituency members. He writes:

"This is not an arcane or technical issue primarily of interest to connoisseurs of electoral reform. Quite the contrary. The single member constituency will remain the linchpin of our electoral system, under which about 80% of members will be elected. So it is crucial that the method of election within these constituencies should be sound in principle, easy to understand and above all capable of commanding the enduring respect of the electorate. I do not consider that AV satisfies these tests.

My colleagues support AV because they think it important that every member gains some measure of majority support from the voters in their constituency. Yet most votes in constituencies are cast for a party, not an individual. Once an election is over, however, there is a long-standing tradition that MPs are available to serve all their constituents. MPs do not do this any less well where they have under 50% of the vote. Indeed they need to work hard to garner future support. This healthy convention diminishes the need for the party from which the member comes to have some form of support from a majority of voters in an individual constituency. In addition there will be MPs within the Top-up areas from parties previously unrepresented in those areas who will be available to any voters particularly wanting to consult an MP from their own party."

He goes on to argue that AV could heighten the tendency to tactical voting and lead to attempts by two parties to marshal their supporters so as to gang up on a third which is precisely what those who are suspicious of electoral reform fear. Certainly, the frequently disproportionate results secured in Australia do not encourage confidence in the system.

Lord Alexander points out that there was no groundswell of enthusiasm for AV in the submissions the commission received. The Conservative party supports the existing system. The Liberal Democrats support STV under which no individual MP normally has majority support. The Electoral Reform Society also advocates STV. But, of course, they may change their positions after considering the Jenkins report. However, he also regards it as significant that Parliament has twice endorsed FPTP for constituency elections under a Top-up system for both the Scottish Parliament and the Welsh Assembly without anyone attempting to amend such proposals to introduce AV.

He also criticises AV on the ground that it comes into play only when a candidate fails to secure a majority of first preference votes. It does not, however, then take account of the second preferences of all voters but only of those who have supported the least successful candidates. So it ignores the second preferences of the voters who supported the two candidates with the highest first preference votes but allows the voters for the third or even weaker candidates to have their second votes counted so as to determine the result. He then gives what he calls a "homespun example" of this illogical approach:

"Suppose within a constituency, Conservatives receive 40% of first preferences. Labour are second on 31% and Lib Dems third on 29%. Lib Dems second preferences happen to be split 15/14 in favour of Labour. The Conservatives are therefore elected with 54% of the total vote (ie, 40%+14%).

But now suppose the position of Labour and Lib

Dems had been reversed on first preferences, with Lib Dems 31% and Labour 29%. If Labour second preferences were split 20/9 in favour of Lib Dems, the Lib Dems would be elected with 51% of the total vote (ie, 31%+20%). So the result would be different depending on which horse was second and which third over Becher's Brook first time round. This seems to me too random to be acceptable."

Press Response

On the whole the press responded favourably to the report. For example, a leading article in *The Independent* headed "Jenkins report must not be sidelined" claimed that the electoral system was unsatisfactory and if the right system could be devised it would breathe new life into our democracy. It could help to restore people's damaged faith in politics, give them more confidence as citizens and make politicians more accountable to their electors. "Lord Jenkins and his colleagues," it declared, "have gone a long way towards designing a system that meets these objectives."

Nevertheless, the paper had some reservations. It thought a strictly proportional system was not necessarily desirable. The direct link between an MP and a locality was valuable but such a system would tend to deliver too much power to small parties, because they would be more likely to hold the balance of power. Furthermore, rather than progressively eliminating the bottom candidate of several and reallocating their vote until somebody had a clear majority, as with AV, which could allow a candidate who starts of in third place to "come through the middle" it would be better to "eliminate all candidates except the top two and reallocate the votes between them, which is in effect what happens in the French two-ballot system."[13]

The Observer also backed the report having written in an editorial a month earlier, on 27 September, "Nobody would design the current system from scratch because it corresponds to no democratic ideal nor works especially well. Elections are won in about 100 constituencies and in the others the voters are effectively disenfranchised. The safe seats, run by a small caucus, are little better than the rotten boroughs. Legitimate government must be the outcome of engaged citizens casting votes that count equally wherever they live, and which would directly determine party strength in the House of Commons."

The Guardian closed a favourable editorial on the report headed, "Well done, Jenkins," with the words, "We welcome it, and believe the burden is now on traditionalists to prove why this change will not improve our politics - and our national life."[14]

The Times, however, was critical. On 7 September, prior to the publication of the report, a leading article headed, "The War of Jenkins' Ear - A guide through the minefield of electoral reform" complained that AV would be biased against the Conservative party and that "it

---

13. 30 October 1998, p. 3.
14. *The Guardian*, 30 October 1998, p. 12.

would be a shocking abuse of power - without precedent in British history - for the government to introduce an electoral system for its own partisan advantage. It would be the moral equivalent of ballot rigging". Any AV method, it said, above all one with some party-list top up would simply substitute a known set of imperfections with even worse faults.

Its leader when the report was published was headed: "TOO CLEVER BY HALF - The Jenkins Commission has not made the case for change". The proposals, it claimed, were selective in their proportionality. The Liberal Democrats would have won 43 additional seats in 1997 under the Jenkins system. The Conservatives a mere three seats more. "There must be the suspicion that the real attraction of an AV Top-up system for the Prime Minister is the prospect that the Conservatives could be excluded from power." Further, the Top-up element drawn from party lists would also create a large number of MPs with no meaningful role. Although the commission insisted that they would have equivalent status to constituency members, it was extremely vague on what functions, if any, such figures would fulfil. The paper also thought that the commission was less than frank in its declaration that coalition government and the disproportionate influence of small parties would be an unusual event under their package. Instead, there was every chance that the Liberal Democrats would hold office on a semi-permanent basis regardless of their performance at the polls.[15] In other words, there might not be a future Conservative or Labour government on its own.

The Daily Telegraph was critical to the point of rudeness. The purpose of the commission, it wrote editorially, was "to obliterate the Labour Party as we know it, to gerrymander the Conservatives into lasting opposition and to frustrate the electorate". It was a fix because the commission could only consider alternatives but not any advantages of FPTP itself. "The system proposed is a muddle. Why should there be two classes of MP? Why should the party machines be given more power? Why should the people of Britain be troubled by all this in the first place?" Because AV with a PR element was "most likely to gratify the ambitions of an old man in a hurry."[16]

Debate

The prime minister immediately, but cautiously, welcomed the report as making a well-argued and powerful case for the system it recommended and as being a modification of the existing Westminster system rather than any full-blown PR system as practised in other countries. The Conservative leader, William Hague, on the other hand, pledged to work with other parties,

---

15. 30 October 1998.
16. 30 October 1998, p. 29.

business leaders and trade unionists to block the changes. "It would be a great mistake," he said, "to move to this ridiculous dog's breakfast."

On 5 November 1998 MPs discussed the report. The home secretary, Jack Straw, told the House of Commons that a referendum before the next election was "less certain" because no new system could be introduced until the election after next. Making clear that he personally favoured the FPTP system he added that "This is not an issue on which there is any need to rush to a verdict". Liam Fox, the then Conservative spokesman on constitutional affairs, said the commission had been rigged to help create an arranged marriage between the Lib Dems and part of the Labour party. He stressed the importance of the link between voters and their MPs. "We all know that what we do and say will be scrutinised by constituents who all have a vote to put us out at the next election, and that would not happen under any form of top-up." He added that under such a system there would be created a new class of MP who would not be answerable to the electorate but to their party bosses.

Gerald Kaufman (Labour) claimed that the report was intellectually shoddy, hopelessly complicated, self-contradictory and biased against the Labour party. Alan Beith, for the Liberal Democrats, insisted AV Top-up would be fairer and would give all parties greater representation in areas where they currently have no MPs. Tony Benn (Labour) was concerned that the Jenkins proposals would undermine the link between voters and their MPs. "Representation," he said, " is that delicate thread which links the people to the government. They want a man you can see, you can argue with and ultimately you can get rid of." Stuart Bell (Labour) said that FPTP had given the country stable government, it gave the constituency link, was accountable and gave the doctrine of mandate.[17]

Implementation

In its manifesto for the 1997 general election the Labour party promised a referendum on electoral reform during its first term in office. In the wake of the very low turnout for elections for the European Parliament in June 1999 Tony Blair abandoned this commitment and told the House of Commons that a new system would not be introduced in time for the next general election.[18] It is no longer clear whether a referendum will be held at all and if it is whether the general public will be asked to vote on the recommendations of the Jenkins Report or some amended form of them.[19] If there is a referendum and the response is favourable the commission concluded that the election after next (perhaps in 2006) is the earliest realistic point at which its proposals could come into operation. The reason it gives for this is the burden

---

17. *The Times,* 6 November.
18. *Ibid.*, 18 June 1999, p. 2.
19. At the time of writing it seems likely that a referendum will be held and that any new system of preference voting will keep the traditional link between MPs and their constituencies.

placed on the boundary commission by the need to reduce by approximately a fifth the number of constituencies.

The questions that remain are: will the government produce a different package from that of Jenkins; if not, will the report's recommendations be put to the people and accepted in a referendum; and if they are what surprises in subsequent elections may the British people inflict on the politicians and indeed on themselves? Jenkins's favourable forecasts of the consequences of AV Top-up may well prove to be unwarranted and unreliable. The report itself concedes that the effects of AV are "disturbingly unpredictable". This may be an understatement, and the burden of proof that change will not result in some disaster which may affect the lives of millions of people should be placed upon those advocating it.

CHAPTER 18

Afterword

The breathtaking changes wrought by modern technology and communications have made the world in which we live today a smaller and more insecure place. It has also made modern government extraordinarily complex and involved. Long gone are the days when a prime minister such as Gladstone could spend a great deal of his time away from government at his country home at Hawarden Castle felling trees; or Asquith, who was able to sit in Cabinet in wartime writing letters to Venetia Stanley. Today a prime minister may have to be in Washington one day, Tokyo the next and Brussels and London on the same day.

Since ordinary citizens cannot run the state themselves on an Athenian model they have to elect representatives to act on their behalf. Detailed control of what the government does is, of course, beyond their capability but they can and do have a healthy general influence on a government's policies and actions which is what the franchise is all about. That is why popular engagement with the franchise is at its highest level when people are concerned about their living standards, unemployment, poverty and war. And their power is ultimately exercised when they put a sitting government out of office. This overriding control safeguards accountability and reduces corruption and it should not be overlooked that such power is an essential ingredient of a democratic society. After all, dictatorships may present themselves to the world as democracies but their people are given no democratic opportunity to change them.

For example, in China, which considers itself more democratic than Britain, the electoral system entails the people at a very local level electing a local committee which in turn elects one of its members to a district committee. Each district committee then elects a member to the provincial committee and so on up to the National People's Assembly. This system of so-called "democratic" centralism gives rise to what is termed the People's Democratic Dictatorship yet only a handful of people vote for anything other than local committees and at all stages the candidates are vetted by the Communist Party. This results in an all-powerful Communist government which cannot be removed by democratic processes.

In the United Kingdom with our present electoral system not all electors gain any electoral benefit from exercising the franchise since large numbers of them never see a candidate of their choice elected. In parliamentary elections sometimes a substantial minority but more often a majority of the electorate are governed by MPs for whom they did not vote. This is one consequence of single-member constituencies and in this the system is not fully democratic. Indeed, Lord Hailsham considers that safe seats in which the candidate is selected by a small caucus are not much different from the old nomination boroughs. He recalls that in 1936 when the chairman of the local party interviewed him he was told that although "I was perfectly acceptable I had no prospect of selection unless I offered £400 a year". The only change was from paying the voter to vote for him to paying the party to select him.[1]

But does proportional representation solve this or create even more problems? We have considered some of the latter in the previous chapter. Is the answer to return to multi-member constituencies of larger areas as existed throughout most of our history? In these each party could put forward several candidates which would give more choice to the electors. It would also go some way to opening up pockets, or sometimes large areas, of the country that have strong leanings towards one party.

Given that the British Constitution is unwritten and systems can be altered more or less at will by Parliament it might be considered surprising that recent discussion about Parliament has not been about the machinery of government - whether it can be changed for a better one - but only about the manner in which the vote can be cast.

But what would be a better one? In the United States many people consider their system to be more democratic than our own. They have two elected chambers and an executive president and the people elect all three. However, in a system of checks and balances the Representatives can block the Senate, the Senate can block the president and in some circumstances the

---

1.   *The Dilemma of Democracy.* 1978.

president can override either House. In contrast, according to Lord Hailsham, in the UK the executive and legislature are intertwined and "the people's will is not adequately protected by its representatives in Parliament."[2] And neither the Congress nor the president ever enjoy the situation where a government in Britain, even with the slimmest majority (occasionally with no majority at all), can carry out their programme in the way they want until the next election.

Switzerland has yet a different system which *they* consider more democratic. They have a very weak federal government, stronger elected cantonal governments and many important decisions are decided by referendums. The Swiss say that the people should decide important issues; the British have traditionally said that is what Parliament is for.

Another form of voting for parliamentary representatives is that employed in Israel. There a pure list system is in use. The electors vote for a party and a particular percentage of the vote (currently 5%) triggers the election of a Knesset member (MK); candidates are elected in order from the party list, the leader, being first on the list, would be elected first. Thus the candidates, chosen by each party and elected from each party, precisely reflect the proportion of votes cast for them. This means that minority groups are represented and to this extent the system is democratic. However, where the system breaks down is that the Knesset membership is so

---

2. *Ibid.*

fragmented that the party with most MKs, which has never had an overall majority, has to enter into *ad hoc* coalitions or do deals with tiny parties having only one or two members and who actually represent only a minute part of the electorate. Hence what is democratic in the polling booth becomes undemocratic in the House when parties representing a small number of people wield undue influence in policy-making, can block legislation and even bring down the government. Thus can representation and democracy part company altogether.

To varying degrees this is a problem that arises with most systems of proportional representation which is why Japan, France and Israel are thinking of changing their systems and Italy is seriously considering adopting First-Past-The-Post.

In Britain the present government is certainly making radical changes. But what is the ideology behind them? It was seen in our Preface that Peter Mandelson was a government minister when he made his speech in Bonn in April 1998 arguing that it might be that the era of pure representative democracy was coming to an end. He also claimed that, "democracy is not the only source of legitimacy for institutions", citing the Bundesbank as an example.

Professor David Marquand, a former Labour MP, has argued that new Labour is faced with a choice. Either it can continue with a highly centralised type of state which its structure and Whitehall encourage. Or, if it wishes to cope with the big issues of a changing Europe, the nature of capitalism and the role of the state, it can attempt to introduce a new pluralist political system with diffused power and responsibility. Marquand favours the pluralist option but believes that such a radical change of outlook "would mean abandoning the dream of a new society engineered from above by a reforming government" and "would mean the end of the victory-at-all-costs, winner-take-all mentality".[3]

For Marquand the new approach would include what appears to comprise a mixture of both old and new policies. These would encompass a local income tax, strengthening local economic development powers, regional assemblies, more democracy for quangos, full proportional representation, radical parliamentary reform and an elected second chamber. Without them, he said, victory in the old sense was no longer worth having. Whether Tony Blair's "third way" takes on board all such ideas is not yet clear although he has already made his mark with devolution for Scotland and Wales and changes in the electoral systems for them, Northern Ireland and elections to the European Parliament. But the results may not be entirely to his liking. He cannot be happy with a coalition in what was a Labour stronghold or where Labour remains the party with the largest number of seats although without an overall majority.

Some of Marquand's proposals, such as an elected second chamber, deserve serious debate but the Labour Party's plans, as put to the royal commission on House of

---

3. In a speech at ESRC's ninth annual lecture, "Must Labour Win?" delivered at the end of October 1998.

Lords Reform, include appointed members of the second chamber, although with no party permitted to have a majority. Perhaps the Labour leaders should recall the words of Edward Gibbon on the reform of the Roman Senate by Augustus when he wrote, "The principles of a free constitution are irrevocably lost, when the legislative power is nominated by the executive".[4] This government is not averse to referendums which by-pass Parliament and suggests a tendency towards the manipulation of public opinion through a plebescitary dictatorship. The referendum is a blunt political instrument that can be easily misused unless it is closely controlled to ensure fairness in the wording of the question(s) put to the vote and the accompanying propaganda.

The veteran MP Tony Benn has a different viewpoint from that of Peter Mandelson. Benn sees "a sustained frontal assault on democracy" and has argued that the former minister's analysis "completely eliminates the idea of representation in politics where people could choose those who would speak for them and to legislate to see that their interests are met through Parliament through the control of the statute book and the budget .... Globalization is just capitalism writ large and we are to be trained by our leaders to adjust our society so as to meet the harsh requirements of that system, based entirely on profit rather than need."[5]

---

4. *The History of the Decline and Fall of the Roman Empire.* i. 79 Folio Society edition 1983.
5. *Tribune.* 3 April 1988.

Another serious problem is the growing emergence of the list system. Involved here are both the selection of Labour Party candidates for Parliament and voting in general elections. In certain internal Labour Party elections one-member-one-vote has been accompanied by trade union block votes. And the introduction of selected lists of candidates vetted by the leadership is now under consideration. The Top-up lists of candidates introduced in elections in Scotland and Wales have resulted in some 40% of members of the Scottish Parliament and one third of those in the Welsh Assembly owing their seats to some extent to their party machines. Indeed, the first leader of the Welsh Assembly, Alun Michael, was defeated at the polls but was "elected" by Top-up. If the recommendations of the Jenkins report are implemented Top-up lists will feature also in elections in England.

For the election of members of the European Parliament in June 1999 Britain was divided into 11 regions, each returning between four and 11 MEPs. Closed lists were used and voters were not allowed to vote for an individual candidate but only for a political party so that candidates were totally insulated from the preferences of the electorate. In the event, only 23% of the electorate voted and all the resulting members of the European Parliament owed their seats to party managers. This was hardly democracy at work.

It is to be hoped that this book's survey of the history of the parliamentary franchise has revealed how the representative function has changed over the centuries and why such alterations were brought about. A few years ago the conclusion of such a survey might have indicated that any further variations in the electoral system in the UK would be merely cosmetic. Instead, suddenly the nature of the discussion of the topic has altered and turbulent waves of opinion surge around us. And who can say what uncharted waters lie ahead?

Appendix 1

Brief Summary of the Provisions of Legislation relating to the Franchise from the 13th Century to the Present Day.

1297   Statute De Tallagio. King Edward I provided that no tax would be levied without the consent not only of barons and higher clergy but also of *"burgesses and the other free men of our realm"*.

1430   Statute limited the franchise in the counties to 40 shilling freeholders. Voters and representatives had to be resident in the county.

1653   Cromwell's "Instrument of Government" increased the threshold of the county franchise to £200 freeholders, provided for triennial Parliaments and more equal electoral districts.

1654   Parliament restored the lower county franchise limit to 40 shillings.

1660   Franchise measures of the Protectorate Parliament annulled.

1694   Triennial Act introduced for three-year Parliaments.

1695   Three Acts of Parliament attempted unsuccessfully to impose a minimum age for voters of 21 and reduce bribery.

1710   County candidates for Parliament required to possess an income of £600 from land and burgess candidates £300. Largely circumvented and not repealed until 1858.

1716   Septennial Act provides for seven-year Parliaments.

1832   The Great Reform Act. The electorate increased from an estimated 435,000 in England and Wales to 652,000, ie, from 3.1% to 4.7% of the population. The number of MPs remained at 658. Fifty-six English boroughs returning one member each lost the franchise. Thirty-six other boroughs lost one member each. Twenty-two large towns were enfranchised and given two members each with 20 more given one member each. The number of county MPs rose from 94 to 159.

1867   Disraeli's Reform Act abandoned the property qualification for the franchise and added 938,000 voters to an existing electorate of 1,056,000 in England and Wales. Working class voters were now a majority in the towns under a new household suffrage based upon a £6 rateable value. Householders who paid their rates via their landlords were also given the vote. The county franchise was based on a £12 rateable value. Forty-five seats were taken from small boroughs. Of these 25 were given to the counties, 15 to new boroughs, a third member each to Manchester, Liverpool, Leeds and Birmingham and a member to the University of London.

1884/5 Gladstone's Reform and Redistribution Acts

extended household suffrage to county voters and raised the United Kingdom electorate from some three million to about five million. Seventy-nine small towns were disenfranchised and 36 lost one of their two seats. Many constituencies became single-member. In Ireland an increase in the electorate from 200,000 to 700,000 voters gave a tremendous boost to Parnell's Nationalist Party.

1911   The Parliament Act reduced the maximum duration of Parliament from seven to five years.

1918   Representation of the People Act provided for 13 million male voters over 21 years of age a six-month's residence qualification and enfranchised 8.4 million women over 30. It redistributed seats to create constituencies of about 70,000, each returning one member. Ten two-member boroughs remained as curiosities. Otherwise the age-old distinction between boroughs and counties vanished. A postal vote for servicemen overseas was introduced.

1918   The Parliamentary Equality of Women Act provided that women could stand as candidates for Parliament.

1928   Equal Franchise Act lowered the voting age for women from 30 to 21 and gave them the same residence qualification as men.

1948   Representation of the People Act abolished University and business votes and removed the six-months residence qualification for both men and women. The servicemen's postal vote was extended to civilian occupations "ex-pats".

1969   Representation of the People Act reduced the minimum voting age to 18.

1989   United Kingdom citizens living overseas for up to 20 years given the postal vote.

1998/9 A devolved Parliament for Scotland and Assemblies for Northern Ireland and Wales introduced with modified systems of proportional representation for elections to them.

Appendix 2

Prime Ministers from 1715 to 1999

October 1715	Robert Walpole *Whig*
April 1717	Lord Stanhope *Whig*
March 1718	Earl of Sunderland *Whig*
April 1721	Sir Robert Walpole *Whig*
February 1742	Earl of Wilmington *Whig*
August 1743	Hon. Henry Pelham *Whig*
Feb.10-12, 1746	Earl of Bath *Tory*
February 1746	Hon. Henry Pelham *Whig*
March 1754	Duke of Newcastle *Whig*
November 1756	William, 4th Duke of Devonshire *Tory*
June 1757	Earl Waldegrave *Whig*
June 1757	Duke of Newcastle *Whig*
May 1762	Earl of Bute *Tory*
April 1763	George Grenville *Whig*
July 1765	Marquis of Rockingham *Whig*
August 1766	Duke of Grafton *Whig*
February 1770	Lord North *Tory*
March 1782	Marquis of Rockingham *Whig*
July 1782	Earl of Shelburne *Whig*
April 1783	Duke of Portland *Coalition*
December 1783	William Pitt *Tory*
February 1801	Henry Addington *Tory*
May 1804	William Pitt *Tory*
December 1806	Lord Grenville *Whig*
March 1807	Duke of Portland *Tory*

October 1809	Spencer Perceval *Tory*
June 1812	Lord Liverpool *Tory*
April 1827	George Canning *Tory*
September 1827	Viscount Goderich *Tory*
January 1828	Duke of Wellington *Tory*
November 1830	Earl Grey *Whig*
July 1834	Viscount Melbourne *Whig*
December 1834	Sir Robert Peel *Conservative*
April 1835	Viscount Melbourne *Whig*
September 1841	Sir Robert Peel *Conservative*
July 1846	Lord John Russell *Whig*
February 1852	Earl of Derby *Conservative*
December 1852	Earl of Aberdeen *Coalition*
February 1855	Viscount Palmerston *Whig*
February 1858	Lord Derby *Conservative*
June 1859	Viscount Palmerston *Liberal*
October 1865	Earl Russell *Liberal*
June 1866	Lord Derby *Conservative*
February 1868	Benjamin Disraeli *Conservative*
December 1868	W.E. Gladstone *Liberal*
February 1874	Benjamin Disraeli *Conservative*
April 1880	W.E. Gladstone *Liberal*
June 1885	Lord Salisbury *Conservative*
February 1886	W.E. Gladstone *Liberal*
August 1886	Lord Salisbury *Conservative*
August 1892	W.E. Gladstone *Liberal*
March 1894	Lord Rosebery *Liberal*
June 1895	Lord Salisbury *Conservative*
July 1902	Arthur Balfour *Conservative*

December 1905	Sir Henry Campbell-Bannerman *Liberal*
April 1908	H.H. Asquith *Liberal*
December 1916	David Lloyd George *Coalition*
October 1922	Andrew Bonar Law *Conservative*
May 1923	Stanley Baldwin *Conservative*
January 1924	Ramsay MacDonald *Labour*
November 1924	Stanley Baldwin *Conservative*
June 1929	J. Ramsay MacDonald *Labour Coalition* from 1931
June 1935	Stanley Baldwin *Conservative*
May 1937	Neville Chamberlain *Conservative*
May 1940	Winston S. Churchill *Coalition*
July 1945	Clement Attlee *Labour*
October 1951	Winston S. Churchill *Conservative*
April 1955	Sir Anthony Eden *Conservative*
January 1957	Harold Macmillan *Conservative*
October 1963	Sir Alec Douglas-Home *Conservative*
October 1964	Harold Wilson *Labour*
June 1970	Edward Heath *Conservative*
February 1974	Harold Wilson *Labour*
April 1976	James Callaghan *Labour*
April 1979	Margaret Thatcher *Conservative*
November 1991	John Major *Conservative*
May 1997	Tony Blair *Labour*

Select Bibliography

A. Manuscript Sources

(1) *British Library Additional MSS.*
Gladstone Papers. 44768.
Place Papers. 27,790/1; ;27,793/6; 27,828;
35,149.
Peel Papers. 40391/2.
*General Convention of the Industrious
Classes.* Papers 34245A.
Miscellaneous. 27,801; 27,837; 30,109; 34,516;
36,466; 38,593.
Parliamentary Writs. (1295).
(2) *Public Record Office*
HO 40/29; 41/13; 42/172; 44/6; 44/24; 52/14;
102/40.
Wellington Despatches. 2nd ser. vii. (1878).

B. Printed Records

Annual Register. 1780; 1788; 1819; 1867.
Cmd. 8023; 8463. (1917).
House of Commons Journals. xi (1693-7): xx (1722-7):
xxii (1732-7): xlviii (1793).
Parliamentary History and Hansard.
(1745-1969).
State Papers. (1640/1).

State Trials. xxii. (1783-94). xxiv. (1794-1818).
CM 4090-1 Independent Commission on the Voting
System. (The Jenkins Report) (1998).

C. Newspapers and Journals

Anti-Suffrage Review. 1910.
Birmingham Journal. 1838.
Daily Universal Register and *The Times*. 1785-8.
Edinburgh Review. 1810, 1867.
Historical Journal. 1963.
Manchester Guardian. 1907, 1908.
Morning Chronicle. 1831.
National Reformer. 1837.
New Statesman. 1913.
Northern Star. 1839, 1941.
Political Register. 1806, 1829.
Poor Man's Guardian.1831.
Prompter. 1831.
Quarterly Review. 1817; 1831.
The Ballot. 1831.
The Daily Telegraph. 1998.
The Examiner. 1830.
The Guardian. 1998.
The Republican. 1831.
The Standard. 1830.
The Suffragette. 1914.
The Times. 1788 -1998.
The Times Literary Supplement. 1998.

Votes for Women. 1908-9.
Westminster Review. 1867.

D. Early Books, and Pamphlets

Atlay, J.B. *The Victorian Chancellors*. (1906).

Bagehot, Walter. *Essays on Parliamentary Reform*. (1883).
Bamford, Samuel. *Passages in the Life of a Radical*. (1841).
Brougham, Henry. *Life and Times*. (1871).

Carlyle, Thomas. *Chartism*. (1839).
Shooting Niagara: And After? (1867).
Chatham, Earl. *Correspondence*. (1771).
Cox, Homersham. *Antient Parliamentary Elections*. (1868). *Whig and Tory Administrations during the last Thirteen Years*. (1868).
Creevey, Thomas. *Papers*.(1905 edn).
Croker, John Wilson. *Papers*. (1884 edn).

Defoe, Daniel. *The Freeholder's Plea against Stock-jobbing Elections of Parliament Men*. (1701).
A Tour through the Whole Island of Great Britain. (1725).
Disraeli, Benjamin. *Sybil, or the Two Nations*. (1845).
Coningsby. (1982 edn).

Eagles, John. *The Bristol Riots, their Cause, Progress and Consequences.* (1832).

Gardiner, S.R. *The History of the Commonwealth and Protectorate.* 3 vols. (1901).

Grey, Sir Edward. *Correspondence with King William IV and Sir Herbert Taylor.* (1867).

Hale, Sir Matthew. *The Original Institution, Power and Jurisdiction of Parliaments.* (1707).
Hardy, Thomas. *Memoir.* (1832).
Hart, Heber L. *Women's Suffrage and National Danger: A Plea for the Ascendancy of Man.* (1897).
Heaton, William. *The Three Reforms of Parliament. A History.* (1885).

Jenks, Edward. *The Constitutional Experiments of the Commonwealth. A Study of the Years 1649-1660.* (1890).
Jephson, H.L. *The Platform: Its Rise and Progress.* (1892).

Kebbel. T.E. *Lord Beaconsfield and other Tory Memories.* (1907).

Lecky, W.E.H. *A History of England in the Eighteenth Century.* (1882-3).
Lowe, R. *Speeches and Letters on Reform.* (1867).

Macaulay, Thomas. *A History of England in the Eighteenth Century*. (1980 edn).

Maitland, F.W. *Township and Borough*. (1898). *The Constitutional History of England*. (1908).

Molesworth, W.N. *The History of the Reform Bill of 1832*. (1866). *The History of England from the year 1830*. 3 vols. (1871).

Murdoch, James. *A History of Constitutional Reform in Great Britain and Ireland*. (1885).

Oldfield, T.H.B. *Representative History*. (1816). *History of the Boroughs*. (1792).

Porritt, E. & A. *The Unreformed House of Commons. Parliamentary Representation before 1832*. 2 vols. (1903).

Russell, Lord John. *The Final Reform Bill*. (1866). *Recollections and Suggestions*. (1875).

Shelley, Percy Bysshe. *The Mask of Anarchy*. (1819).

Sparrow, Joseph. *Reform not Revolution*. (1831).

Stubbs, William. *The Constitutional History of England in its Origin and Development*. 3 vols. (1884). *Select Charters*. (1921).

Trevelyan, G.O. *The Life and Letters of Lord Macaulay*. (1876).

E. Modern Books and Articles

Bassett, A. Tilney. *Gladstone's Speeches.* (1916).

Black, Jeremy. *Pitt the Elder.* (1992).

Blake, Robert. *Disraeli.* (1966).

Brailsford, H.N. *The Levellers and the English Revolution.* (1976).

Briggs, Asa. ed. *Chartist Studies.* (1959).

The Age of Improvement. (1969).

Brock, Michael. *The Great Reform Act.* (1973).

Butler, J.R.M. *The Passing of the Great Reform Bill.* (1914).

Butler, D.E. *The Electoral System in Britain 1918-1951.* (1953).

Butler, D.E. *The Electoral System in Britain Since 1918.* (1963).

Cannon, John. *Parliamentary Reform 1640-1832.* (1973).

Clanchy, M.T. *Early Medieval England.* (1997).

Clark, G. Kitson. *The Making of Victorian England.* (1962).

Cole, G.D.H. *A Short History of the British Working-Class Movement 1789-1947.* (1966).

Cole, G.D.H. and Filson, A.W. *British Working Class Movements. Select Documents 1789-1875.* (1967).

Cole, G.D.H and Postgate, Raymond. *The Common People: 1746-1938.* (1938).

Colley, Linda. *Britons.* (1994).

Cowling, Maurice. *1867 Disraeli, Gladstone and Revolution - The Passing of the Second Reform Bill.* (1967).
Mill and Liberalism. (1990).
Crossman, Richard. *Diaries of a Cabinet Minister 1964-1970.* (1979).

Derry, John W. *Charles James Fox.* (1972).
Politics in the Age of Fox, Pitt and Liverpool - Continuity and Transformation. (1990).
Dickinson, H.T. *Liberty and Property. Political Ideology in Eighteenth-Century Britain.* (1977).
Dictionary of National Biography.

Ehrman, John. *The Younger Pitt.* (1969).

Fulford, Roger. *Votes for Women: The Story of a Struggle.* (1957).

Gosnell, Harold F. *Democracy: The Threshold of Freedom.* (1948).
Gwyn, W.B. *Democracy and the Cost of Politics in Britain.* (1962).

Hailsham, Lord. *The Dilemma of Democracy.* (1978).
Hammond, J.L. & Barbara. *The Village Labourer.* (1911).
Hobsbawm, E. & Rude, G. *Captain Swing.* (1969).
Holdsworth, Sir William. A *History of English Law.* 17 vols. (1966).

Holton, Sandra Stanley. *Suffrage Days. Stories from the women's suffrage movement.* (1996).
Hostettler, John. *Thomas Wakely - An Improbable Radical.* (1993).
Thomas Erskine and Trial by Jury. (1996).
Hovell, Mark. *The Chartist Movement.* (1925).

Jenkins, Roy. *Gladstone.* (1995).
Johnson, Paul. *A History of the American People.* (1997).
Jones, Andrew. *The Politics of Reform, 1884.* (1972)
Jones, David. Chartism and the Chartists. (1975).
Jones, David J.V. *The Last Rising: The Newport Insurrection of 1839.* (1985).

Keen, M.H. *England in the Later Middle Ages: A Political History.* (1997).
Knowles, C. H. *Simon de Montfort.* (The Historical Association). (1965).
Kraditor, Aileen S. *The Ideas of the Woman Suffrage Movement, 1890-1920.* (1965).

Lewis, Jane. (ed). *Before the vote was won: arguments for and against women' suffrage.* (1987).
Lonton, M. and Southcott, M. *Making Votes Count.* (1998).

Magnus, Philip. *Gladstone.* (London 1963).
Marshall, Dorothy. *The Rise of George Canning.* (London 1938).

Miller, Edward. *The Origins of Parliament.* (The Historical Association) (1960).

Namier, Lewis. *The Structure of Politics at the Accession of George III.* (1957).

O'Gorman, Frank. *Voters, Patrons and Parties. The Unreformed Electoral System of Hanoverian England 1734 - 1832.* (1989).

O'Toole, Fintan. *The Life of Richard Brinsley Sheridan.* (1997).

Pankhurst, Christabel. *Unshackled.* (1959).

Pankhurst, E. Sylvia. *The Suffragette Movement.* (1931).

Pankhurst, Emmeline. *My Own Story.* (1914).

Park, Joseph H. *The English Reform Bill of 1867.* (1920).

Pasquet, D. *An Essay on the Origins of the House of Commons.* (1925).

Perkin, Harold. *The Origins of Modern English Society 1780-1880.* (1978).

Phillips, John A. *The Great Reform Bill in the Boroughs. English Electoral Behaviour, 1818 - 1841.* (1992).

Pinto-Duschinsky, Michael. *"Send the Rascals Packing".* TLS. (1998).

Pollard, A.F. *The Evolution of Parliament.* (1934).

Porter, Roy. *England In the Eighteenth Century.* (1998).

Pugh, Martin. *Women's Suffrage in Britain 1867-1928.* (1980).
The Evolution of the British Electoral System 1832-1987. (1988).
Women and the Women's Movement in Britain 1914-1959. (1992).
Electoral Reform in War and Peace 1906-18. (1978).

Radzinowicz, Sir Leon. *A History of English Criminal Law.* (1974).
Raeburn, Antonia. *The Militant Suffragettes.* (1973).
Ross, J.F.S. *Elections and Electors. Studies in democratic representation.* (1955).
Rover, Constance. *Women's Suffrage and Party Politics in Britain, 1866-1914.* (1967).

Seymour, C.S. *Electoral Reform in England and Wales. The Development and Operation of the Parliamentary Franchise 1832-1885.* (1915)
Shannon, Richard. *The Age of Salisbury, 1881-1902: Unionism and Empire.* (1996).
Speck, W.A. *Stability and Strife. England 1714-1760.* (1977).
Stewart, Robert. *Henry Brougham - His Public Career 1778-1868.* (1986).

Taylor, A.J.P. *English History 1914-1945.* (1965).
The Times, Past, Present, Future. (1985).
Thompson, E.P. *The Making of the English Working Class.* (1968).

Vallance, Elizabeth. *Women in the House. A Study of Women Members of Parliament.* (1979).

Veitch, G.S. *The Genesis of Parliamentary Reform.* (1913).

Vernon, James (ed). *Re-reading the constitution. New narratives in the political history of England's long nineteenth century.* (1996).

Wallas, Graham. *The Life of Francis Place.* (1918).

Watson, J.Steven. *The Reign of George III 1760-1815.* (1960).

West, Julius. A *History of the Chartist Movement.* (1920).

Woodward, E.L. *The Age of Reform: 1815-1870.* (1954).

Wright, Sir A. Unexpurgated Case against Woman Suffrage. (1912).

Ziegler, Philip. *Melbourne. A Biography of William Lamb, 2nd Viscount Melbourne.* (1976).

Index